THRESHOLD
EDITIONS

MERCURY
RADIO ARTS

Also by Glenn Beck

COWARDS

WHAT POLITICIANS, RADICALS, and the MEDIA REFUSE to SAY

Written and Edited by
GLENN BECK and **KEVIN BALFE**

Writers: Scott Baker, Deneen & Tom Borelli,
LTG (Ret.) William G. Boykin, Kevin Freeman, David Harsanyi,
David Horowitz, Dr. M. Zuhdi Jasser, Sylvia Longmire,
Barry Rubin, Brian Sack, Ben Shapiro, Ira Stoll, Mark Tooley
Art & Design: Paul E. Nunn, Mark Mabry
Design: Timothy Shaner

THRESHOLD
EDITIONS

MERCURY
RADIO ARTS

New York   London   Toronto   Sydney   New Delhi

College of the Ouachitas

Threshold Editions/ Mercury Radio Arts
A Division of Simon & Schuster, Inc.
1230 Avenue of the Americas
New York, NY 10020

First Threshold Editions/Mercury Radio Arts hardcover edition June 2012

THRESHOLD EDITIONS and colophon are trademarks of Simon & Schuster, Inc.

GLENN BECK is a trademark of Mercury Radio Arts, Inc.

For information about special discounts for bulk purchases, please contact
Simon & Schuster Special Sales at 1-866-506-1949 or business@simonandschuster.com.

The Simon & Schuster Speakers Bureau can bring authors to your live event.
For more information or to book an event, contact the Simon & Schuster Speakers
Bureau at 866-248-3049 or visit our website at www.simonspeakers.com.

Designed by Timothy Shaner, nightanddaydesign.biz

Manufactured in the United States of America

10 9 8 7 6 5 4 3 2 1

Library of Congress Cataloging-in-Publication Data

Beck, Glenn.
  Cowards / Glenn Beck.
     p. cm.
  1. United States—Politics and government. I. Title.
JK31.B43 2012
320.520973—dc23   2012015507

ISBN 978-1-4516-9347-8
ISBN 978-1-4516-9483-3 (ebook)

To Gandhi, Martin Luther King,
Dietrich Bonhoeffer, and all those
who emulate their courage in
some small way, like Alveda King,
Ted Nugent, Jerry Boykin, and
M. Zuhdi Jasser

Agree or disagree with any of
them, these people will never
say the things they do not
believe, no matter the cost.

They are the opposite of cowards.

ACKNOWLEDGMENTS

Special thanks to . . .

The **LISTENERS**, **READERS**, and **GBTV PIONEERS**—you give me hope every single day.

My amazing wife, **TANIA**, all my **PARENTS**, and my beautiful **CHILDREN**, who always teach me something new and make me understand what we are fighting for.

Everyone at **MERCURY RADIO ARTS** and **GBTV**, including those at our sister companies, **THEBLAZE.COM** and **MARKDOWN.COM**. You are showing the world the incredible things that can happen when you combine a dream with hard work and talent.

All the important **CONTRIBUTORS** and **RESEARCHERS** who helped bring this book to life, including **STU BURGUIERE**, **ELIZABETH HURLEY**, **SHARONA SCHWARTZ**, **KENT LUNDGREN**, **ZACK TAYLOR**, **DAVID BRODY**, and **MARTHA WEEKS**.

All those at **SIMON & SCHUSTER** who may have a case against me for torture. You deal effortlessly with the craziest book production schedules in the industry, and you have my unending gratitude. This includes **CAROLYN REIDY**, **LOUISE BURKE**, **JEAN ANNE ROSE**, **MITCHELL IVERS**, **ANTHONY ZICCARDI**, **LIZ PERL**, **EMILY BESTLER**, **AL MADOCS**, **JOY O'MEARA**, **SALLY FRANKLIN**, and those who work tirelessly behind the scenes to put this book in your hands.

Everyone at **PREMIERE RADIO NETWORKS** and **CLEAR CHANNEL** who help my voice reach millions every day, including **MARK MAYS**, **JOHN HOGAN**, **JULIE TALBOTT**, **DAN YUKELSON**, and **DAN METTER**.

The talented and hardworking people behind the scenes at **NEP** and **CRM** and all the other companies that have helped GBTV become the amazing success story it is.

Everyone else whom I owe so much of my personal and professional success to, including: **GEORGE HILTZIK**, **BILL O'REILLY**, **BRIAN GLICKLICH**, **MATTHEW HILTZIK**, **JOSH RAFFEL**, **JON HUNTSMAN**, **DUANE WARD**, **STEVE SCHEFFER**, **DOM THEODORE**, **RICHARD PAUL EVANS**, **GEORGE LANGE**, **RUSSELL M. BALLARD**, **KEN SWEZEY**, and **JOSH SESSLER**, along with **ALLEN**, **CAM**, **AMY**, **MARY**, and the whole team at **ISDANER**.

CONTENTS

"A lie told often enough becomes the truth."
— Lenin

"Cowards can never be moral."
— Mahatma Gandhi

George Orwell once said, "In a time of deceit, telling the truth is a revolutionary act." Consider this book a revolutionary act. After all, in this world, at this time, it's not those who incite street riots who are the revolutionaries, it's those who tell and seek the truth.

We live in a country where the establishment is infested with cowards; people who are not only unwilling to find solutions, but who are often too spineless to even acknowledge that a problem exists. They are far more enamored with power, or ratings, or their personal agendas than with the truth. I'm talking about politicians, yes, but also academics, the mass media, movement leaders, business leaders—and anyone else who keeps perpetuating the lie that everything will be fine if we just listen to them.

They are wrong. Everything is not fine—it hasn't been for a very long time.

The cowards want us to believe that the two-party political system is working, when, in reality, it hasn't offered American voters a genuine choice in a very long time. We complain election after election about not having a candidate who truly represents our values, and yet nothing ever changes. We keep playing the game, electing the same progressives and then feigning outrage when they back off from their bold campaign promises and instead turn into the same mealy-mouthed weasels they replaced. They hide the fact that there is another option, another way of looking at the world—one much more closely aligned with the Constitution—because it threatens their monopoly on power.

The cowards want us to believe that the public education system is adequately preparing our children for their futures in an increasingly competitive world. It isn't.

The cowards want our kids to believe that capitalism has failed. It hasn't.

The cowards want us to put all facts and common sense aside and instead believe that our economy is not being targeted by terrorists and other nations. They want us to ignore the fact that powerful people like George Soros are willing and able to bring down entire currencies and change entire countries.

The cowards want us to look the other way as progressive activists disguised as religious leaders, like Jim Wallis, hijack our churches by turning legitimate policy debates into issues of morality rooted in the Bible.

The cowards want us to sit back and accept that the mainstream media is hostile and condescending toward traditional values. They think it's okay that stories about celebrities or murder are sensationalized and put at the top of newscasts while stories of real importance are ignored or buried.

The cowards want us to believe that the cartel violence along our southern border is contained and is not a threat to Americans. They want to minimize the threat of radical Islam and dismiss well-established goals, like spreading the Islamic caliphate and shariah law, as conspiracy theory. Cowards prioritize political correctness over the truth.

All of this must change. We've spent decades playing by the rules, only to find out that the game itself has been rigged all along. After all, you cannot have a legitimate debate when the moderators—the political and media elite—have a vested interest in the outcome.

The cowards have had their way for far too long. By concealing themselves in the darkness, they've advanced an agenda that has brought America to the brink. Only the bright sunlight of truth can expose them for who they really are.

It is my sincere hope that, with your help, this book helps to usher in those first, bright rays of light.

Dallas, Texas 2012

Chapter One

STEP RIGHT UP!
THE PROGRESSIVE SHELL GAME

66 I am impatient with those **Republicans** who after the last election rushed into print saying, 'We **must broaden the base** of our party'— when what they meant was to **fuzz** up and **blur** even more the **differences** between ourselves and our opponents. 99

—Ronald Reagan, 1975

I'M SURE you've noticed how little choice there seems to be in politics. I hear it over and over again from people who call in to my radio show and tell me that they don't see any point in voting since both candidates are equally terrible.

They're often right. In 2008, our choice for president was between a Republican who wanted to spend billions to "combat" global warming and a Democrat who wanted to spend hundreds of billions to do the same thing. In 2004, it was between the incumbent George W. Bush, whose embarrassing conservative record we'll cover later, and John Kerry—a man who, by some accounts, had been the most liberal member of the Senate for multiple years.

If it seems like no "real" conservative or libertarian candidate for president ever makes it very far it's because they don't. They are derided and marginalized by the establishment and mainstream media until their names become toxic. By the time the power base is done with a candidate who might pose a threat, he's become the punch line to a joke, the plot of a *Saturday Night Live* skit, or the first thing that pops up on Google when you search for "homophobia" or "racist" or "idiot."

None of this is happening by chance. It's a shell game, and the progressives who run our political parties, our universities, and our media treat the rest of us like tourists in Times Square. It may occasionally look as if libertarians and small-government candidates have a chance to win the prize—but that's just the way they set up the con. The illusion of victory is omnipresent, but it's just that— an illusion. A con can't ever really be beaten.

THE SHELL GAME TURNS 100

The Big Con started right around 1912. America was given a "choice": Woodrow Wilson or Theodore Roosevelt. The New Freedom or the New Nationalism. Progressive or Progressive.

That was the year that Republican became Democrat and Democrat became progressive. Later, after progressives finally had their hands on our wallets, they stopped calling themselves progressives and took the name "liberal" instead. When people caught on to that, the left changed the names to protect the guilty once again.

Progressives realized long ago that if you rig the game of politics against the small-government option, then you end up with a series of candidates who increasingly blur the line between the parties. Eventually the parties themselves become meaningless—empty vessels that simply serve to funnel money and power through the system. With very few exceptions, our elections are really no longer about whether to grow or cut government's size and power, but rather *by how much* they should grow. We debate double-digit increases in social program spending versus single-digit increases. We debate how many new billion-dollar entitlements we should add instead of whether these programs should even exist in the first place. We debate whether teachers unions and the U.S. Department of Education should have more or less power, rather than whether the federal government should have any role in local education at all. All of this is part of the con, and it's worked to absolute perfection. With very few exceptions even the

The Con, Revealed

Hillary Clinton actually described these bait-and-switch word games pretty well during a 2007 debate after she was asked if she would define herself as "liberal."

You know, it is a word that originally meant that you were for freedom, that you were for the freedom to achieve, that you were willing to stand against big power and on behalf of the individual.

Unfortunately, in the last 30, 40 years, it has been turned up on its head and it's been made to seem as though it is a word that describes big government, totally contrary to what its meaning was in the 19th and early 20th century.

I prefer the word "progressive," which has a real American meaning, going back to the progressive era at the beginning of the 20th century.

"boldest" of conservative politicians submit budgets and bills that, a hundred years ago, would've been too far left for even a Democrat to propose.

Whenever candidates or groups raise their hand and question these debates, invoke the Constitution, or propose "radical" ideas like a balanced budget amendment, shutting down overreaching and ineffective federal agencies, or adhering to the Tenth Amendment, they are ostracized. Why do you think the Tea Party was immediately branded as a bunch of racists and birthers? It's because they posed a real threat of waking voters up to the fact that Americans are being presented with a never-ending series of false choices. The progressive establishment can't allow real diversity to stand.

The only hope we have of changing this is by first educating people as to how this happened and who's behind it—and then by presenting a better way forward. That's what the first two chapters of this book are all about: the virus—progressivism; and the antibiotic—commonsense libertarianism. Yes, we have plenty of other issues to solve, and many of them are covered in this book, but if we don't start by treating the underlying disease then none of that will matter.

So, let's take a giant step back, get out of the weeds of the twenty-four-hour news cycle and cable channels and Twitter attacks, and ask ourselves this simple but important question: How did we ever get to the point where the conservative/libertarian point of view does not even get a seat at the table?

THE RINO—AN ANCIENT SPECIES

It's pretty easy to spot the people who don't really fit into the Republican Party. A lot of times these are the same people who frequent the Sunday morning talk shows or are media darlings. I'm talking about people like Arlen Specter, John McCain, and Lindsey Graham. But these types of Republicans are nothing new.

Theodore Roosevelt was one of the first RINOs (Republican in Name Only) in American history. Yes, I know, Roosevelt was brave and strong. He explored the world. He strung up rustlers in the Wild West. He wrote more history books than most people ever read. He edited a magazine. (Even if Newt Gingrich were around back then, Teddy Roosevelt would still have been the smartest guy in the room.)

All of this made Roosevelt incredibly dangerous when he decided to get on board the Progressive train. And the longer he rode those rails, the more radical he got. His "Square Deal" was one thing. It started the ball rolling. It got the nose of big government under the Constitution's tent by regulating business and

They Really Said It

You know, my hero is a guy named Teddy Roosevelt.

—JOHN MCCAIN AT A PRESIDENTIAL
DEBATE IN OCTOBER 2008

And for government to not leave guarantees that you don't have the ability to change, no private corporation has the purchasing power or the ability to reshape the health system, and in this sense I guess I'm a Theodore Roosevelt Republican. In fact, if I [was] going to characterize my—on health where I come from, I'm a Theodore Roosevelt Republican and I believe government can lean in the regulatory leaning is okay.

—NEWT GINGRICH

the banks. But then Roosevelt's progressivism got increasingly more toxic. After he left the White House, he unveiled something he called the "New Nationalism."

There's a reason Barack Obama took time out in December 2011 from pretending he was FDR or JFK or Harry Truman or Lincoln (and from golf, too, come to think of it) to channel Roosevelt at Osawatomie, Kansas. Osawatomie is where, in 1910, Roosevelt gave a speech that would sound right at home in today's Democratic Party. "We should permit [wealth] to be gained only so long as the gaining represents benefit to the community," Roosevelt told a crowd of thirty thousand listeners. "This, I know, implies a policy of a far more active governmental interference with social and economic conditions in this country than we have yet had, but I think we have got to face the fact that such an increase in governmental control is now necessary. . . ."

Two years later, Roosevelt doubled down, turning from rogue elephant to Bull Moose and running for president on his own Progressive Party ticket. The *New York Times* explained that Roosevelt's 1912 Progressive Party convention was at best a gathering of "a convention of fanatics." How bad was Roosevelt's 1912 campaign? It made people think that Woodrow Wilson was conservative. That's bad, but what's far worse is that Roosevelt is the president who some prominent modern-day Republicans, like John McCain and Newt Gingrich, still look up to.

Roosevelt certainly wasn't alone in being a progressive Republican; the GOP was infested with these guys. In 1912, Roosevelt's Progressive running mate was California governor Hiram Johnson, a big-time Progressive who hated Japanese immigrants. You know who worshipped Johnson? Earl Warren—the same guy who, as the Republican governor of California during World War II, helped FDR ship the Japanese in his state to internment camps.

Then there was Nebraska's progressive senator George W. Norris, who served nine congressional terms (five in the House and four in the Senate)

Sometimes the Truth Slips Out

I am keenly aware that there are not a few men who claim to be leaders in the progressive movement who bear unpleasant resemblances to the lamented Robespierre and his fellow progressives of 1791 and '92.

—THEODORE ROOSEVELT

as a "Republican." Norris was the very model of a RINO. Not only did he endorse FDR in 1932; in 1928 he had also endorsed Democrat Al Smith. Norris also sponsored FDR's Tennessee Valley Authority and Rural Electrification Act (both alongside segregationist Mississippi anti-Semitic congressman John Rankin)

Bipartisan Progressives

I guess it's not really surprising that when Henry A. Wallace (another former progressive Republican) and his communist-controlled Progressive Party staged their national convention in 1948, they hung a huge portrait of the late former supposed Republican George Norris from the rafters.

and was very pro-Soviet ("Russia is more in accord with the United States . . . than most any other foreign nation").

Another big-time Republican progressive was Wisconsin's Senator Robert La Follette Sr. "Fighting Bob" La Follette actually wanted to be the national Progressive standard-bearer in 1912, but two things stood in his way: Teddy Roosevelt, and a nervous breakdown he suffered while delivering a speech in Philadelphia that year. (It must

have been really stressful keeping up the small government charade.) In 1924, La Follette finally embraced who he really was, leaving the GOP and running for president as a Progressive against Calvin Coolidge. His platform included nationalizing the country's big industries, an idea that was so good it resulted in an endorsement from the Socialist Party of America.

AN UGLY HISTORY

In his 1796 Farewell Address, George Washington put on his spectacles and looked right into the future when he warned us about the dangers of political parties, or factions:

> *The alternate domination of one faction over another, sharpened by the spirit of revenge, natural to party dissension, which in different ages and countries has perpetrated the most horrid enormities, is itself a frightful despotism. But this leads at length to a more formal and permanent despotism. The disorders and miseries which result gradually incline the minds of men to seek security and repose in the absolute power of an individual; and sooner or later the chief of some prevailing faction, more able or more fortunate than his competitors, turns this disposition to the purposes of his own elevation, on the ruins of public liberty.*

It's hard to find a better example of the "absolute power of the individual" or the "ruins of public liberty" than the way early progressives looked at the weakest members of our society. These people, many of whom are emulated and respected by modern-day politicians, weren't just busy trying to control big business or monetary policy; they also wanted to control society—from cradle to grave. In some ways that's just the natural evolution of their ideology; once somebody thinks they know best about a bunch of things like regulating the snot out of the economy, they think they know best about *everything*.

"Everything," in this case, included determining who was good enough to live, die, and breed.

That was what the Progressive Era eugenics movement was all about. Crippled? No children for you. The wrong race? Ditto. Have special needs? You're an embarrassment to society and you'll get none of our attention or care. That's right—the people who advertise themselves as the ones who care most about the "least of us" are actually the people who preferred that the least of us didn't exist.

One of the big players in the eugenics movement was a guy named Madison Grant. Since Grant was named after two presidents, he thought he was really great—and, more than that, he thought that *you* weren't really great at all. In 1916 Grant wrote a huge bestseller titled *The Passing of the Great Race*. It contained gems like this:

> *Mistaken regard for what are believed to be divine laws and a sentimental belief in the sanctity of human life tend to prevent both the elimination of defective infants and the sterilization of such adults as are themselves of no value to the community. The laws of nature require the obliteration of the unfit and human life is valuable only when it is of use to the community or race.*
>
> *As the percentage of incompetents increases, the burden of their support will become ever more onerous until, at no distant date, society will in self-defense put a stop to the supply of feebleminded and criminal children of weaklings.*

The Passing of the Great Race was translated into German in 1925, and guess who was a big fan? Yep, that's right. "The book is my Bible," Adolf Hitler wrote to Madison Grant.

So, what's this got to do with this chapter? Just this: Madison Grant and Theo-

66 The laws of **nature** require the obliteration of the **unfit,** and human life is **valuable** only when it is of use to the **community** or race. **99**

—Madison Grant, writing in a book endorsed as "fearless" by Theodore Roosevelt dore Roosevelt were great friends. And when *The Passing of the Great Race* came out, this is what Roosevelt wrote to Grant: "The book is a capital book: in purpose, in vision, in grasp of the facts that our people must need to realize. . . . It is the work of an American scholar and gentleman, and all Americans should be grateful to you for writing it."

Senator McCain, is your hero really "a guy named Teddy Roosevelt"?

DAMN HOOVER

Back to the national picture. There were three Republican presidents of the 1920s: Warren G. Harding, Calvin Coolidge, and Herbert Hoover. Harding and Silent Cal were true conservatives: they cut spending and taxes; they reduced the national debt; they vetoed bad legislation; their policies fostered growth and prosperity. They got it right.

Herbert Hoover was something else entirely. In 1912, Hoover bolted the Republican Party to support Theodore Roosevelt's Progressive Party ticket. He served in Woodrow Wilson's wartime administration and oversaw the nation's food supply. In 1918, he joined in Wilson's call to elect a Democratic Congress. In 1920, Franklin Roosevelt (another Wilson appointee) even supported Hoover as the *Democratic* candidate for president—and angled to be his running mate.

Because Hoover was a progressive, he reacted exactly how you'd expect when the stock market crashed in October 1929. Like most elected officials today, Hoover simply didn't trust the free market to correct the situation. Instead, he waded into the Great Depression with his own version of TARP and stimulus plans.

Cal vs. Herb

It's not all that surprising that Hoover looked to the government after the '29 crash. After all, this is the guy about whom Calvin Coolidge said "for six years that man has given me unsolicited advice—all of it bad."

It was Hoover's Republican big government response that set the stage for FDR's even-bigger-government New Deal. Hoover's programs cost so much that, in 1932, presidential hopeful FDR blasted Hoover for "presiding over the greatest spending administration in peacetime in all of history." He charged the Hoover administration with "fostering regimentation without stint or limit." Speaker of the House John Nance Garner, FDR's running mate that year, charged that Hoover was "leading the country down the path of socialism."

"We might have done nothing," Hoover said, defending his big-government, big-spending, little-results efforts. "That would have been utter ruin. Instead we

Regulation! Taxes! Stimulus! Infrastructure! Vote Hoover!

[B]efore a year [of the Depression] would pass, Hoover had done damage . . . on three fronts: by intervening in business, by signing a destruction tariff, and by assailing the stock markets. . . . Hoover proceeded undaunted. He ordered governors to increase their public spending when possible. He also pushed for, and got, Congress to endorse large public spending projects: hospitals, bridges. . . . By April 1930 the secretary of commerce would be able to announce that public works spending was at its highest level in five years.

—AMITY SHLAES IN *THE FORGOTTEN MAN: A NEW HISTORY OF THE GREAT DEPRESSION*

met the situation with proposals to private business and to Congress of the most gigantic program of economic defense and counterattack ever evolved in the history of the Republic. . . . No government in Washington has hitherto considered that it held so broad a responsibility for leadership in such times."

Sound familiar? Many years later, after another economic panic, George W. Bush, another Republican president, would claim that he "abandoned free-market principles to save the free-market system . . . to make sure the economy doesn't collapse."

The GOP went into the fetal position after the Great Depression left Republican officeholders in the breadlines. Alf "the Kansas Sunflower" Landon, the GOP's hapless 1936 nominee, set the standard for all the "me too" Republican nominees who have followed him. *Just elect us*, these guys have said for years. *We won't repeal anything the Democrats have done. Elect us, and we'll run progressive programs better than the Democrats ever could.*

In 1940, Wall Street utilities attorney Wendell Willkie followed Landon. Willkie may have been the RINO-est Republican presidential candidate of all time considering that he'd been a registered Democrat until just before emerging as the 1940 long-shot GOP nominee. After his 1940 loss to FDR, Willkie pursued an obnoxious career of lecturing Republicans to be even less conservative than they already were.

In 1944 rumors began to fly that Willkie might turn his coat again and endorse FDR for a fourth term. Unfortunately, Willkie died before that might have happened, but we do know this: Willkie had a secret meeting that July with a Roosevelt emissary about realigning all the progressive/liberal elements into a single party in 1948.

Even Taft?

Just how dismal were the 1940s and '50s for conservatives in the GOP? To a lot of people, the conservative alternative to duds like Wendell Willkie, Tom Dewey, Harold Stassen, and Earl Warren was Ohio senator Robert A. Taft, a guy they called "Mr. Republican." But even Taft was, on occasion, a little squishy. Listen to these words from his colleague Richard Nixon: "As a matter of fact, Taft was a progressive. . . . [H]e had very progressive, advanced views on aid to education, on health care, and on housing."

IKE, BARRY, AND TRICKY DICK

Some might say that everything changed for the better after Tom Dewey's embarrassing 1948 defeat; that the GOP turned away from progressivism. But that's simply not true.

Dwight Eisenhower captured the GOP nomination in 1952 by defeating the more conservative (caveats apply) Senator Robert Taft of Ohio. Compared to what would follow Ike, his administration looks pretty darn good, but compared to what it might have accomplished, it left a lot to be desired.

The truth is that Ike's eight years looked very much like what Tom Dewey's "unity" administration might have looked like had he won. Think about it: Dewey's campaign manager became Ike's attorney general; Dewey's foreign policy adviser became Ike's secretary of state; Dewey's running mate Earl Warren became chief justice of the Supreme Court. It's no wonder that Arizona's Barry Goldwater blasted Ike for running a "dime store New Deal."

Barry Goldwater.

"Mr. Conservative" captured the GOP nomination in 1964, but, let's face it, he was the only bright light around at that point for conservative Republicans. There was, however, an avalanche of liberal, progressive RINOs: New York governor Nelson A. Rockefeller, Pennsylvania governor William W. Scranton, Michigan governor George W. Romney, and senators like Jacob Javits, Tom Kuchel, Kenneth Keating, John Sherman Cooper, Margaret Chase Smith, Leverett Saltonstall, Clifford Case, and George Aiken.

And that's not counting Prescott Bush, Chuck Percy, Mark Hatfield, Edward Brooke, or even John Lindsay, who soon became mayor of New York City and drove "Fun City" into the ground. In other words, it was a liberal Republican field day. Goldwater was the exception, not the rule. And with the rest of the RINO bunch manning the ship, we didn't stand a chance of stopping LBJ's "Great Society."

After Goldwater was betrayed by party progressives in 1964, Republicans lost their nerve. The conservative recapture of the GOP fell apart. The Washington establishment decided to play it safe. Read our lips: No new Goldwaters! And certainly, they weren't interested in that actor-governor out in California—Ronald Reagan. Nope, the GOP wasn't going to buy into any of that c-r-a-z-y free enterprise, small government stuff anymore. It was going to play it safe—that was how you won elections. Or so we were told.

In 1968, the GOP decided to nominate Richard Nixon again. Now, Dick Nixon wasn't only a retread (think Bob Dole, John McCain, or Mitt Romney); he was one seriously bad president—and one really bad example of a progressive republican.

Liberals hated Richard Nixon. They didn't go for his style. They resented the way he helped expose Stalinist agent Alger Hiss in the late 1940s. But, if they were smart, they should've embraced him: down deep he was their compatriot on some very important issues.

Conservatives, on the other hand, cut Nixon a lot of slack for a very long time. They shouldn't have. They fell for the argument that "the enemy of my enemy is my friend." But Richard Nixon was never a friend of conservatism; he just used the rhetoric and the movement to his own advantage. He played conservatives—and Republicans—for suckers. And Barry Goldwater was one of the biggest suckers of all.

Yes, Richard Milhaus Nixon really was Tricky Dick.

Nixon not only *didn't* repeal Lyndon Johnson's Great Society, he went out of his way to put the entire program on steroids. Nixon never balanced a budget (even LBJ did it in 1968–69), but he did create the Environmental Protection Agency and proclaimed Earth Day. He signed OSHA and an Emergency Unemployment Act into law. He recognized Communist China (a policy that I would venture to say has now had a few unintended consequences) and he spent more on social programs than on defense. In fact, Nixon wanted to spend more with his "Family Assistance Program," which would have provided a "guaranteed income" to tens of millions of Americans.

Under Nixon, Medicaid's spending skyrocketing 120 percent. He also wrecked what was left of the gold standard and devalued the dollar. And, when inflation ran riot, he instituted wage-and-price controls.

Spiro Agnew, Nixon's vice president, was actually an eastern establishment Rockefeller-type Republican who only mouthed conservative words to keep Nixon's Republican base at ease. Liberal Senate minority leader Hugh Scott got it right when he boasted: *"The conservatives get the rhetoric; we [the liberals] get the action."*

New York Times columnist James Reston said of Nixon in 1970: "He is at a critical point in his career. He has been trying to liberate himself from his conservative and anti-Communist past, and work toward a progressive policy at home and a policy of reconciliation with the Communists abroad. . . ."

Reston got it only half right. Nixon never really was a conservative; he was

No Explanation Necessary

I will be prepared to put on an aggressive and vigorous campaign on a platform of progressive liberalism designed to return our district to the Republican Party.

—RICHARD M. NIXON, RUNNING FOR CONGRESS IN 1946

always—you guessed it—a progressive. And his favorite president was—you guessed right again—Woodrow Wilson. In fact, while Ronald Reagan placed a portrait of Calvin Coolidge in the Cabinet Room, Nixon hung portraits of Wilson—and Theodore Roosevelt—in his own private office.

INTO THE BUSHES

I've met George H. W. Bush and George W. Bush. They are both decent, kind, courteous people. But neither of them did a very good job with bringing a true conservative philosophy to the Oval Office.

The GOP had come a long way under Ronald Reagan. This new and improved party might not have accomplished everything that conservatives wanted (it never could, for example, figure out how to balance a budget or abolish Jimmy Carter's Department of Education), but it seemed to be finally taking us away from the progressive track that Teddy Roosevelt had laid for the country all those years ago.

Reagan's conservatism, however, never seemed to be good enough for the first president Bush. He was too busy ridiculing "voodoo economics" or introducing his own brand of watered-down, progressive "kinder, gentler conservatism." Before you could say "Read my lips, no new taxes," Bush Sr. had blown an 89 percent approval rating and received a pathetic 37.5 percent in the 1992 election.

It was pretty much the same with George H. W. Bush's son when he took over eight years later. George W. had marketed his own brand of politics as "compassionate conservatism." He campaigned for the White House without promising to abolish *any* federal agencies—something that was odd for a true small government politician. Conservatives should have seen through this act (we've seen it enough times to know how it ends), but we didn't. There was so much concern about beating Al Gore (for good reason, I should add) that no one really stopped to think about Bush himself.

George W. not only abandoned the traditional GOP promise to eliminate the federal Department of Education, he imposed a whole *new* level of Washington bureaucratic control on local schools with his "No Child Left Behind"

Vladimir Milhaus Lenin?

There are many strange things about Richard Nixon, but this is among the strangest: When Nixon rolled out his abandonment of the gold standard, a rise in the tariff, and wage-and-price controls, he could have named his program anything. He could have called it "the New Progressivism." He could have called it "the Great, New, Fair, Square Deal-Frontier-Society." Instead he called it "the New Economic Policy"— the name Soviet dictator Vladimir Ilyich Lenin gave to the economic policy he instituted in 1922.

act. He also doubled federal education spending (amazing fact: Bush spent more on education than on Iraq) and grew federal spending 68 percent overall.

For years on end, a Republican Congress spent like Charlie Sheen in a Vegas nightclub, and Bush generally stood by and accepted it. He issued just twelve vetoes over his two terms, the lowest total since Warren Harding—which isn't even a fair comparison considering that Harding died in office during his only term.

> **Voodoo Election Returns**
>
> **H**ow bad did George H. W. Bush's "kinder, gentler conservatism" stink up the lot in his 1992 reelection campaign? This bad: Bush ended up with 37.5 percent of the vote. In 1932, colorless old Herbert Hoover, running at the depth of the Great Depression, got 39.7 percent! Bush got exactly 1.0 percent more than hapless Alf Landon did in 1936 when Landon won a whopping 8(!) electoral votes.

George W. nearly doubled our national debt, taking it from $5.768 trillion to $10.626 trillion. He oversaw creation of the $700 billion blank-check TARP program, the first stimulus, and a $180 billion Medicare drug benefit program.

In 2009, the Mercatus Institute ran the numbers on George W. They aren't pretty:

 Bush increased spending more than any of his seven predecessors (LBJ, Nixon, Ford, Carter, Reagan, GHWB, Clinton).

 In Bush's last term discretionary spending skyrocketed 48.6 percent.

Adjusted for inflation, Bill Clinton's budget rose by just 11 percent. Bush's budgets soared by 104 percent.

 The number of federal subsidy programs expanded by 30 percent. When Bush left office the number of programs had grown to 1,816.

My point with all of this is not to add to the George W. Bush bashing—he obviously did plenty of very good things—but simply to underscore that he was not even close to being a conservative president. A Republican? Sure. A guy who kept us safe during one of the most dangerous times in American history? Absolutely. But a real, small government, constitutional conservative? No way.

FOOL ME ONCE...

At this point some people may be thinking that I believe there's absolutely no difference between Republicans and Democrats.

No, not at all. There is absolutely a difference between the way Michele Bachmann, Jim DeMint, and Mike Lee view the world as opposed to the way Nancy

Pelosi, Debbie Wasserman Schultz, and Barbara Boxer view it. What I *am* saying, however, is that those on the right who stand for real conservatism are relentlessly attacked and marginalized and, therefore, never really even make it into the running for the West Wing. You only have to look back to how Sarah Palin was treated once she had a chance at making it to Washington to see how this works in practice.

I am also saying that even those who claim to carry the conservative torch can backfire once they are exposed to the glitter and glamour found along the Potomac. No candidate is a sure thing to be conservative or moral or honest or constitutionally focused just because they wear the label "Republican." Richard Nixon and Spiro Agnew weren't any of those things. Teddy Roosevelt was no small government conservative. George III interfered less in our educational system than George W did.

Courting Disaster

The rationale of those who tell us to ignore our gut and vote Republican usually boils down to something like this: *No matter how bad Republicans really are, conservatives have to vote Republican so that we can place conservative justices on the U.S. Supreme Court.* But guess what? Democrats are told the same thing! I'm not sure that either side is really all that happy with the results.

There have been plenty of Republican SCOTUS nominees who were so atrocious they didn't even get confirmed: Clement Haynsworth, G. Harold Carswell, Douglas H. Ginsburg, and Harriet Miers. And then there's the nightmare of GOP nominees who actually do get confirmed: Ike's disastrous choices of Earl Warren (a payback for help at the 1952 convention) and William J. Brennan (chosen solely to woo northeastern votes in Ike's 1956 reelection bid), Nixon's catastrophe of the cranky and unprofessional Harry Blackmun (he gave us *Roe v. Wade*), Gerald Ford's pick of John Paul Stevens, and George H. W. Bush's stupefying selection of the liberal nonentity David Souter.

With selections like that, who needs Democrats?

We're told that we have to forgive the GOP for the Nixons and McCains that it hands us from time to time; that we have to turn a blind eye to what's wrong with the Republican Party. The "smart people" in charge tell us that we just have to keep our mouths shut, turn off our brains, and rally around the elephant. Sorry if I'm not thrilled by the idea of standing in line to pull the lever for a party that couldn't seemingly care less about governing by the values it pretends to stand for.

There are also those who make a more fundamental argument about why none of this matters: old-fashioned conservatism's time has passed. I hear it all the time; people say that the modern GOP has to move on and adapt. They say it has to expand beyond its traditional base, be a big tent, be progressive—maybe not as progressive as Barack Obama, but smart and tough when it comes to using government as a tool to help people. If you want to win, they say, then you have to move toward the middle—offer a little something to everyone.

Be more like McCain and Romney and less like Palin and Santorum.

Nope, sorry, not buying it. Decades of evidence are in to show us exactly what we get when we compromise our values to win elections: more government, more spending, more taxes, more regulations, more bureaucracy, more interference by Washington in our daily lives. If that's what winning means then you'll excuse me if I'm not excited about continuing that trend. If turning my back on my principles is a prerequisite to winning elections, then, I hate to say it, but I'd rather lose. I'd rather not be in power than have to justify using that power to do things that I'm fundamentally opposed to.

But perhaps the biggest problem for those of us who care about the future of liberty is that most people don't understand that we are being offered false choices; that John McCain as the standard-bearer of the Republican Party in a presidential election is indicative of how the conservative/libertarian chair has been taken from the table.

The truth is that we are the mark—the sucker—in a national shell game. The ball—which represents real small government, constitutional candidates—seems like it's always there, ready to be discovered, when, in reality, the operator is palming it. It doesn't matter which shell you choose or how many times you play or how closely you pay attention—the ball will never be where you think it is.

You will lose every time.

That is why understanding history is so vital to understanding the current political playing field. What the establishment is doing today is what progressives originally did when they took the chair away from constitutionalists and said: Here's your choice: Theodore Roosevelt or Woodrow Wilson; John McCain or Barack Obama. Which is it going to be?

Sorry, that's not a fair choice—and so it's time that we call the shell game what it really is: a scam. I don't know about you, but I don't participate in scams, I expose them. And that's what we need to do now: expose the system as not just flawed, but rigged; expose the "two-party" system as a one-party monopoly; and, most important, show America that there is another choice. We just have to pull our chair back up to the table. 🐔

Beck Quotes a Socialist!

I'd rather vote for what I want and not get it, than vote for what I don't want and get it.

—EUGENE V. DEBS, SOCIALIST CANDIDATE FOR PRESIDENT IN 1900, 1904, 1908, 1912, AND 1920.

Chapter Two

THE LIBERTARIAN OPTION
ENDING THE PROGRESSIVE SCAM

> "Where **morality** is present, laws are unnecessary. Without morality, laws are **unenforceable.**"

—Anonymous

CAN ANYONE NAME a modern-day politician who has actually given us more freedom and less government, or who has made our lives happier and more prosperous?

Yeah, that's what I thought.

We all hear a lot of talk from politicians about their deep concern for the ideals of the Founders—even President Barack Obama pays lip service to streamlining and shrinking government—but when it comes to action, those who *actually* believe in the core principles of the Constitution always come away disappointed.

Always.

As journalists Nick Gillespie and Matt Welch explain in *The Declaration of Independents: How Libertarian Politics Can Fix What's Wrong with America*: "[W]e are held hostage to an eighteenth century system, dominated by two political parties whose ever-more-polarized rhetorical positions mask a mutual interest in maintaining a stranglehold on power." And the only way to end this stranglehold is to disconnect government from our morality, from our prosperity, and from our lives in general.

Most of you reading that last sentence are probably nodding your heads in agreement. It sounds great—maybe even easy; after all who *wants* government in their lives? The problem is that human nature is a very worthy adversary. To disconnect from government we also have to strip away all of the feel-good rhetoric and lofty promises made by politicians and instead demand real change and real accountability. We have to stop supporting the newest "savior" politician and stop hitching our futures to the best-run campaigns or the most charismatic establishment candidates because they are "most electable." We have to stop being distracted by the gotchas and rumormongering of the mass media, which cares more for its own ratings than the future of our country. But, most of all, we have to stop thinking about *politics* and start concentrating on *ideas*. Electoral maps, delegate counts, and brokered conventions may all be fun for political insiders on twenty-four-hour news channels to dissect and debate, but they do nothing to change our actual course as a country.

Lip Service

Speaker of the House Nancy Pelosi came up with an interesting angle to celebrate the passage of Obamacare. Democrats, she claimed, "honor the vows of our founders, who in the Declaration of Independence said that we are 'endowed by our Creator with certain unalienable rights, that among these are life, liberty and the pursuit of happiness.' This legislation will lead to healthier lives, more liberty to pursue hopes and dreams and happiness for the American people. This is an American proposal that honors the traditions of our country."

When the National Labor Relations Board decided that it could dictate by fiat where companies could move and produce their goods, nixing Boeing's decision to build its Dreamliner 787 fleet in union-free South Carolina, Senate Majority Leader Harry Reid claimed that the NLRB "acts as a check on employers and employees alike" and was consistent with the "spirit of checks and balances" the Founding Fathers had envisioned.

And Barack Obama, during his inaugural address, also invoked the Founders, saying that their "ideals still light the world, and we will not give them up for expedience's sake."

It all goes to prove that while it's very easy to quote the Founders' words, it's much harder to actually govern by them.

YOU JUST MIGHT BE A LIBERTARIAN

I'm proud to say that I'm a libertarian—and you might be one, too. In fact I believe that most Americans are libertarian at heart. Most Americans understand individual struggle and individual reward. Even though we are teaching them that everybody gets a trophy, most still understand that the government usually screws things up. But let's get away from the words and labels for a minute and instead talk about ideas.

When you boil it down, libertarians believe that government is best when it governs least. We don't believe government should try to make life more "fair" or force you to lose weight or "nudge" people into wanting to use solar panels. We believe that citizens should be making those decisions for themselves. In other words, a libertarian is an antiprogressive. Like the Founding Founders, libertarians are classical liberals, people who believe that limited government, the rule of law, individual liberty, freedom of religion (not *from* religion), speech, press, and assembly, and free markets represent the most moral kind of government.

Libertarians also understand a fundamental truth about this country: the most pressing problem we face isn't a lack of fairness, or private-sector corruption in the business world, or unfettered capitalism, or a diminishing work ethic, or China, or fill-in-any-other-issue-here. No, the most pressing problem we face is that the balance of power in this country has tilted toward the political class. Turning that around will require rethinking everything we've been conditioned to believe about how Washington and the two-party system work.

When most people think of a "libertarian" they think of . . . I don't know . . . a cult of hippies who barter their heroin for prostitutes. In other words, people tend to not take them very seriously. Part of the problem is that many Americans just don't understand what it means to be a libertarian. If they did, they might quickly come to the realization that they're actually one of them.

CNN has run a poll for nearly two decades asking Americans the same question: "Some people think the government is trying to do too many things that should be left to individuals and businesses. Others think that government should do more to solve our country's problems. Which comes closer to your own view?"

In 2011, a record number of people reported that they believed government is doing too much. That number has been tracking higher and higher—from around 40 percent in 2000 to over 60 percent today. Another recent poll, this one by Rasmussen, found that a majority of likely voters are wor-

Going in the Wrong Direction

According to the *Wall Street Journal*/Heritage Foundation "Freedom Index," the United States' economic freedom score dropped to 76.3, which puts us in tenth place worldwide. The score is 1.5 points lower than last year, "reflecting deteriorating scores for government spending, freedom from corruption, and investment freedom." In the Cato Institute's Economic Freedom of the World index the United States also placed tenth. Cato noted that the United States "has suffered one of the largest declines in economic freedom over the last 10 years." In other words, if you like small government and a free economy, we're going in the wrong direction.

WARNING: ADULT CONTENT

Yes, we all know that libertarians also understand a thing or two about irrelevance and unelectability. I'm sure you can visualize a typical libertarian presidential stump speech: "Ladies and gentlemen, if you elect me president I swear on my sacred honor to do absolutely nothing for my fellow Americans. I want you to do it all for yourselves!"

Of course, that's not the reality. While liberal policy works great for bumper stickers ("I Support Teachers, Not the Koch Brothers"), libertarian policy works great in the real world. Unfortunately, you can't put a libertarian's view of foreign policy or the government safety net on the back of your Prius—and that makes it a lot harder to break through the "gotcha!" world of sound bites and tweets that we now live in.

ried that the federal government is doing too much rather than too little when dealing with economic troubles.

Of course, simply having a desire for Washington to "do less" doesn't automatically make a person a libertarian. Far from it. But when you dig deeper into the polls, you realize that a majority of voters have, economically speaking, very strong libertarian beliefs. For example, among all voters in the Rasmussen poll, 77 percent say they want government to cut deficits. Seventy-one percent say they want government to cut spending. Fifty-nine percent say they want the government to cut taxes.

That's a nice start.

Though long-term polling shows that there was a temporary spike in the public's acceptance of government intervention after 9/11, concerns about the police state and antiterror measures have recently reached all-time highs. More voters seem to be turning toward the idea of individual freedom in almost every category they were asked about—from the police state to the government being the arbiters of morality.

But the most visible sign that libertarians are entering the mainstream isn't a poll, it's a person: Texas congressman Ron Paul, quite possibly the most popular libertarian politician in modern American history. Congressman Paul has raised millions of dollars and has deeper support from young, enthusiastic voters than perhaps anyone else in America. And, no offense, but I doubt we can attribute his success to his electric personality or political skills. No, it must be something else, like his ideas, his message, or his love for, and unwavering defense of, the Constitution.

Young people are getting excited about liberty. But I think it's even more than that. I think voters are also looking for something pure, something real, something consistent—something outside the partisanship we see every day.

And these voters are different from most. Blind allegiance to a party or the "presumptive nominee" is not part of their equation. For example, fewer than 50 percent of Republicans who voted for Ron Paul in the 2008 GOP primary ended up supporting John McCain in the general election. It turns out that Ron Paul is pretty popular among those who consider themselves independents—and that also happens to be a pretty good place to find libertarians.

Since the last presidential election more than 2.5 million voters have decided that neither the Democrats nor the Republicans are making much sense. I think the only thing shocking about that is that it took them this long to figure it out.

When *USA Today* analyzed the trend, it found that the number of registered Democrats had declined in 25 of the 28 states where voters have to register by party. Republicans lost voters in 21 states and the number of independents has increased in 18 states.

This trend becomes even clearer when you look at eight swing states where party registration is required. These are the battleground states that hold the key to elections—and they're changing. The *USA Today* report shows a decline of 800,000 in registration for the Democrats, while Republicans' dipped by 350,000. Voters who identify themselves as independents have increased by 325,000.

I'm giving you all of this data to make a simple point: the two parties just aren't doing the job—and people are finally beginning to realize that there's got to be another way.

There is.

Small-Tent Ideology

It's odd that people instantly acknowledge that the Democratic Party, for example, is a "big tent" under which people with views of all stripes can reside. You can have a "Blue Dog" right next to a radical—and no one blinks an eye. Same thing on the Republican side—Jim DeMint can share the stage with John McCain and everyone gets it. Unfortunately, that same perception doesn't seem to translate to libertarians.

The reality is that there are "small *l*" libertarians and "big *L*" libertarians. Small *l* libertarians believe in the basic tenets of liberty and try to make those ideas work within the framework of political reality. Let's make it easy and call them "commonsense libertarians." A "big *L*" Libertarian, on the other hand, is a purist who demands the most stringent interpretation of libertarian thought. They are, you might expect, what the media focuses on most—and they are also completely irrelevant when it comes to politics.

NO, YOU DON'T HAVE TO SMOKE CRACK TO BE LIBERTARIAN

I can hear it now: *That's all wonderful, Glenn, but I am definitely not a libertarian! Libertarians believe in legalizing crack and prostitution, they're isolationists and crackpots, and conspiracy theorists—not to mention antiwar activists and apologists for Islamic radicalism. Like you said, Ron Paul is a libertarian and he basically wants to shut down our army!*

The key to understanding the libertarian argument is to realize that most libertarians don't believe simply in personal freedom at all cost; they believe in personal freedom at a very significant cost: responsibility.

Take alcohol, for example. Libertarians would not be in favor of banning alcohol, of course, but just because they don't want to ban it does not mean they think that drink-

Agree to Disagree

Republicans Jim DeMint and Marco Rubio disagree on how the United States should approach immigration policy, but no one doubts that they are both "conservatives." Conservatives argue about gay marriage, economic policy, defense spending, and just about everything else under the sun. We've all seen how contentious the Republican primaries can be (and have listened to the media tell us how the Republican Party is fighting itself to the death). If there are pro-choice Republicans and pro-life Democrats, why can't there be libertarians who disagree on some policies but agree to concentrate on the fundamental issues that actually matter?

ing every night is a great idea. Put it this way: there are few things I love more than freedom of speech, but that doesn't mean I love everything (or *anything*, actually) that someone like Van Jones has to say. Just because you want something to be legal does not mean you have to personally embrace it.

Most people hear this argument and immediately go to the worst possible examples, like black tar heroin or underage prostitution. That's because we've all been conditioned by the media and the two-party establishment to think that way. When you hear "Republican" you don't immediately think of "banning abortions even in the case of incest." While that is a view that *some* Republicans may have, it is neither prevalent enough, nor important enough, to be allowed to define the entire party. Yet we allow that to happen with libertarians.

So, let's get this out of the way right up front: Yes, some libertarians want to legalize drugs. Within that group some want to legalize every drug that man can create. Others would prefer to focus on a narrower list. But the truth is that none of that matters because legalizing drugs is not an important part of the libertarian agenda. In my mind, it's not even a small part of the agenda. It's irrelevant, inconsequential—a diversion.

Of course, legalizing drugs gets a lot of attention because it makes for great sound bites and helps to make the entire party look insane—but it's not at all relevant to the larger cause of freedom. Deciding you don't want to be a libertarian because some sliver of the party wants to be able to smoke weed is like deciding that you don't want to be a Republican because some sliver of the party wants to outlaw alcohol. Who cares? Neither has any relevance to the future of America and, by the way, neither is going to happen.

Regardless of where you stand, legalization of fill-in-your-vice-here is not anything that we should be debating. It not only does a disservice to the country, but it also helps continue the false media narrative that has been built about libertarians over the years. Surely we have more vital things to talk about, anyway. Things we can agree on. We have watched so many liberties evaporate over the last few decades that it's almost embarrassing to hear people give any time to the "should we legalize heroin?" nonexistent debate.

What we *should* be giving time to are issues like the government takeover of health care, restoring religious and market freedoms, reducing regulations that prevent people from starting and growing businesses, getting monetary policy under control, and cutting the growth of the welfare state.

We should also be explaining to Americans that libertarians offer the only real alternative to a system that has been completely infected by progressivism. Democrats offer virtually no policy idea that doesn't expand the welfare state or the regulatory burden or give Washington more control over our everyday lives. Republicans usually aren't far behind.

When Newt Gingrich was asked about Wisconsin congressman Paul Ryan's efforts to reform entitlement programs, he didn't say it was "about time we got rid of socialistic programs and replaced them with market-based alternatives." Instead he attacked them as "right-wing social engineering." John McCain has cosponsored bills in support of "cap-and-trade" and against gun rights. Plenty of Republicans have supported bailouts and higher taxes and hordes of new regulations—the very things that used to be supported only by Democrats.

All of this has provided libertarians with an opportunity to cut through the nonsense and take their message directly to the people. The drug "debate" is nothing but a red herring; let's not get distracted.

YOU DON'T HAVE TO BLAME AMERICA TO BE A LIBERTARIAN

I've already mentioned how popular Ron Paul is, but have I mentioned what a lost opportunity Ron Paul is for the libertarian cause?

First, the good: If I were president, the first thing I would do is name Congressman Paul as

Where'd You Put My Drugs?

A recent Gallup poll asked Americans about the things they believed were important for the president and Congress to deal with in the next year. Here are the issues that people believe are "Very" or "Extremely" important:

The economy—93 percent, Unemployment—89 percent, Federal budget deficit—84 percent, Corruption in government—83 percent, Education—79 percent, Health care—78 percent, Terrorism—76 percent, Social Security—78 percent, Medicare—71 percent, Situation in Afghanistan—71 percent, Gas and home heating prices—68 percent, Illegal immigration—64 percent, Taxes—66 percent, Situation in Iraq—62 percent, Environment—59 percent.

You'll notice that there is no item called "crack consumption" or "heroin needle exchange program" that makes it into the top 15. My guess is that they probably don't make it into the top 100, either.

The Two-Party Train

Just in case you're the kind of person who needs actual data before you'll believe an argument, here are some statistics from the Heritage Foundation's 2012 Index of Government Dependence. If this doesn't prove that the two parties are taking us to the same place at different speeds, I don't know what does. Here are some of the lowlights:

- The number of people dependent on some federal government programs grew by 7.5 percent in two years under the Obama administration. That's the largest increase since the Carter administration.
- 67.3 million Americans rely on some federal program.
- Spending on dependency programs now eats up more than 70 percent of the federal budget.
- In 2009, 49.5 percent of Americans paid no federal income taxes, up from 14.8 percent as recently as 1984.
- 34.8 million Americans were not represented on a federal taxable income return in 1984. Today that figure is 151.7 million.

my Treasury secretary. For me, he's the only candidate who's run for president in recent years who is completely serious about slashing spending, reducing the size and role of government, and taking on the Federal Reserve.

And, man, would it be a fun ride. A Beck administration would lean heavily on Ron Paul to make numerous decisions regarding the economy—and as a bonus, Secretary Paul would drive everyone else nuts. As you can imagine, the Fed would be audited or shut down entirely on day one. Departments would be slashed. The establishment would be in hysterics. Good times.

But, as much as I absolutely love Ron Paul's views on economic policy, I can't stand his positions on foreign affairs. In fact, I believe most of what he proposes is downright dangerous—and, more important, it is not reflective of how most libertarians think. And for commonsense libertarians that should be pretty exciting: if you can combine real libertarian thought with smart and precise foreign policy, you'd have a candidate who might actually have a chance at the Oval Office.

Two weeks after 9/11, while Americans were still grappling with grief in the wake of the worst attack on U.S. soil in our history, Ron Paul was on the floor of the U.S. House of Representatives blaming the United States for terrorism. Paul claimed that the Muslim world had seen our defense of Kuwait during the First Gulf War "as an invasion and domination by a foreign enemy which inspires radicalism" and that terrorists "react as some Americans might react" if a foreign country had invaded them.

And his mind didn't change much with the passage of time. Six years later he was at a presidential debate when this exchange occurred:

PAUL: Have you ever read the reasons they attacked us? They attack us because we've been over there; we've been bombing Iraq for ten years.

Q: Are you suggesting we invited the 9/11 attack?

PAUL: I'm suggesting that we listen to the people who attacked us and the reason they did it. . . . If we think that we can do what we want around the world and not incite hatred, then we have a problem. They don't come here to attack us because we're rich and we're free. They come and they attack us because we're over there.

That's obviously a ridiculous stance, but since I'd prefer not to get ten thousand emails from Ron Paul supporters claiming that I'm trashing their guy (I'm not; I'm just trying to illustrate the difference between him and true, small-*l* libertarianism), I want to be precise about his foreign policy. Paul describes himself as a noninterventionist, not an isolationist. In an interview with CNN's Wolf Blitzer, he explained: "An isolationist is a protectionist that builds walls around the country. They don't like to trade. They don't like to travel about the world. And they like to put sanctions on different countries. . . . Nonintervention is quite a bit different. It's what the Founders advised to get along with people, trade with people, and to have—practice diplomacy, rather than getting—having this militancy of telling people what to do and how to run the world, and building walls around our own country."

It's a great-sounding argument and I understand where it comes from; we're as war-weary as we are broke. If we don't pull our military back, the argument goes, there will be no country left to defend because we'll collapse under the weight of our own debt. This is the perfect storm that I've been talking about for almost a decade now and, as a result, there are no good choices left.

> **Google It**
>
> **I**'ll have to mobilize my research team, but I'm pretty sure that Islamic radicals were targeting Americans long before we showed up in Iraq. The Islamists' ransacking our embassy in Tehran in 1979 comes to mind, as does the 1983 truck bomb attack on the American barracks in Beirut in which 241 American soldiers were murdered. It was the deadliest single-day death toll for the United States Marine Corps since Iwo Jima.

But you have to look at this from another angle. We can survive even the worst economic depression if we strengthen people and communities. But we cannot survive being blindsided by a large-scale attack from Islamic extremists. That is a clear and present danger, an existential threat to our country. So you have to make a decision: where do you focus? You can't do it all. Is the Fed more dangerous than Islamist extremism? Maybe in the long term—they both take away from our freedom—but only one has the chance of taking us down overnight.

I don't want to be the "policeman of the world" any more than Ron Paul does, but that doesn't mean we can simply shut our eyes and pretend that the world no longer has any evil in it. We can't fall into the same trap that our politicians so often do and react so far in the opposite direction that we make America less safe and less able to defend herself. The world may have changed, but not the fact that there are many people who would like nothing more than for this country to no longer exist.

I'm only bringing up Ron Paul's foreign policy to point out that this view is a recurring theme with *him*, not necessarily with libertarianism. There is nothing inherently libertarian about not being willing to fight for freedom or protection, and there is certainly nothing libertarian about blaming America for violence perpetrated by others. There is no reason that libertarians can't make the argument that the United States has both a moral right and a national obligation to defend itself—and the liberty of its citizens—from threats that develop around the world.

Yet most of the media, and many voters, are under the impression that Ron Paul's brand of libertarian isolationism is the position that all libertarians hold—as though Paul is somehow the national spokesperson for the cause.

Our Founders—who wrote the very Constitution that Paul says he gets mandates from—were keenly aware that they lived in a growing, interconnected world. One of the intellectual heroes of the Revolutionary War, Thomas Paine—a pretty libertarian guy by any standard—once wrote that "the cause of America is in a great measure the cause of all mankind." We can't just ignore the events shaping the world, even if they are happening in another part of it.

In some ways it's frustrating that we still have to have this conversation. Yes, I know that every situation is unique, but what would this world look like if we had

Following the Founders

The Founders advised us to trade and get along with other nations—and, for the most part, we do. Trade is one of the cornerstones of a healthy, free society. But they never advised us to be suckers. How would they have handled the idea that a country thousands of miles away could build a weapon that could be used against American citizens? How would they have approached a scenario in which sea routes that make "free trade" possible were threatened by a navy controlled by radicals?

Actually, we already to know the answer to that last question. In the early nineteenth century President Thomas Jefferson sent navy ships to the Barbary states of northern Africa to fight Muslim pirates who were blackmailing and terrorizing Americans. He realized that to protect American interests we had to take the fight to the enemy. Clearly, that concept of intervention was not a foreign idea to our Founders.

never intervened in World War II? The Jews left in Europe would have been completely destroyed and perhaps millions of Chinese and Slavs (and many others nationalities) would have been massacred and enslaved. Sooner or later we would have had to confront Hitler or else we'd succumb to him ourselves. And sometimes sooner is better; sometimes it's true that an ounce of prevention (although, in the case of war, it's a lot more than an ounce) is worth a pound of cure.

If you reread Ron Paul's description of his own foreign policy, you'll notice one phrase that really sticks out: "practice diplomacy." You'll be hard-pressed to find anyone who disagrees, but you'll also be hard-pressed to find anyone who doesn't think that's what America does. Even Ron Paul must understand that sometimes, however, it simply doesn't work. Ask Hitler. Ask bin Laden. Ask Saddam. We've been working diplomatically with the U.N. and others to promote change in Iran and North Korea for how long now? If we, as a nation, don't defend the welfare and lives of our citizens, there will be no freedom to protect.

And it's not like the U.S. just started protecting its interests abroad when George W. Bush was elected; we've been doing it from the beginning. Almost immediately after our independence we found ourselves in an undeclared quasi-war when the French began terrorizing our ships and trade routes. And it was Founding Fathers like Thomas Jefferson and James Madison—not exactly a cabal of neoconservatives, I might add—who sent American marines overseas to protect our interest. Is Paul suggesting that those guys weren't libertarian enough?

I agree that America should not be the world's babysitter. I agree that we should not be in a war without declaring it. I agree that we should not have military bases all over the world (over 650 at last count). I agree that we should take a close look at our foreign aid every year. So, yes, there must be commonsense limits to our national defense, but libertarians do not need to be isolationists.

CAN'T WE ALL JUST GET ALONG?

When the Tea Party movement was getting off the ground, David Kirby, a policy analyst at the libertarian Cato Institute, became somewhat skeptical about the mainstream media's portrayal of these activists. Were they really a bunch of angry, far right-wing, bloodthirsty racists? Shockingly, no. "Many political scientists and political pundits who have not examined the data," Kirby wrote, "wrongly conclude the Tea Party is the GOP's base of extreme fiscal and social conservatives."

Kirby spoke with Tea Party supporters at the Virginia Tea Party Convention in 2010 and published his results on Politico.com. Instead of raging hatemongers, Kirby found a conservative move toward more pure libertarian ideas—especially regarding free markets.

Most legitimate national surveys have confirmed that result, finding that the Tea Party is libertarian leaning, but socially conservative. The bone of contention between libertarians and conservatives, in general, has always been whether or not government should be promoting traditional values in society.

One of the most misunderstood aspects of libertarianism is that people confuse policy and morality. Government can't make you moral. It can't make you thin. It certainly can't make you sober.

Remember, the Founders believed that there was a major difference between "liberty" and "license." Friedrich von Hayek put it best when he explained, "Liberty not only means that the individual has both the opportunity and the burden of choice; it also means that he must bear the consequences of his actions. . . . Liberty and responsibility are inseparable."

In contrast, "license" is having liberty without any regard for rules of personal conduct or morality. There is a big difference. Liberty means recognizing the consequences of actions. License, as the most famous example goes, means yelling fire in a crowded movie theater. Libertarians believe in liberty, not license.

Ronald Reagan, the most revered modern conservative politician, said, "If you analyze it, I believe the very heart and soul of conservatism is *libertarianism*. . . . The basis of conservatism is a desire for less government interference or less centralized authority or more individual freedom and this is a pretty general description also of what libertarianism is."

William F. Buckley Jr., one of the founders of the modern conservative movement and the founder of *National Review*, referred to himself as a "libertarian journalist." Barry Goldwater, the godfather of political conservatism, was essentially a libertarian and, still today, remains a political hero to many modern-day libertarians. Yet all of these people, and many others like them, were stalwart social conservatives when it came to traditional values.

The initial success of the Tea Party bodes well for the future of the movement, as does the historic 2010 congressional victories by Republicans. That was, without a doubt, the most libertarian class of elected officials in history. Congressmen like Rand Paul and Mike Lee are libertarians who understand that, without the strong moral underpinnings of faith, freedom can't work.

> **"** I believe the very **heart** and **soul** of **conservatism** is **libertarianism**. **"**

There is another area of overlap between conservatives and libertarians as well: conservatives who want to preserve traditional values understand that dependency is not helpful to the cause. Being self-sufficient is the best antidote to moral decay. Senator Jim DeMint, one of the leading conservative voices in the Republican Party, has been arguing that voters need to take a more libertarian view of the world. When asked about how cultural conservatives could get along with libertarians he explained:

I think the new debate in the Republican Party needs to be between conservatives and libertarians. We have a common foundation of individual liberty and constitutionally limited government. We can rationally debate some of the things we disagree on. Because I don't think the government should impose my morals or anyone else's on someone else. At the same time, I don't want the government purging morals and religious values from our society. We can find a balance there.

He's absolutely right—but not only *can* we find a balance there, we *must* find one. And it shouldn't be that difficult: libertarians agree that government intrusion is bad for the family and that government doesn't strengthen families or our belief in God. For example, since the "War on Poverty" started we not only have more poverty; we also have destroyed the educational system and we're breaking apart families—all because of bad government policy. You know what the best way for a kid to escape poverty is? Ben Franklin nailed it: to not make them "easy" in it, to show them by example that there is a better way but that it will take hard work and per-

Stand Up for Privacy

To understand just how far libertarians have come *within* the Republican Party, let's look at the Patriot Act. For years, Republicans were champions of the antiterrorism legislation on the grounds that it made America more secure.

But, over time, things have changed, due in no small part to libertarian-minded politicians like Senator Rand Paul and Mike Lee, who are not afraid to question even those policies that their base finds acceptable. Senator Lee, for example, said:

The concept that regardless of how passionately we might feel about the need for certain government intervention, we can't ever allow government to be operating completely unfettered. . . . We voted against it because we love America, because we believe in constitutional limited government, because we want to make it better, we want to make this something that can, at the same time, protect Americans but without needlessly trampling on privacy interests, including many of those privacy interests protected by the Fourth Amendment.

Whether you support the Patriot Act or not, this kind of view is healthy for America and has been missing for a while since neither party has made personal liberty and privacy a priority.

sonal sacrifice. Libertarians, like conservatives, believe that prosperity fosters more self-reliance, stronger families, and more moral societies.

Overall, there is much more that binds libertarians and conservatives together than what keeps them apart. With that in mind, I want to quickly go through a few issues—some minor, some major—and dispel some of the myths about what being a libertarian means you're supposed to believe.

YOU CAN LOVE ISRAEL AND BE A LIBERTARIAN

Many libertarian purists oppose providing any and all foreign aid. I agree that it's probably time we revisited the topic. Who are we giving aid to and why? But what makes me suspicious of too many other "libertarians" is that they seem to direct most of their criticism at one nation: Israel. Why would we be so overly concerned with the aid we send to the one nation that embraces the tenets of liberty and has been our most reliable ally?

Many libertarians falsely view Israel as the aggressor in the Middle East and have succumbed to the liberal inclination to always believe that the less powerful are victims—as if being less powerful makes you right. Some libertarians falsely believe that if the United States wasn't in the Middle East then Israel would be more likely to deal with Arab nations themselves and peace would be within reach.

History tells us a different story, though. It tells us that Israel has tried to form healthy diplomatic relationships with all of its enemies and, with few exceptions, has been rebuffed. But what is most incredible is that a philosophy that claims to honor freedom would take the side of groups and nations that deny their citizens that basic right.

YOU DON'T HAVE TO BELIEVE IN THE GOLD STANDARD TO BE A LIBERTARIAN

President Richard Nixon took America completely off the gold standard over forty years ago. From that point on, America would no longer use "hard money," a fact that has likely unleashed government spending and helped usher our national debt to unprecedented levels. Since 1971, the total amount of U.S. public debt held in the United States has risen over 500 percent (after adjusting for inflation).

But a return to the gold standard—as some libertarians like to promote—is a pipe dream. We seem to forget that even when we had the gold standard, the United States went though a serious depression and many recessions, along with years of deflation. Economic growth seemed to explode after we began turning away from gold.

Then there's the small matter of gold being a precious metal and a limited resource. By my quick math, we would have to invade every county in the world and steal all their gold just to pay off our national debt.

What people who like the gold standard idea are reacting to is out-of-control government spending. They figure that if you tie politicians' hands by not allowing us to print and inflate our money then fiscal sanity will follow. But there are other ways to do that, policies that would be effective and, just as important, could actually pass through Congress. I'm talking about things like a balanced budget amendment with future spending caps, term limits, and the like. (I covered these issues in depth in my book *Broke*.) These are not new ideas but they are absolutely things that both conservatives and libertarians should be able to embrace.

YOU DON'T HAVE TO BELIEVE IN OPEN BORDERS TO BE A LIBERTARIAN

Many libertarians believe in open borders. Not just relaxed immigration laws, but lawlessness. Sorry, that's not going to work for me. I can understand the emotional arguments, the "free trade" arguments, etc.—but there is nothing libertarian about rewarding those who break the law.

Milton Friedman, the great libertarian economist, once observed that America "cannot simultaneously have free immigration and a welfare state." I'm not sure why more libertarians don't understand this concept, especially since it's already happening. Allowing foreigners to take advantage of a system in which nearly half of Americans don't pay any federal income tax is a libertarian nightmare.

BEING A LIBERTARIAN DOESN'T MAKE YOU SELFISH

One of the most consistent attacks on libertarians is that they are somehow selfish and hateful. For example, Van Jones, the former Obama administration green jobs czar recently said that libertarians "hate the people, the brown folk, the gays, the lesbians, the people with piercings . . ."

Progressives aren't the only ones who label libertarians that way. Conservative *Washington Post* columnist and former George W. Bush chief speechwriter Michael Gerson once wrote that libertarians promote "a freedom indistinguishable from selfishness." Economist Jeffrey Sachs wrote, "Libertarians hold that individual liberty should never be sacrificed in the pursuit of other values or causes. Compassion, justice, civic responsibility, honesty, decency, humility, respect, and even survival of the poor, weak, and vulnerable—all are to take a back seat."

This argument is so stupid that it's actually laughable. It's like calling someone you disagree with a racist, sexist, or Islamophobe. I like to call it the "EZ Chair" argument because these people are so lazy that they resort to the most stereotypical line of attack possible.

It's really ironic that those who support government taking the hard-earned money of private individuals—money that could go toward creating jobs, giving to charity, and sending children to school—and throwing it into one wasteful project after the next are the ones out there calling *other* people selfish.

It is common for the left, and even many Republicans, to confuse charity and coercion. It's why politicians call the money they steal from taxpayers and spend "investments." A libertarian believes in social cooperation, not social coercion. A libertarian believes in real charity rather than coercion that funnels their money to wherever government thinks it's best served.

In his book *Who Really Cares? The Surprising Truth About Compassionate Conservatism*, Arthur Brooks finds strong evidence that charitable giving is influenced by "strong families, church attendance, earned income (as opposed to state-subsidized income), and the belief that individuals, not government, offer the best solution to social ills—all of these factors determine how likely one is to give."

It turns out that those who believe in classical liberalism tend to give a lot more. Brooks found that "conservative" house-

Now in the EZ Chair: Jeffrey Sachs

Here's how the EZ Chair argument might work in reverse: Jeffrey Sachs is an elite of the highest order, a guy who sits in the cozy confines of his Columbia University office (where he attempts to "solve" man-made global warming) without having any clue how the real world works. He's spent so much time collecting degrees and being part of a university faculty that the idea that people might actually want to work for a living probably makes him queasy. He's probably written a bunch of scholarly books with high-minded titles implying how smart he is (like "The End of Poverty") and I bet he's so "accomplished" that he has three versions of his biography listed on his website: short, medium, and long so that you can select which version you want by how much time you have to read about how perfect he is.

holds gave an average of 30 percent more money to charity than liberal house-holds—even though liberals make approximately 6 percent more. How's that for "selfish"?

Those who believe that the government, or some federal program, can ever take the place of individual compassion are clearly short on another ingredient that's imperative for success: intelligence.

THE PLAN

Libertarians are not going to be able to change minds overnight. In fact, that's part of the problem: we want Americans to move much faster than they ever will. We don't understand how people could know so little about history that they're falling for the same tricks all over again. We can't fathom how people *willingly* hand over their rights and power to a heartless, soulless, brainless entity.

But libertarians have to understand that there is no quick-fix, Jiffy Lube, thirty-minute solution. The *only* strategy that has any chance to succeed is to dismantle and reverse-engineer the entire system, brick by brick, until it's back down to its foundation. Only then can it be built back up the right way. Think about what would happen if you tried to just instantaneously legalize drugs or rip away programs or entitlements that people have been dependent on for generations. Riots if we're lucky, revolution if we're not. Either way, libertarian policy would not be high on the agenda at that point.

For decades Americans have been raised to believe that entitlement programs are their God-given right. The only way to overcome that is to teach principles, morals, ethics, and personal responsibility again. That takes time, and I know we're running out of it, but there's no other choice—the system has been rotted to the core over the past hundred years. We have to restore it piece by piece, but we first have to make sure that people and families and communities are strong enough to handle it.

About five years ago I was going to write a book called *The One-Hundred-Year Plan*, about this exact topic. Nobody wanted it. *Oh, that's too long of a time,* they told me. *No one wants to read about a hundred-year plan; we'll all be dead by then! Can't you give us something that will work by the next election?*

No! Don't you see that's exactly how we got here and why things only keep getting worse? A long time ago a group of people got together and thought outside of the box to develop a hundred-year plan that would make the Constitution essentially irrelevant. They knew they would never see the results in their lifetimes, but that was okay; they just wanted to plant the seeds.

Those are the people that libertarians must now become. We've got to think like the Chinese or early-twentieth-century American Progressives, not like political tacticians, campaign managers, or cable news executives who live and die by every daily poll, delegate count, or Nielsen rating.

None of this will be easy. In fact, it may not even be possible—a hundred years of decay is a lot to overcome. But we've got to try.

You are holding the first step in your hands right now. It's the truth. About America, about the threats we face, and about those who are working hard every day to take away our exceptionalism. Only when people truly understand what progressivism has brought us—an educational system that churns out kids who can't think for themselves, a government that won't face the truth about Islamists' agenda for the world, and a media that is complicit in it all—will they be willing to join the fight.

Chapter Three

GEORGE SOROS
THE PUPPET MASTER
PULLS ALL THE STRINGS

"Everybody says that I have a lot of power. But what does that power consist of? . . . Can I influence governments? I am beginning to be able to. . . ."

—George Soros, 1995

SOME PEOPLE seem like they were born to play puppet master. (I believe it was the profound philosophers Tears for Fears who said "everybody wants to rule the world.") Of course, not everybody has the resources to actually pull it off. Not everybody wants to force others to live the way they think is best. Not everyone wants to line their pockets while they manipulate society for their own benefit.

The fact that we all think our ideas are the best ones makes sense. If you thought something else would work better, you'd possibly change your mind. That's why I believe that one of the most impressive feats accomplished by the founders of this country was to recognize their own imperfection. They created the most brilliant foundation for a country in world history—yet they were smart enough to realize that they might not have thought of everything.

They had a free ride to grab as much power as they wanted in a brand-new country where they were heroes. Yet they spent all of their time devising ways to prevent anyone—including themselves—from ever claiming too much of it. They recognized that only God could grant rights that were self-evident. The federal government would protect those rights, and cede the rest to the states. If something in the Constitution needed to be tweaked, there was the constitutional-amendment process.

All of this resulted in a framework that has been able to handle more than two hundred years of a burgeoning nation's experimental existence, simply and effectively. It is now the globe's longest-lasting constitution.

Our Constitution declares that sovereignty shall rest in the people.

Our Declaration proclaims that "all men are created equal."

I've read both of those documents many times and nowhere in them can I find anything that acts to qualify the above two tenets of society. No "but's," no "except for's," no "unless they really want to's." That's why it's surprising to see that some people have determined that they are above the law; that their money and influence should somehow afford them more rights, powers, and influence than others.

One of those people is a billionaire named George Soros.

BIRTH OF A BILLIONAIRE

George Soros was born to Tividar and Erzebat Schwartz, nonpracticing Jews, in Budapest, Hungary, on August 12, 1930. According to Soros, his mother was "quite anti-Semitic, and ashamed of being Jewish." Soros's father was an attorney by profession, but his main focus seemed to be the promotion of Esperanto, a "universal" (aka "completely made up") language created during the 1880s. Proponents believed that if the world would share one language, we could eventually achieve one world government and get rid of this silly idea of national sovereignty.

In 1936, two years after Hitler came to power and the attacks on Jews intensified, Soros's father decided to sever the family's Jewish roots altogether and change his surname to Soros, a future-tense Esperanto verb meaning "will soar."

Lessons in Esperanto

Marioneto majstro—(n) puppet master

When the Nazis occupied Budapest in 1944, Soros's father purchased forged papers identifying the family as Christians and bribed a fascist Hungarian government official named Baumbach to claim George as his Christian godson. Baumbach took the young Soros, then fourteen, on at least one of his trips to take the possessions of a Jewish family that had been forced to leave the country.

In December 1998, Soros appeared in a segment of CBS's *60 Minutes* and was asked by Steve Kroft about that experience:

KROFT: I mean, that's—that sounds like an experience that would send lots of people to the psychiatric couch for many, many years. Was it difficult?

SOROS: Not—not at all. Not at all. Maybe as a child you don't—you don't see the connection. But it was—it created no—no problem at all.

KROFT: No feeling of guilt?

SOROS: No.

KROFT: For example that "I'm Jewish and here I am, watching these people go. I could just as easily be there. I should be there." None of that?

SOROS: [W]ell, actually, in a funny way, it's just like in markets—that if I weren't there—of course, I wasn't doing it, but somebody else would—would—would be taking it away anyhow. And it was the—whether I was there or not, I was only a spectator, the property was being taken away. So the—I had no role in taking away that property. So I had no sense of guilt.

In 2000 Soros wrote a foreword to a book by his father, which had originally been published decades earlier. In it, Soros recalled the Nazi occupation of Hungary and described his life during that time in a way that has come across as odd to many people. "It is a sacrilegious thing to say," he wrote, "but these ten months were the happiest times of my life. . . . We were pursued by evil forces and we were clearly on the side of the angels because we were unjustly persecuted; moreover, we were trying not only to save ourselves but also to save others."

Soros had made very similar comments a couple of years earlier in the *60 Minutes* segment:

It was, actually, probably the happiest year of my life. For me, it was a very positive experience. It's a strange thing because you see incredible suffering around you and the fact you are in considerable danger yourself. But you're fourteen years old and you don't believe that it can actually touch you. You have a belief in yourself. You have a belief in your father. It's a very happy-making, exhilarating experience.

WARNING: **ADULT CONTENT**

Since this story doesn't lend itself well to a sound bite, let me be clear: No one is trying to make the case that a fourteen-year-old child was evil for trying to survive. The point is that Soros endured horrors in his childhood that most people can't even fathom. These are events that would change the life of anyone who experienced them. How Soros has dealt with these events, in a way that he himself admits most see as "sacrilegious" and "strange," is an undeniably important window into his thought process.

When the communists swallowed Hungary in 1947, the Soros family relocated to England, where George attended the London School of Economics. In his third year there, he selected the Viennese philosopher Professor Karl Popper as his "tutor."

Soros would later adopt Popper's idea of an "Open Society" as a vision of a future governed by universal standards and relativist principles, as opposed to "closed" societies that were based on absolute or "self-evident" truths. The one part of Popper's philosophy that Soros found objectionable later in life? His admiration for the United States. Popper said his first trip to America "tore me forever out of a depression caused by the overwhelming influence of Marxism in postwar Europe." He went back twenty-five times, gushing "each time I have been more deeply impressed."

Soros found that optimism to be fleeting:

> *Who would have thought sixty years ago, when Karl Popper wrote* Open Society and Its Enemies, *that the United States itself could pose a threat to open society? Yet, this is what is happening, both internally and externally.*

What the Constitution Ought to Be

In his 2003 book, *The Bubble of American Supremacy*, Soros wrote that the principles of America's Declaration of Independence "are not self-evident truths but arrangements necessitated by our inherently imperfect understanding." In 2010, the Open Society Institute, which Soros founded, was one of the principal sponsors of a conference on "The Constitution in 2020," the purpose of which was to produce "a progressive vision of what the Constitution ought to be." He also described the "bubble of American supremacy" as the greatest threat to world peace.

In 1956, Soros moved to New York City. At the time, he admits, he "did not particularly care for the United States. . . . [They] were, well, commercial, crass, and so on." He had devised a "five-year plan" to save half a million dollars and then return to Europe. Somewhere along the way that plan evidently changed and Soros instead became a citizen. Five hundred grand, after all, was thinking small, and George Soros always thinks big.

He eventually found himself as a portfolio manager at the investment bank Arnhold and S. Bleichroeder and established the "Double Eagle Fund" with $4 million in capital, including $250,000 of his own money. Four years later, the Double Eagle Fund changed its name to the "Soros Fund." By 1985, the fund had again been renamed, this time to the "Quantum Fund." It was worth more than $1 billion.

"[A] global open society requires affirmative action on a global scale."

To turn $4 million into $1 billion, you have to be smart, and Soros has never had trouble being amazed by his own brilliance. When an interviewer once told him, "There are some people who believe it's possible to be too smart in this business and that the smartest people are rarely the most successful investors," Soros responded simply: "I hope you are wrong."

Soros built his fortune not only with smarts, but with an ethical relationship with the rest of humanity that some would call . . . disconnected. Others, like me, for instance, would call it borderline *malbonega* (that's Esperanto for "evil").

Soros was a speculator who, by his own account, was not constrained by scruples. One of his more notorious exploits was his short-selling of the British pound, forcing a devaluation of the British currency. For those of you who aren't glued to CNBC, that basically meant that Soros was rooting for the British currency to take a nosedive. He was right, and he pocketed a billion dollars off the trade.

"When I sold sterling short in 1992," he wrote in his book *The Crisis of Global Capitalism: The Open Society Endangered*, "the Bank of England was on the other side of my transactions and I was taking money out of the pockets of British taxpayers. But if I had tried to take the social consequences into account, it would have thrown off my risk/reward calculation, and my chances of being successful would have been reduced."

It's like a truck driver saying, "Sure, I felt the bumps. But if I stopped to think about the fact that each bump was a human being that I was running over, I would have never made the delivery on time."

Soros would argue that there is no morality necessary in financial markets because markets themselves are amoral. The British pound, for example, would've been devalued anyway—his trade only sped that process up. Or, as the truck driver would say, "Those people would have eventually died at some point anyway."

It's twisted logic, and it's not necessarily been left in his past. In 2010, as the euro was under immense pressure due to the financial crises in countries like Greece, Ireland, and

Lessons in Esperanto

Man egema—(*adj*) Having an intense and selfish desire for something, especially wealth or power. Greedy.

The Ultimate Insider

Markets might not have morals, but they do have rules. In 2005, Soros was fined $2.9 million after a French court convicted him of insider trading in connection with a takeover bid for the bank Société Générale.

Portugal, a British newspaper reported that "[a] secretive group of Wall Street hedge fund bosses are said to be behind a plot to cash in on the decline of the euro. Representatives of George Soros's investment business were among an all-star line up of Wall Street investors at an 'ideas dinner' at a private townhouse in Manhattan, according to reports."

I guess this proves that playing with economies, and the lives of the taxpayers who participate in them, never gets dull—no matter how much money you have.

IT'S NOT ABOUT THE MONEY

Regardless of morals, Soros was not content with simply accumulating wealth. He had a far more grandiose ambition: to change the world. To achieve this goal he began investing his wealth in tax-exempt organizations whose purpose was not to produce products for people's consumption, but to produce propaganda for their minds.

These investments began in earnest in 1984 with the creation of the first of his "Open Society Foundations" in Hungary. That was followed in the ensuing years by a series of foundations that he established throughout Eastern Europe and Central Asia. In 1993, Soros established the flagship of his network, the New York–based Open Society Institute (OSI). The stated mission of these foundations was "to build vibrant and tolerant democracies whose governments are accountable to its citizens," a slogan as believable as a rat-infested diner claiming it serves the "World's Best Coffee."

Soros appointed Aryeh Neier as director of both the Open Society Institute and the entire global network of Soros foundations. Neier, a former sixties radical, spent fifteen years as an operative of the ACLU, including eight years as its national executive director. Neier was also the founder and executive director of Human Rights Watch, a group famous for absurdly making the United States and Israel the chief targets of its "human rights" protests.

Soros claims that he has donated over $7 billion to his Open Society organizations and he has successfully organized other billionaires to follow his example. Among those that have received his money:

Franchise Opportunities Available

Today, the Open Society Foundations funded by Soros and run by Neier are active in more than seventy countries around the world and his Open Society Institute is a $1.9 billion operation.

- Organizations that oppose America's post-9/11 national security measures, such as the ACLU and the Bill of Rights Defense Committee, which has persuaded the governments of more than four hundred American cities to pledge noncompliance with the Patriot Act;
- The Center for Constitutional Rights, founded by four longtime supporters of communist causes, which has condemned the "immigration sweeps, ghost detentions, extraordinary rendition, and every other illegal program the government has devised" in response to "the so-called War on Terror";
- Organizations that promote "open borders" and full citizenship rights for illegal aliens such as the American Immigration Council and the Immigrant Legal Resource Center, which tries to shield illegal aliens from the law;
- Organizations such as the Sentencing Project, which attacks the American prison system as racist;
- The Gamaliel Foundation and the Midwest Academy, whose radical instructors train political organizers, Barack Obama among them, to fight for "social, economic and racial justice";
- The pseudo-anarchist Ruckus Society ("actions speak louder than words");
- The Ella Baker Center for Human Rights, an organization founded by self-declared (former, if you listen to him) communist Van Jones.

Because his overall goal is the transformation of American society, Soros has also made donations—really *investments*—in an astonishing number of media organizations and activist groups:

- NBC, ABC, the *New York Times*, and the *Washington Post*;
- The *Columbia Journalism Review* and ProPublica;
- The Center for Public Integrity, the Center for Investigative Reporting, the *Lens*, the Columbia School of Journalism, the National Federation of Community Broadcasters, the National Association of Hispanic Journalists, the Committee to Protect Journalists, the Organization of News Ombudsmen, National Public Radio, the socialist American Prospect Inc.;

Lessons in Esperanto
Iluzio—(*n*) A deceptive appearance or impression. Illusion.

The far-left media organizations the Nation Institute, Pacifica Foundation, Independent Media Center, Media Fund, Independent Media Institute, and Media Matters For America;

Left-wing religious organizations such as Catholics in Alliance for the Common Good; Sojourners, whose founder, Jim Wallis, merits a chapter of his own; People Improving Communities through Organizing; and Catholics for Choice, a nominally Catholic organization that "believes in a world where everyone has equal access to . . . safe and legal abortion services";

Global Exchange, whose founder, Medea Benjamin, is a pro-Castro radical who created Iraq Occupation Watch for the purpose of encouraging American troops to desert. In December 2004, Benjamin announced that Global Exchange would be sending aid to the families of terrorist insurgents who were fighting American troops in Iraq.

The Tides Foundation, which receives cash from individuals, groups, and other foundations and then funnels it to designated left-wing recipients. Having given more than $400 million to "progressive nonprofit organizations" since 2000, Tides is the chosen vehicle for many progressives to donate cash to questionable organizations without leaving their fingerprints on it.

Various groups supporting drug-legalization and needle-exchange programs. In 1996, former Carter administration official Joseph Califano called Soros "the Daddy Warbucks of drug legalization."

Groups promoting physician-assisted suicide such as the Project on Death in America (PDA), whose purpose was to provide "end-of-life" assistance and to enact public policy that would "transform the culture and experience of dying and bereavement." Over a nine-year period, the Open Society Institute gave $45 million to PDA.

Leftist organizations whose perspectives are "internationalist" and who see American sovereignty as an obstacle to their goals, such as the United Nations Foundation and the Coalition for an International Criminal Court, which sought to subordinate American criminal justice to an international prosecutor. Soros once wrote: "In short, we need a global society to support our global economy." "The sovereignty of states must be subordinated to international law and international institutions."

MAN OF ACTION

George Soros is not a man who simply thinks big; he puts his ideas, and his money, into action. Soros showed just how serious he was about global regime change by deploying his Open Society Institutes, and the cluster of socially involved organizations he had built around them, in efforts to overthrow the governments of several countries, while also banking loads of cash on the side.

Right around the turn of this century, Soros began to target Central Asian countries that were former members of the Soviet bloc. These nations were generally in a state of disintegration under the pressures of American military and economic power. Among the regimes in Europe that Soros himself took credit for overthrowing were those in Serbia, Croatia, and the former Soviet republic of Georgia, where, according to the *Los Angeles Times*, he played an "important role" in preparing the country for a revolt against their president. "I'm delighted by what happened in Georgia," Soros said, "and I take great pride in having contributed to it."

Soros's preferred method in these countries was to set up Open Society Institutes, which had a broad mandate to influence and infiltrate social institutions and media outlets, and to fund activist organizations that could organize street protests charging the existing regimes with corruption and other crimes. Franjo Tudjman, the late president of Croatia who fought a long (and, ultimately, losing) battle with Soros, described his opponents this way:

> *[Soros and his allies] have spread their tentacles throughout the whole of our society. . . . [Their aim is to] control of all spheres of life . . . setting up a state within a state. . . .*

Soros not only admitted to this subversion, he in fact became addicted to the experimentation:

> *When you try to improve society you affect different people and different interests differently and they are not actually commensurate, you very often have all kinds of unintended adverse consequences. So I had to experiment. And it was a learning process. The first part was this subversive activity, disrupting repressive regimes. That was a lot of fun and that's actually what got me hooked on this whole enterprise. Seeing what worked in one country, trying it in the other country.*

That image in your mind of an evil billionaire dictating world events while maniacally laughing from his midtown penthouse apartment with a furry white cat on his lap may not be that far off. These methods were effective in small, poor countries, but America presented much larger problems. So he went right to the top.

Around the time that George Soros launched the Open Society Institute, he also forged a close relationship with Bill and Hillary Clinton, the new president and first lady. "We actually work together as a team," he boasted. When the Clintons took office in early 1993, they faced the daunting task of cultivating a productive relationship with the collapsed Soviet empire, which was attempting to rise from its ruins. Soros was chosen to serve as a key adviser on the project.

Jeffrey Sachs, a Harvard professor whose work Soros had previously funded through one of his foundations, was tapped to head the economic team to oversee Russia's transformation to a market economy. Soros worked closely with Sachs, and the pair held such enormous sway over Russian president Boris Yeltsin that Soros once quipped "the former Soviet Empire is now called the Soros Empire."

That new empire turned out to be massively corrupt. An enormous money-laundering scheme, which came to be known as "Russiagate," led to the diversion of $100 billion out of the country and the transfer of valuable public properties into private hands for a fraction of their value.

The mess was eventually investigated by the U.S. House Banking Committee and Soros was called to testify. He denied any responsibility but did admit that he had used insider access in a deal to acquire a large portion of Sidanko Oil. Soros further acknowledged that some of the missing Russian assets had made their way into his personal investment portfolio and conceded that the Sidanko deal "was part of the crony stuff that was going on." House Banking Committee chairman Jim Leach later characterized the entire sordid affair as "one of the greatest social robberies in human history."

Lessons in Esperanto

Egoista—(*adj*) Lacking consideration for others; concerned chiefly with one's own personal profit or pleasure. Selfish.

Think about the significance of this for a moment. The Soviet Union's opportunity for transition to a free-market economy could have been the knockout blow in a century-long battle between capitalism and communism. If capitalism were to have worked in the former Soviet Union, capitalism could work anywhere. There would be no more plausible arguments to be made for socialism and communism. With all of that on the line, the man with his fingers deep in the cookie jar was none other than George Soros. It's no wonder that the Soviet transition was so messy, corrupt, and for a select few, very, very profitable.

SHADOW PARTY

Another area of close collaboration between the Clintons and Soros was the campaign to socialize the American health-care system. The defeat of Hillarycare convinced Soros that he would have to change the political process if progressive ideas were to triumph. The key would be to create the illusion of a mass movement so that members of Congress would feel that everywhere they looked—academic institutions, the business community, religious groups, the media—there was a clamor for reform.

Lessons in Esperanto

Propagando—(*n*) Information, especially of a biased or misleading nature, used to promote a particular political cause. Propaganda.

Soros poured millions into the illusory mandate effort, mobilizing the institutions he had funded and recruiting other philanthropies, such as the Pew Charitable Trust, to get behind his crusade. He also contributed money to Senator John McCain, the politician leading the reform efforts—which paid off in 2002 with the passage of the McCain-Feingold Act.

The new campaign finance law banned "soft" money, stripping the two major political parties of their financial base. This funding vacuum provided Soros with the perfect opportunity to create a "Shadow Party," which would funnel massive amounts of capital into organizations that would assume the role that political parties traditionally played in electoral campaigns. These organizations (which are used by both parties) are called 527s and they would be tasked with conducting the political "air war" through media buys and the "ground war" through get-out-the-vote efforts.

An equally important impetus behind Soros's creation of the Shadow Party was the September 11, 2001, terrorist attacks upon the United States. Soros did not see these attacks as indications that religiously motivated enemies had declared war on the West. Instead he complained about "American supremacy" and "growing inequality between rich and poor, both within countries and among countries." His solution was, naturally, to subordinate American sovereignty to the will of the rest of the world. He wrote that "[a] global open society requires affirmative action on a global scale."

Soros took advantage of that perceived opportunity in a big way. There was no official press release when the Shadow Party was born on July 17, 2003, at Soros's estate in Southampton, Long Island. But it was a momentous event, creating the largest and most powerful political juggernaut in American history. Among those present at its founding were former secretary of state Madeleine Albright, former White House chief of staff John Podesta, Carl Pope, executive director of the Sierra Club, and Andy Stern, former head of the SEIU public employees union, along with billionaires like Progressive Insurance mogul Peter B. Lewis.

The Shadow Party, which would spend hundreds of millions of unofficial dollars on the 2004 presidential campaign, consisted of a network of seven 527 organizations. The ground war was orchestrated by a variety of people and groups, including leaders of the left-wing government unions and the Center for American Progress, headed by Podesta. The air war was run by the Media Fund, headed by Clinton operative Harold Ickes, and MoveOn.org, the Internet fund-raising and agitation group created by West Coast billionaire Wes Boyd.

September 11: An "Unusual Opportunity"

Like other progressives, Soros believed that you should never let a serious crisis go to waste. In his mind, 9/11 provided an opportunity to move his agenda forward much faster than might otherwise be possible. He wrote:

September 11 has shocked the people of the United States into realizing that others may regard them very differently from the way they see themselves. They are more ready to reassess the world and the role that the United States plays in it more than in normal times. This provides an unusual opportunity to rethink and reshape the world more profoundly than would have been possible prior to September 11.

Soros regarded the "war on terror" that President Bush had declared as the heart of the problem and promised to devote every penny he had to defeat Bush in the 2004 elections. "America under Bush is a danger to the world," he declared in 2003. "And I'm willing to put my money where my mouth is." Based on the election results, I guess Soros *bezonas pli monon*. (In case you're still not fluent in Esperanto, that means: "needed more money.")

Another component, "America Votes," referred to by one of its staffers as a "monster coalition," was designed to coordinate the efforts of all the left-wing groups working at the grassroots level to defeat Bush—from ACORN to the Planned Parenthood Action Fund, from the Sierra Club to the American Federation of Teachers and the Service Employees International Union.

True to his word, Soros contributed $23,700,000 of his personal funds to the campaign effort during the 2004 elec-

Lessons in Esperanto

Malnobla—(*adj*) Deserving contempt. Despicable.

tion cycle. The Campaign Finance Reform Act, which Soros had engineered, and which was marketed to the public as legislation that would take money *out* of the political system, had instead resulted in an avalanche of money coming *into* politics—and the lion's share of that money was directed by Soros himself.

When the ballots were counted in the 2004 elections, the Shadow Party came within a few thousand votes in Ohio of pulling off a victory. But, even in defeat, its alteration of the American political landscape was profound.

By pushing campaign finance reform, Soros had cut off the Democrats' soft money supply; by forming the Shadow Party, he had provided the Democrats with an alternative source of funding—one that he, and the institutions he created, controlled; and by controlling the money, George Soros was finally in a position to define the agenda of the party.

Lessons in Esperanto
Malprospero—(*adj*)
Lack of success.
Failure.

But most important of all, by controlling campaign resources, Soros was able to begin purging those campaigns of the small minority of moderates who remained. The polarization of the political parties, and of America as a whole, was about to be fully unleashed.

AN UNHOLY ALLIANCE

In April 2005, Soros called another summit of the wealthy and powerful to prepare for the next presidential campaign. Seventy well-heeled progressive activists met in Phoenix to form the Democracy Alliance.

The Alliance would become the most exclusive of all the Shadow Party institutions. Members were obligated to pay an initial $25,000 fee, plus $30,000 in yearly dues, and were also required to donate at least $200,000 annually to groups endorsed by the Alliance. This was a gathering of the top 1 percent of the top 1 percent. Donors were to "pour" these requisite donations into four different categories: leadership, civic engagement, ideas, and media.

Over the next three years, the Democracy Alliance established subchapters in all fifty states. Just two months after the Democratic Party won control of both houses of Congress in the 2006 midterm elections, Soros and then-SEIU president Andrew Stern created a PAC called "Working for Us," whose goal was to eliminate Democratic Party moderates and to "collaborate with those who worked so hard to elect a progressive Congress, including state and local activists, the netroots and progressive organizations."

A year after its formation, the Democracy Alliance launched a 527 initiative called the "Secretary of State Project." The idea was to win secretary of state elections in crucial "swing" states where the margin of victory in the 2004 election cycle had been 120,000 votes or less. At this point you might be thinking that Soros and the Alliance had gone senile. Who targets secretary of state elections?

But there was a method to their madness: The secretary of state is the chief election officer of each state. They are responsible for certifying candidates and election results. Are you starting to see why Soros was interested?

One of the project's first successes came in Minnesota where Mark Ritchie, an activist supported by ACORN, was elected secretary of state with the Alliance's help. Two years later, when Norm Coleman, the incumbent Republican senator, finished 725 votes ahead of Democratic challenger Al Franken, the thin margin of victory triggered an automatic re-count. With Ritchie presiding, and ignoring what John Fund from the *Wall Street Journal* described as a series of "appalling irregularities" (in one case, at least 393 convicted felons voted illegally in two particular Minnesota counties), Coleman's lead gradually dwindled. "Almost every time new ballots materialized or tallies were updated or corrected, Franken benefited," wrote Matthew Vadum. When the recount was over, Franken had eked out a 312-vote lead and was officially declared the victor.

> **Alliance or Empire?**
> **W**orking for Us published the names of what it called the "Top Offenders" among congressional Democrats who failed to support such leftist priorities as "living wage" legislation—a socialist program to raise the minimum wage to potentially unlimited levels— the proliferation of government labor unions, and a single-payer government-owned health-care system.

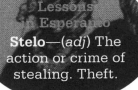

Lessons in Esperanto

Stelo—(*adj*) The action or crime of stealing. Theft.

The Democracy Alliance had bought itself a United States senator.

HOPE AND CHANGE

Later that week, Soros announced that he would support Obama for the Democratic Party's presidential nomination. The Obama campaign was soon staffed, funded, and promoted by personnel from the forces Soros had welded into the Shadow Party juggernaut: the left-leaning public employees unions, the progressive billionaires, and the ACORN radicals from Project Vote.

When Obama was elected, members of the Soros coalition immediately began showing up in high-level jobs in the new administration:

- Van Jones, who headed the Soros-funded Ella Baker Center for Human Rights, spent six months as the new president's "green jobs czar" before revelations about his background forced him to resign and take up a position at the Soros-funded Center for American Progress.
- Carol Browner was named by Obama as his "environment czar." Browner was a board member of the Alliance for Climate Protection, the Center for American Progress, and the League of Conservation Voters, all funded by Soros.
- David Axelrod, Obama's campaign manager, and recipient of over $200,000 from the Shadow Party's Media Fund, was appointed as the president's political adviser. He was later named the media and communications director of Obama's 2012 reelection campaign.
- Anna Burger, vice chair of the Soros Democracy Alliance, and top SEIU executive, was appointed to the President's Economic Recovery Advisory Board.
- Kevin Jennings, founder of the Gay, Lesbian and Straight Education Network, a Boston-area organization that Soros helped fund, was named "safe school czar."
- Andy Stern, who headed the SEIU, the second-largest labor organization in America, and a key figure in the Shadow Party through America Votes, was among the most frequent visitors to the White House in Obama's first term.

Almost everywhere you looked in the new administration you would find members of the Soros inner circle, beneficiaries of the Soros "charities," and operatives from the Shadow Party. And, not coincidentally, as soon as the Obama administration took over, the White House began to roll out policies that had George Soros's fingerprints all over them.

Just a few days after the election, Soros said:

I think we need a large stimulus package which will provide funds for state and local government to maintain their budgets because they are not allowed by the Constitution to run a deficit. For such a program to be successful, the federal government would need to provide hundreds of billions of dollars.

Shortly thereafter, in one of the first acts of his presidency, Obama announced, and the Democratic Congress passed, a monumental 1,071-page, $787 billion economic stimulus bill.

Energy is another area where Soros has taken a key interest. Obama's tax-based policy proposal to reduce Americans' consumption of fossil fuels through "cap-and-trade" was a strategy that, after being proposed and perfected by the nonprofits that Soros funded, was incorporated into the Shadow Party campaigns. Under cap-and-trade regulations, companies are subject to taxes or fees if they use more "dirty" energy than the government wants them to. Some economists have predicted that such legislation, if enacted, would impose colossal costs on businesses—costs that would be passed on to consumers, who would pay anywhere from several hundred to several thousand more dollars each year in energy costs. But to Soros, the taxpayers' money would be well spent. "[D]ealing with global warming will require a lot of investment," he said, emphasizing that it "could be the motor of the world economy in the years to come," while admitting that it "will be painful."

When Soros was asked in 2008 whether he was proposing energy policies that would "create a whole new paradigm for the economic model of the country, of the world," he replied simply, "Yes."

During his 2008 presidential campaign, Obama had a comparable moment of candor: "[U]nder my plan of a cap-and-trade system, electricity rates would necessarily skyrocket," he conceded. "Because I'm capping greenhouse gases, coal power plants, you know, natural gas, you name it, whatever the plants were, whatever the industry was, they would have to retrofit their operations."

The cap-and-trade policies being pushed by Obama and Soros were also a favorite of Obama's "regulatory czar," Cass Sunstein, a leftist law professor and longtime proponent of "distributive justice." Under Sunstein's idea of justice, which sounds eerily similar to Soros's post-9/11 "affirmative action on a global scale" comment, America would transfer much of its own wealth to poorer nations as compensation for the alleged harm that U.S. environmental transgressions have caused. In language echoing Soros's own pronouncements, Sunstein wrote:

Lessons in Esperanto

Kiel i tiu Guy ganjo post diranta i tiu?—(*question*) How did this guy win after saying this?

It is even possible that desirable redistribution is more likely to occur through climate change policy than otherwise, or to be accomplished more effectively through climate policy than through direct foreign aid.

Translation: climate change regulation might be the best way to accomplish the redistribution of wealth that we want anyway. It might even be better than just handing the money to foreign countries for nothing. Yet conservatives are crazy for being skeptical of the left's intentions with environmental policy.

SOROS-CARE

The biggest Obama agenda item of all—Obamacare—was also a Soros crusade.

Soros had devised his own ideas for reform, many of which found their way into Hillarycare through what he called "the Project on Death." The Project's boilerplate mission was compassionate—to embed hospices and "palliative" care in U.S. health policy—but its practical objective was to ration care. Those who are very sick and won't see much improvement in their condition are, after all, very expensive to take care of. Some might even call them a burden on the system.

Following the defeat of Hillarycare and the failure of the Project on Death to gain traction, Soros created a new coalition, a vast network of organizations to promote socialized medicine. The new umbrella group was called "Health Care for America Now" (HCAN) and it became the primary lobby for the plan that would seek to lock up a sixth of the American economy into a government-controlled operation.

HCAN's strategy, to impose a system of government health insurance that would eventually culminate in a single-payer plan, became the strategy of the Obama White House. The path to this goal would be paved by a public option—a government insurance agency to compete with existing insurers.

An agency like this would have a couple of nice things going for it: It wouldn't have to turn a profit; and it could do whatever it liked to its private competitors. Increase its competitors' taxes? Sure, why not. Add thousands of pages of new regulations to make it almost impossible for them to operate? Naturally! The truth—which HCAN and the others understood very well from the start—is that a "public option" would inevitably force private insurers out of the industry and leave the government as the only alternative.

This strategy was outlined by Professor Jacob Hacker, speaking at the Soros-funded Tides Foundation: "Someone once said to me this is a Trojan Horse for single-payer, and I said, well it's not a Trojan Horse, right? It's just right there. I'm telling you."

Hacker lauded the HCAN approach: "One of the virtues of it, though, is that you can at least make the claim that there is a competitive system between the public and private sectors." He added that while it would lead to a single-payer government health-care system eventually, it wouldn't "frighten people into thinking they are going to lose their private insurance."

ISRAEL: "VICTIMS TURNING PERSECUTORS"

If Obamacare was the crown jewel of the president's domestic agenda, his unprecedented hard line toward Israel and appeasement of Palestinian radicals was a signature statement of his foreign policy. It was also, not coincidentally, another initiative in which Soros played a heavy hand.

Soros's antipathy for Israel had now seemingly developed into a full-blown hostility. Just as he perceived American policies to have provoked the anti-American attacks by Islamic jihadists on 9/11, so too did he regard the Jews and the state of Israel as the primary cause of anti-Semitism. He has referred to Israel's conflict with the Palestinians as a case of the "victims turning persecutors," even though the source of the conflict is the sixty-year Arab war of aggression to erase the Jewish state. While Hamas, the terrorist party in control of Gaza, calls for the extermination of the Jews, Soros argues that the key to a Mideast peace is "bringing Hamas into the peace process."

To promote his anti-Israel views, Soros helped fund a left-wing lobby called "J Street" at the outset of the Obama administration. Like other Soros groups, J Street positions itself as a counter to what Soros considers to be a malignant "conservative" organization, in this case the American Israel Public Affairs Committee—an organization, by the way, overwhelmingly made up of Democrats.

Lessons in Esperanto
Frenezeco—(n) Extreme foolishness or irrationality. Insanity.

J Street has called for "a new direction for American policy in the Middle East" and has cautioned Israel not to be too combative against Hamas—despite that group's avowed hatred for Jews, their refusal to recognize the Jewish state, and their eight thousand unprovoked rocket attacks on civilian targets in Israel.

According to J Street, the Mideast conflict is perpetuated chiefly by Israel: "Israel's settlements in the occupied territories have, for over forty years, been an obstacle to peace." While this is an enormously complex issue, the reality is that these settlements are an obstacle only to those who do not want a Jewish presence in a Muslim state.

The Soros/J Street positions mark a break with sixty years of American policy toward Israel, but they are largely indistinguishable from those of the Obama White House. Obama signaled his comfort with J Street's agendas when he sent his then-national security adviser James Jones to deliver the keynote address at the organization's annual conference in October 2009, and when he objected to Jewish settlements in Jerusalem, which is the capital of the Jewish state.

Soros, knowing that his comments on Israel made him controversial in the Jewish community, initially tried to conceal his support of J Street from the public for fear that it might alienate other potential backers of the organization. But, in September 2010, the *Washington Times* penetrated the veil, revealing that from 2008 to 2010, Soros and his two children had given a total of $750,000 to J Street and that the organization's Advisory Council includes a number of individuals with close ties to Soros operations.

When the streets of Cairo erupted in February 2011, and Obama hesitated as Mubarak tried to hold on to power, Soros wrote an op-ed piece in the *Washington Post* urging Obama to embrace regime change and welcome the entrance of the outlawed Muslim Brotherhood, an Islamic cult that has spawned twelve terrorist organizations including al-Qaeda and Hamas. "President Obama personally and the United States as a country have much to gain by moving out in front and siding with the public demand for dignity and democracy . . . ," he wrote. "[D]oing so would open the way to peaceful progress in the region. The Muslim Brotherhood's cooperation with Mohamed ElBaradei, the Nobel laureate who is seeking to run for president, is a hopeful sign that it intends to play a constructive role in a democratic political system. . . .

"The main stumbling block is Israel. . . . Israel is unlikely to recognize its own best interests because the change is too sudden and carries too many risks. . . ."

In other words, according to Soros, America—which considered the reigning Mubarak regime to be an ally for forty years despite its faults—and Israel, a nation under siege from Muslim extremists, are the real obstacles to peace in the Middle East. On the other hand, the Muslim Brotherhood—the fountainhead of Islamic terrorism—is the key to peace.

That logic must cost billions of dollars, because I don't get it.

AN INCESTUOUS AFFAIR

In Soros's anti-Israel, pro–Muslim Brotherhood *Washington Post* op-ed, he inadvertently outlined the way he does business to anyone with the curiosity to notice: "The American Israel Public Affairs Committee," he wrote, "is no longer monolithic or the sole representative of the Jewish community."

This, of course, was correct—since the creation of J Street. In essence, George Soros is citing an organization funded by George Soros as evidence that there are voices out there that support the opinions of George Soros.

The Key to Peace?

Just so we're all on the same page about the Muslim Brotherhood, Yusuf al-Qaradawi, the Brotherhood's most important cleric (who is often portrayed as a moderate in the Western media), once said: "Throughout history, Allah has imposed upon the [Jews] people who would punish them for their corruption. The last punishment was carried out by Hitler. By means of all the things he did to them—even though they exaggerated this issue—he managed to put them in their place. This was divine punishment for them. Allah willing, the next time will be at the hand of the believers [i.e., Muslims]."

Some will call this successful political activism. Some will call it a conspiracy. I call it incestuous. When Israel is the question, Soros has J Street as the answer. When government health care is the question, Soros has HCAN as the answer. When the Obama administration's attempt to force Catholic organizations to provide contraception was the question, Soros had Media Matters to answer, claiming "Faith leaders . . . agree with the regulation." Their backup for that claim? A statement from the group Faith in Public Life, cofounded by Jim Wallis, and funded, you guessed it, by George Soros.

Almost everybody wants to play puppet master. Some people are just a lot better at it than others.

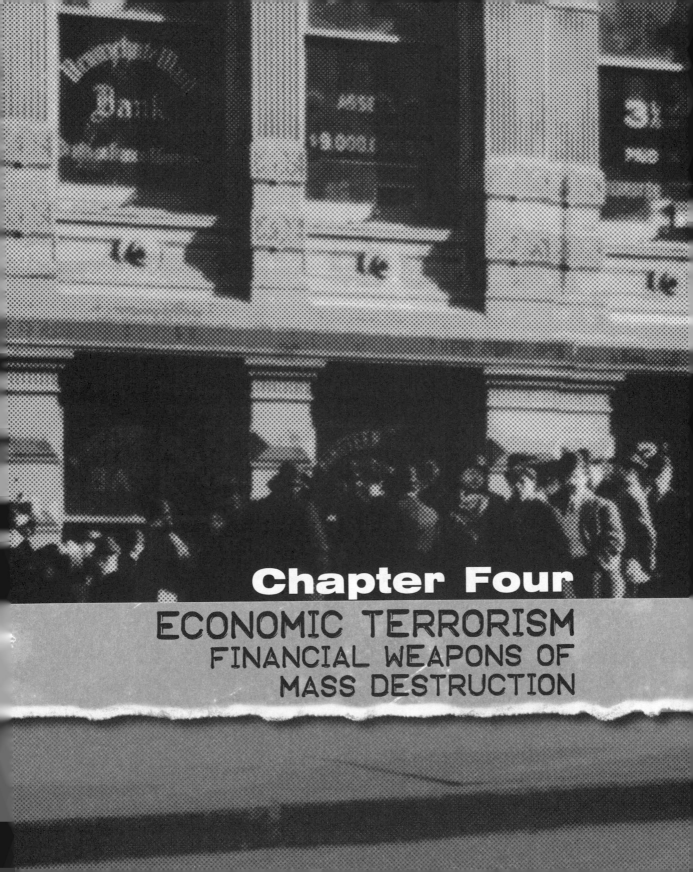

Chapter Four

ECONOMIC TERRORISM
FINANCIAL WEAPONS OF MASS DESTRUCTION

" [Al-Qaeda's supporters] are aware of the cracks in the Western financial system as they are aware of the lines in their own hands. **"**

—Osama bin Laden, 2001

BY EARLY 2009 the global economy had lost close to $50 trillion from its peak. Of that decline, $13 trillion came from America. Blue-chip financial institutions that had survived the worst of the worst collapsed before our eyes. The world had nearly been plunged into a second Great Depression.

It was in this environment that a financial analyst named Kevin D. Freeman was commissioned by the Pentagon to analyze the economic crisis in light of the threats posed by Osama bin Laden and the Chinese People's Liberation Army. He was asked to answer several questions: Could terrorist organizations or enemy nations execute a significant attack on our financial markets? Could these groups really succeed in crashing our stock market? Could they debase our currency?

The answers, as you will see, are all yes. Yet, despite the compelling evidence of outside manipulation that Freeman published in his Pentagon report, *Economic Warfare*, his findings were generally ignored. "Nobody wants to go there" was the response from one anonymous government official to the *Washington Times* when asked why the threat wasn't being taken seriously.

Freeman has told me personally that government officials threatened to classify his report and punish him with jail time if he dared to publicly discuss his research on how our enemies might harm our economy.

They are cowards.

It's time to shine a light on Freeman's findings—and the threat of financial terrorism in general. This isn't some conspiracy theory or academic research: this is very real. Remember, terrorists didn't have bombs or guns on 9/11—just better imaginations. The same applies here. The size of our economy is both our greatest strength and greatest vulnerability. Our enemies don't need bombs or guns to target it—just better imaginations.

MONEY: THE WORLD'S OLDEST WEAPON

Economic warfare is nothing new; we've seen it used many times throughout history:

- Under the biblical Joseph's direction, the Egyptian pharaoh stored grain and cornered the market. This made the Egyptians dominant over the entire region without ever raising a sword. According to the Bible (Genesis 41:57, 47:13–26), the Egyptians were able to force all the surrounding countries to exchange money, livestock, land, and possessions for the food Joseph had stored.
- Napoleon was also a big fan of economic weaponry. He waged something of a currency war by only accepting gold for the sale of French goods to Britain.
- FDR created a "Board of Economic Warfare" and instituted a blockade of oil against Japan, cutting off 90 percent of their oil imports and setting off a chain reaction that eventually led to the attack on Pearl Harbor.Once World War II began, the Germans counterfeited British currency in the hopes of destroying their economy.
- Eisenhower threatened to liquidate our holding of British bonds (which would've likely forced them to devalue their currency) if they did not withdraw their troops from the Suez Canal.
- OPEC used an oil embargo against the United States and Israel in 1973.
- The Reagan administration worked with the Saudis to lower the price of oil and break the "Evil Empire" of the Soviet Union.
- George Soros used financial markets to short the British pound and "break the Bank of England."
- The North Koreans have been counterfeiting hundred-dollar bills.

🐓 The United States has undertaken an economic warfare approach against Iran, attempting to get them to abandon their nuclear efforts by cutting off access to the international payments systems, thereby straining their economy and ability to sell oil on world markets.

Given that history, it would be naïve to think that others are not plotting to use these same techniques against America one day.

UNRESTRICTED WARFARE

As it turns out, that plotting actually began over a decade ago.

In 1999, the Chinese People's Liberation Army (PLA) asked two senior colonels to war-game how to defeat the military superiority of the West—namely, the United States. At that point in time, this probably seemed like an impossible task. America was dominant in almost every respect. The nation that had shoved Saddam Hussein out of Kuwait in forty-two days had also reinvented the global economy with the Internet and the Information Age. The American budget was in its best shape in years, with some even saying that our national debt could be extinguished within a decade.

For those who were intent on making the next century a Chinese one, this was a nightmare. So they got creative. The result was a new doctrine—a strategy for taking on the West that would have nothing to do with nuclear arsenals or laser-guided bombs. Roughly translated, it was called "Unrestricted Warfare."

In the document explaining these tactics, the colonels made the case that a new approach to warfare was needed to derail the West, a kind of warfare that wouldn't demand new technology, only "lucid and incisive thinking." They knew that Americans would be so caught up in making the latest stealth fighter or cruise missile that we wouldn't notice a weapons-grade financial crisis. As they put it, we are "slaves to technology in [our] thinking."

The colonels wrote that "a single man-made stock-market crash, a single computer virus invasion, or a single rumor or scandal that results in a fluctuation in the enemy country's exchange rates or exposes the leaders of an enemy country on the Internet, all can be included in the ranks of new-concept weapons."

The colonels made some other interesting observations as well, especially when looked at with the benefit of hindsight. For one, they directly identified Osama bin Laden more than two years before he became infamous:

Whether it be the intrusions of hackers, a major explosion at the World Trade Center, or a bombing attack by bin Laden, all of these greatly exceed the frequency band widths understood by the American military. The American military is naturally inadequately prepared to deal with this type of enemy psychologically, in terms or measures, and especially as regards military thinking and the methods of operation derived from this.

They also identified George Soros by name and compared him to bin Laden:

[W]e began to get an inkling of a non-military type of war which is prosecuted by yet another type of non-professional warrior. . . . [H]is or her faith is by no means inferior to Osama bin Laden's in terms of its fanaticism. Moreover, he or she does not lack the motivation or courage to enter a fight as necessary. Judging by this kind of standard, who can say that George Soros is not a financial terrorist?

[W]hen people revise the history books on twentieth-century warfare in the early 21st century, the section on financial warfare will command the reader's utmost attention. The main protagonist in this section of the history book will not be a statesman or a military strategist; rather, it will be George Soros.

Were they right? Is financial warfare the way future battles will be fought? Only time will tell for sure, but it certainly makes sense. There is even some evidence showing that many of these tactics have already been tried or tested by our enemies in various forms. But before we get to that, let's go back to the Chinese PLA strategy report, which offers a succinct road map for bringing down the West without ever firing a bullet:

[I]f the attacking side secretly musters large amounts of capital without the enemy nation being aware of this at all and launches a sneak attack against its financial markets, then after causing a financial crisis, buries a computer virus and hacker detachment in the opponent's computer system in advance, while at the same time carrying out a network attack against the enemy so that the civilian electricity network, traffic dispatching network, financial transaction network, telephone commu-

nications network, and mass media network are completely paralyzed, this will cause the enemy nation to fall into social panic, street riots, and a political crisis.

That's a pretty comprehensive strategy, so let's go through some of the key components, one by one.

THE PLAN: PART ONE
Muster larger amounts of capital.

The best estimate is that the Chinese currently hold a staggering $3 trillion in foreign reserves—virtually all of it accumulated since the year 2000. Most politicians and government officials tell us that there's nothing to see here, but no one really knows how much of that money has made its way into the global capital markets.

Another way to look at capital accumulation around the world is through something called Sovereign Wealth Funds. These are vehicles in which foreign governments invest capital overseas. They have swelled to an estimated nearly $5 trillion in size, of which nearly $3 trillion is owned by oil-producing states (more than $1 trillion by China). Of the top twenty non-Chinese Sovereign Wealth Funds, all but five are connected to the Middle East or Russia. The vast majority of this wealth has been accumulated since the year 2000 and, it goes without saying, much of it has come directly from the pockets of Americans who buy oil, gas, or products made in China.

That's a staggering amount of wealth, but it may not even be all they have. The truth is that it's very difficult to get a good handle on just how much capital our enemies have amassed because they keep that information as confidential

The Chinese Need America; Why Would They Ever Hurt Us?

The only way to answer that question is by asking another question: Which Chinese are you talking about?

Those in China who depend on exports to the United States wouldn't want any harm to come to their Wal-Mart customers, but the PLA is a different story. They don't have customers or experts; their only agenda is world domination. Consider this account from Kevin Freeman's book *Secret Weapon* and then decide how much the PLA cares about American consumers:

"It is indeed brutal to kill one or two hundred million Americans," General Chi said in 2005. "But that is the only path that will secure a Chinese century." Chi even took a poll to determine whether the "people [of China] would rise up against us if one day we secretly adopted resolute means to 'clean up' America." Eighty percent of those polled approved the secret methods. Why then would they shy away from economic warfare?

General Chi is Chi Haotian, the former minister of national defense for China (1993 to 2003) and a highly respected figure in their military today as vice chairman of the Central Military Commission. In other words, he's not exactly some low-level soldier speaking out of school.

as they keep their other military secrets. Nations realize that wealth in itself is a weapon. We don't advertise the number and locations of our nuclear weapons, or the latest stealth bomber project we're working on—so why would other countries advertise their wealth?

As an example of how far off these numbers can be, let's look at the estimates of the "personal" fortune held by Muammar Gaddafi. As recently as February 2011, it was estimated that he had "several billion" dollars. The reality? Experts believe that Gaddafi had secretly stashed away as much as $200 billion in Western markets—four times the estimated wealth of Warren Buffett. That would make him the richest person to have ever lived.

THE PLAN: PART TWO
Launch a sneak attack against its financial markets.

In the 1980s, the Soviet economy was extremely reliant on oil revenues. When prices collapsed, so did their economy, and, eventually, the entire government followed. What many people don't know (and others dispute) is that, by working with the Saudis, the United States helped to set these dominoes in motion. It's somewhat ironic that a Cold War that took the world to the brink of nuclear annihilation may have been ended not with guns and bullets but with dollars and rubles.

Unfortunately, we're on the exact opposite side of that issue now. As the world's largest *consumer* of oil, the United States is vulnerable to oil manipulations in the other direction. Higher oil prices are, after all, essentially a tax on consumers, with the majority of that money leaving the country. According to Ross Devol, chief research officer at the Milken Institute, "Each 50 cent increase in the price of gasoline adds almost $60 billion to annual consumer bills" for Americans.

If you consider the fluctuations in the price of oil over the last decade alone, that money can really add up. Oil was about $20 a barrel in 2000, $50 in early 2007, and as high as $147.50 in mid-2008. That spike from 2007 to 2008 alone—which took just eighteen months—meant an estimated $1 trillion in additional dollars was paid by the West.

Despite Wall Street denials, there was actually a serious financial component to the increase in oil prices. According to MIT professor of economics Richard Eckaus, "Hedge funds are very active in the oil market and their activity, along with other speculators, has raised the volume of oil transactions far above the volume warranted by ordinary commercial transactions." When *60 Minutes* correspondent Steve Kroft asked Petroleum Marketers Association president Dan Gilligan if there was manipulation going on, he answered: "I can't say. And the reason I can't say it, is because nobody knows. Our federal regulators don't have access to the data. They don't know who holds what positions." Kroft went on to explain that federal law doesn't give the public the ability to find out who is buying and selling oil contracts.

Our enemies have, of course, realized this. Muslim Brotherhood spiritual adviser and Islamic theologian Yusuf Qaradawi has often spoken of "the weapon of oil," or *Silah al Naft*. According to Walid Phares, a former professor of Middle East Studies at Florida Atlantic University and a Fox News analyst, "For years now, Salafist websites and al-Qaeda spokespersons have loudly called for an 'oil Jihad against infidel America and its lackeys.' Online material is still circulating. But more revealing are the official speeches by Osama bin Laden and his deputy on the 'absolute necessity to use that weapon.'" And that's exactly how Islamic extremists view oil—as a weapon.

Another way to sneak-attack financial markets is by using a technique called a "bear raid" to bring down vulnerable companies. According to Dictionary.com, a bear raid is "an attempt to force down the price of a security or commodity by sustained selling." This practice is illegal, but it can still occur when traders work together to lower the price

Rock, Paper, Oil?

A high-stakes economic warfare drama has been playing out between the United States and Iran—but it's inadvertently exposing one of our greatest vulnerabilities. Essentially, to punish Iran for their continued nuclear development, we are depriving them of access to the U.S. dollar. That is a serious threat and has serious implications for their economy. The problem is that when all is said and done, the world may actually prefer to have their oil rather than our paper. That is certainly what the market has told us as the price of oil in dollars has risen sharply.

Put it this way: Iran has broken ranks with the rest of the world and is now trading oil for other currencies, and even gold. If the rest of the world sees that strategy turn out well, there will be a massive target painted on the back of the dollar.

In the game "rock, paper, scissors," scissors beats paper. But won't oil also beat paper? Do we really want to be so arrogant as to believe that the world prefers American paper to oil from any source? American paper (whether in the form of currency or Treasury debt) has, after all, continued to grow exponentially while the amount of available oil reserves has been reasonably stagnant by comparison. In addition, oil has enormous practical use and the demand for it will grow over the long term. But our paper? Every major nation in the world, including our most trusted trading partners, has begun to question (some publicly, some privately) its long-term usefulness as the world's reserve currency.

Iran believes this will eventually spell the end for the dollar. Depending how these behind-the-scene monetary tactics play out, the rest of the world may agree.

of a stock. If successful, the bear raid creates panic in the wider market, thereby making the problem much worse. Bear raids generally involve short selling and its evil twin, "naked short selling."

Some people try to deny that bear raids happen, but the New England Complex Systems Institute, an independent academic research institution, proved not only that they exist, but that a bear raid was perpetrated against Citigroup right at the beginning of the market crash. The researchers calculated that the "probability of these two events [the abnormal volume of short positions taken out and subsequently closed] occurring six days apart is . . . 4 billion years." In other words, this was not normal trading activity: this was a prototypical bear raid.

This idea of a foreign enemy attacking our financial markets may seem like a conspiracy theory, but it's actually something they've spoken about pretty openly. Aside from the Chinese PLA, there have also been some eye-opening quotes from bin Laden and other prominent terrorists through the years that demonstrate their focus on attacking our economy.

Was the Flash Crash a Weapons Test?

On May 6, 2010, the Dow Jones Industrial Average fell nine hundred points in about six minutes before recovering. This has been dubbed the "flash crash" and it wiped out about $1 trillion in wealth in about the time it takes to eat a bowl of cereal. Reports on the cause of the crash have blamed everything from computer algorithms to high-frequency traders, but Kevin Freeman believes it was something else entirely: a weapons test.

Just a few months after the 9/11 attacks, bin Laden said, "If their economy is destroyed, they will be busy with their own affairs rather than enslaving the weak peoples. It is very important to concentrate on hitting the U.S. economy through all means possible."

A year later, al-Qaeda's second in command, Ayman al-Zawahiri, continued that theme, saying, "We will also aim to continue, by the permission of Allah, the destruction of the American economy."

On the seventh anniversary of the 9/11 attacks, levels of short selling and credit default swaps began to spike. By September 15, 2008, Lehman Brothers had vanished—its share price had fallen to $0.21 after trading over $30 just a few weeks earlier. It was a very public implosion, one that set off a chain reaction of devastation in the financial markets—but most people don't know that there was something else, something much more serious, going on behind the scenes that very same day. Speaking on C-SPAN several years ago, Pennsylvania congressman Paul Kanjorski revealed that the financial system was much closer to disaster than anyone realized:

Here are the facts and we don't even talk about these things: At 11 in the morning the Federal Reserve noticed a tremendous draw-down of money market accounts in the United States, to the tune of $550 billion was being drawn out in the matter of an hour or two. The Treasury opened up its window to help and pumped $105 billion in the system and quickly realized that they could not stem the tide. We were having an electronic run on the banks. They decided to close the operation, close down the money accounts and announce a guarantee of $250,000 per account so there wouldn't be further panic out there. . . . If they had not done that, their estimation was that by two o'clock that afternoon, $5.5 trillion would have been drawn out of the money market system of the United States, it would have collapsed the entire economy of the United States, and within 24 hours the world economy would have collapsed. . . . It would have been the end of our economic system and our political system as we know it.

CREDIT DEFAULT SWAPS

Imagine some stranger buying fire insurance on your home . . . and then buying a box of matches.

Credit default swaps (CDS) are essentially "side bets" between two parties as to whether or not some other party will default on a debt. Here's how they work, in very simple terms:

Your friend Steve takes out a personal loan that you're pretty sure he won't be able to pay back. You buy a CDS from Susan that will pay you should Steve default. Simple

---

Financial Weapons of Mass Destruction 101

SHORT SELLING (or "shorting") means borrowing shares of a stock and selling them. Of course, since you borrowed shares, you will have to give them back at some point. To do that, you buy the shares back on the open market (which is called "covering") and pay back the "loan." If the price of the stock went down after you sold, you would cover at a lower price and make a profit. If the price went up, you would lose money. This is all legal and regulated and helps create a dynamic marketplace.

NAKED SHORTING is the same as regular shorting except that the seller doesn't have the "inconvenience" of ever actually borrowing shares before selling them. Basically, the investor instructs the broker to sell what he does not have. The buyer is given an IOU that, for all intents and purposes, looks and functions like real shares. Unlike regular short selling, with naked shorting there is no limit to the number of shares you can sell since you are only selling IOUs anyway.

Naked shorting was illegal (and it still is). The rules just aren't always enforced and the perpetrators aren't always caught. According to estimates from Susanne Trimbath, a trade settlement expert, somewhere between 30 percent and 70 percent of the decline in Lehman stock during the year it failed was linked to naked short selling.

enough, right? Yes, except for three things. First, you are not the one who lent the money to Steve in the first place—you actually have no part in the primary transaction. Second, you can buy as many CDS policies on Steve as you want. You could buy so many, in fact, that at some point it would be in your best interests if Steve defaulted. Which brings us to the third point: What if you could help force Steve's hand? What if you were his boss and fired him, leaving him unable to pay back his debt?

Wall Street used CDS to hedge against very big companies like Lehman Brothers, Bear Stearns, General Electric, and Citigroup. Some people who were buying CDS were also shorting the stock of those companies, thereby helping to cause, and subsequently profit from, their demise.

How much money would it take to cripple a major company? General Electric CEO Jeff Immelt was quoted as saying that "'by spending 25 million bucks in a handful of transactions in an unregulated market' traders in credit default swaps could tank major companies."

No wonder Warren Buffett has called them "financial weapons of mass destruction."

Drastic measures were taken by the Bush administration in late 2008 to try to stem the tide. The bear raids were essentially over by the end of the year, but the stock market kept falling through March 2009. And while the collapse didn't put an end to our financial system, it came awfully close.

Can You Spare a Dollar?

If Kevin Freeman is right, the battlefield has shifted from our markets to our currency and Treasury. The goal now seems to be to destroy the value of the U.S. dollar and undermine our credit rating (though we're doing a pretty good job at that all by ourselves).

In response to the financial market collapse and recession we've dramatically increased the national debt while also pumping trillions of dollars into the system. If all of that weren't enough, the BRIC (Brazil, Russia, India, and China) countries are only too happy to hit us while we're down. A recent *Washington Post* report detailed how, during their 2011 summit, they called for "a restructuring of the World War II–era global financial system and an eventual end to the long reign of the U.S. dollar as the world's reserve currency."

THE PLAN, PART THREE
After causing a financial crisis, bury a computer virus.

Over the past decade, we have uncovered attempts by foreign hackers to infiltrate our infrastructure and telecommunications systems, NASA, the stock market, and several key utilities. These attacks have really ramped up over the last five years. Security vendor McAfee recently published a report revealing that one group of hackers had penetrated the systems of seventy-two companies and organizations in fourteen countries, stealing "national secrets, business plans and other sensitive information." More ominously, McAfee reported that "the attackers are likely a single group acting on behalf of a government."

The intrusions have reached NASA, including our satellite systems, and NASDAQ, whose systems control a major stock market. In fact, some experts, like former counter-terrorism czar Richard Clarke, believe that "every major company in the United States has already been penetrated by China."

These intrusions demonstrate the potential for hackers to take over our communication capabilities and potentially crash our stock market on command. Mike McConnell, former director of national intelligence and former director of the National Security Agency, said, "We know, and there's good evidence . . . of very deliberate, focused cyber-espionage to capture very valuable research and development information, or innovative ideas, or source code or business plans for their own advantage."

McConnell is likely talking about the Chinese, but other countries also engage in cyber-espionage—like Russia. Consider, for example, the case of Sergey Aleynikov, a Russian national who walked out the door with Goldman Sachs trading codes in 2009. Aleynikov transferred the codes, worth millions of dollars, to a computer server in Germany and, according to prosecutors, could have then disseminated them to anyone in the world. Aleynikov was convicted of stealing trade secrets, and though the conviction was later overturned, the vulnerability was clearly exposed.

And then there are the groups like Anonymous, which has clearly shown the ability to cause mayhem:

Computer hacking group Anonymous has launched a cyber-attack on the Greek Ministry of Justice website, and warned of plans to target a

The Enemy of My Enemy . . .

In the summer of 2008, Russian operatives allegedly approached the Chinese with a "disruptive scheme" to surgically target the American economy. According to then Treasury secretary Hank Paulson, the Russians proposed to high-level Chinese officials that "together they might sell big chunks of their [Fannie Mae and Freddie Mac] holdings to force the U.S. to use its emergency authorities to prop up these companies."

The Russians have denied this proposal was made, but they did, in fact, dump over $65 billion worth of these bonds in 2008. Fortunately, the Chinese, who held nearly $500 billion of those bonds, did not sell. If they had joined the Russians, who knows just how much more damage and panic may have been caused to our economy.

further 300 ministry and media sites. . . . It is the latest in a series of attacks by the self-styled "hacktivist" group, which has unleashed havoc on several European governments during the past month, and targeted America's Justice Department in retaliation for the closure of file-sharing website Megaupload.

In a message left on the Greek Justice Ministry's website, the group threatened to take down "all the media in Greece":

We know EVERYTHING, We have your PASSWORDS, We are watching YOU. NEXT TARGET WILL BE ALL THE MEDIA IN GREECE. (ertTV, etc)

WE HAVE MOST OF THE MEDIA WEBSITES ADMIN PASSWORDS.

We are Legion. This is JUST the BEGINING [sic].

Do you think these kinds of threats help or hurt the people of Greece as they deal with a historic economic crisis?

We are watching this "checkmate" strategy play out in Greece right now, but it is planned for the United States soon. Maybe sooner than we think, when you consider that George Soros is, as usual, right at the center of America's version of the Greek street protests: Occupy Wall Street.

Sound Familiar?
The final step in the PLA's "How to Destroy a Superpower" road map? *". . . cause the enemy nation to fall into social panic, street riots, and a political crisis."*

Soros told *Newsweek* that Occupy "is an inchoate, leaderless manifestation of protest," but that it will grow. It has "put on the agenda issues that the institutional left has failed to put on the agenda for a quarter of a century."

When the interviewer asked Soros if riots on the streets of America are inevitable, he had a hard time containing his enthusiasm. "'Yes, yes, yes,' he says, almost gleefully."

It appears that we have now come full circle. The destruction of America was strategized by the Chinese PLA, which cited George Soros as a model. The plan starts with amassing capital and it ends with riots in the streets. And now, here we are, near the final stages of that plan, and we have who else but George Soros explaining how American riots are inevitable.

BIN LADEN: FINANCIAL TERRORIST?

Osama bin Laden was fixated on our stock market prior to 9/11. He had such a vast knowledge of it, in fact, that he was even accused of short-selling American stocks prior to the attacks. In the month following 9/11, bin Laden talked about the economic damage his attacks had inflicted:

> *According to [the Americans'] own admissions, the share of the losses on the Wall Street market reached 16 percent. They said that this number is a record. . . . The gross amount that is traded in that market reaches $4 trillion. So if we multiply 16 percent with $4 trillion to find out the loss that affected the stocks, it reaches $640 billion of losses.*

> "[Bin Laden] said the American economy is like a chain. If you break one—one link of the chain, the whole economy will be brought down. So after [the] September 11 attacks, this operation will ruin the aviation industry, and in turn the whole economy will come down."
>
> —SAAJID BADAT, A CONVICTED AL-QAEDA TERRORIST WHO MET WITH BIN LADEN SHORTLY AFTER 9/11

Given how savvy bin Laden was about economics, I wonder, why is it so hard for some people to imagine that al-Qaeda has targeted our economy through bear raids on our stock market? It makes perfect sense.

If bin Laden had read the PLA's *Unrestricted Warfare* (something that is not at all far-fetched given how extensively he was mentioned in it and given that, by all accounts, bin Laden was something of an egomaniac), then he was aware of the Chinese PLA strategy to take on the West. He would've learned, for example, that if he took his fanaticism and combined it with the tactics and money of a financier like George Soros, he would have a "hyper-strategic weapon" capable of defeating the United States. Is there any doubt that he would jump at that kind of opportunity?

Lawsuit Alert
No, George, I'm not saying that you teamed up with bin Laden. You can call off your dogs now.

It's also interesting, if not exactly conclusive, that when bin Laden was killed by SEAL Team 6, a "strategy concept" for an attack on Europe's economy was discovered inside his compound. According to the report, the document did not list "concrete targets" (meaning that this was not about sending bombers into a stock market), but no other information was given. Unsurprisingly, it doesn't look as though anyone in the mainstream media has been interested enough in that report to bother following up.

Whether this document means that al-Qaeda was close to executing an economic attack is not clear, but what is clear is that we've been pretty slow to catch on. While bin Laden always saw this as an economic war, and himself as a financial terrorist, we've always seen it as a conventional war—one that would be fought in a very conventional way. As *Foreign Policy* magazine put it, "[I]t is not apparent that American planners clearly saw the link between al-Qaeda's war and the U.S. economy even after bin Laden boasted of it on the world stage."

Wait, doesn't that sound a bit like the Chinese commentary from *Unrestricted Warfare*?

However, the Americans have not been able to get their act together in this area. This is because proposing a new concept of weapons does not require relying on the springboard of new technology; it just demands lucid and incisive thinking. However, this is not a strong point for Americans, who are slaves to technology in their thinking.

The Myth of the Cave-Dwellers

I hear it all the time. *These people live in caves in Third World countries; I'm really supposed to believe that they can bring down the most sophisticated financial system in the history of the world?*

In a word: yes.

First, the whole premise is pretty naïve. These are, after all, the same "ignorant cave dwellers" who were able to breach airport security in multiple cities, take over multiple aircraft, inflict massive damage on the Pentagon, and bring down the World Trade Center. You'll excuse me if I'm ready to give them a little bit of credit in terms of their intelligence, patience, and ability to plan.

The reality is that many of those who hate America have university degrees from some of the best-known schools in the world. A study by Peter Bergen and Swati Pandey at the New America Foundation found that "two-thirds of the 25 hijackers and planners involved in 9/11 had attended college" and that of the seventy-five terrorists the authors investigated, two had earned Ph.D. degrees and two others were working on theirs.

Do we really want to be the country that, once again, looks back and asks *How could this have happened?* Wouldn't it be much better to connect the dots, imagine the unimaginable, and take whatever precautions are necessary to ensure that our economy—a great source of our strength—does not become the source of our collapse?

There are plenty of people who would've called you a fear-mongering conspiracy theorist before 9/11 if you'd suggested that terrorists were plotting to destroy the World Trade Center using commercial planes as missiles. Those same people are all too happy to launch those same insults now when it comes to the prospect of economic terrorism.

I have an idea. Let's stop listening to those people and instead start listening to the only things that we should really trust: our own instincts and common sense.

Chapter Five

THE AMERICAN DREAM IS A LIE

" So you, too, want to own a little home of your own? You, too, have dreamed of a vine covered cottage . . . roses, green shutters . . . a fireplace . . . a well kept dog on a well kept lawn. A home of your own. That, probably more than anything else, is the American dream. "

—Associated Press, 1947

POLITICIANS really seem to enjoy dropping the phrase "the American Dream" on us during election time.

Guess what? They support it. So do I. And why shouldn't I—I've lived it, or at least my definition of it.

I'm a baker's son from a small town in western Washington State. I never graduated from college. I was a Top 40 morning deejay for years. Yet, here I am, doing what I love, making a good living—and living a good life. If that's not "the American Dream," I don't know what is.

Do you?

There is no shortage of people trying to tell us what they think the Dream *should* be, or trying to claim the phrase as their own. To the Occupy Wall Street crowd, for instance, "the American Dream" usually means a free college education, free birth control, a guaranteed job, and free housing. To the Tea Party, it usually means the opposite—nothing free and no guarantees, but equality of opportunity for everyone.

Some seem to think that we've lost the American Dream somewhere along the way. President Obama's book *The Audacity of Hope*, for example, sports the subtitle "Thoughts on Reclaiming the American Dream." But if we're *reclaiming* something, wouldn't it be helpful to know what it is and who's taken it?

Of course—but those questions are much easier to ask than they are to answer. And that's the whole point—the "American Dream" itself is a big lie; a marketing slogan to sell a vision for America that is solely based on the political rhetoric of whichever party or politician or activist group wants to harness it.

American Dream 2.0

Occupy supporters will often make the claim that they are simply trying to get back the equality of opportunity that has allegedly gone missing in America. But, if you dig deeper, you find out quickly that they really don't just want opportunity, they want guarantees. Take, for example, this post from Occupy supporter Madonna Gauding:

> [T]he Occupy Wall Street movement is gaining momentum because most Americans now understand that the American Dream is only for the wealthy and well connected. But, the Occupy movement is demanding more than equal opportunity. We are questioning the American religion of free market capitalism, and the extreme individualism that fueled the corporate takeover of America. We are exploring a new morality, one that acknowledges our interdependence with each other, and insists, no matter how much the right screams "socialism" that the least among us deserve to have their basic needs met.

Make no mistake, it's the free market and capitalism that are on trial here; the very things that have powered the American Dream since the beginning.

But that wasn't always the case. In fact, decades ago, when the term was first coined, it wasn't about ideology or material things at all—it was about the embodiment of an idea.

DREAMING UP THE DREAM

It's 1930—the stock market has crashed, and Americans are beginning to realize that the Roaring Twenties might be gone forever. Author James Truslow Adams, who'd won the Pulitzer Prize ten years earlier for his book *The Founding of New England*, was in the midst of writing a one-volume history of the country and was obsessed with this concept of "the American Dream." He was so obsessed, in fact, that he actually wanted to use it as the title of his new book. But his publisher had other ideas. They figured that nobody wanted to spend three bucks on a book about a dream, so a new title won out: *The Epic of America*.

But just because he was forced to change the title didn't mean he'd lost his obsession. So here's what Adams, in the midst of a major economic crisis, had to say about the Dream:

The American Dream is that dream of a land in which life should be better and richer and fuller for every man, with opportunity for each according to ability or achievement. It is a difficult dream for the European upper classes to interpret adequately, also too many of us ourselves have grown weary and mistrustful of it. It is not a dream of motor cars and high wages merely, but a dream of social order in which each man and each woman shall be able to attain to the fullest stature of which they are innately capable, and be recognized by others for what they are, regardless of the fortuitous circumstances of birth or position.

It has been a dream of being able to grow to fullest development as man and woman, unhampered by the barriers which had slowly been erected in older civilizations, unrepressed by social orders which had been developed for the benefit of classes rather than for the simple human being of any and every class. And that dream has been realized more fully in actual life here than anywhere else, though very imperfectly even among ourselves.

Two things are immediately clear. First, to Adams, the "Dream" was about equality of opportunity ("each according to ability or achievement"); and second, that it had nothing to do with material things ("not a dream of motor cars and high wages").

But here's the most shocking part: Adams himself was not exactly viewed as a libertarian. In other sections of *The Epic of America* he wrote about income inequality and saving the Dream by cracking down on business interests. It's a fairly progressive message, with a lot of carping about the wealthy running the country and whining about the "intellectual worker or artist" falling behind "the "rising

wage scale" of average workers. As one historian put it, Adams was "a typical liberal intellectual: a debunker of patriotic myths, a denouncer of Puritanism and Babbitry, a somewhat supercilious observer of the political scene."

Imagine that—a "typical liberal" in the 1930s had a more conservative vision of the Dream than many actual conservatives do today. Of course, being a "liberal" back then didn't mean what it does now—both parties, while having different ideas for the country, were still soundly rooted in traditional American principles. Adams was no exception. One source said this about his earlier book: "[Adams] put forth his idea of the cardinal American values: work, morality, individualism, fiscal responsibility, and dedication to duty. These were the values he saw present in the character of the early New Englanders. 'Americans love property but hate privilege' was his supporting theory."

Work. Morality. Individualism. Fiscal responsibility. Duty. Property.

Those ideals are okay with me—and maybe that's why the idea of an "American Dream" caught on like wildfire. It was, at least at the beginning, uniquely mainstream American. The Dream may not have had a dictionary definition, but each person could insert their own hopes and aspirations onto its blank canvas and strive for a better life.

But that's not where the story ends.

When you get right down to it, the popularity of the phrase "the American Dream" really doesn't have a darn thing to do with James Truslow Adams. He was just the messenger. He doesn't deserve any more credit for people believing in "the American Dream" than Warren Harding does for Americans long revering their "Founding Fathers" (did you know that Harding actually invented that phrase in 1916?). Adams and Harding merely named something that tens of millions of people, generation after generation, already passionately believed in.

IN PURSUIT OF THE DREAM

Putting aside the specific term "the American Dream," just how far back does this *idea* really go? Nobody knows for sure, but some scholars think it all started with the French political philosopher Alexis de Tocqueville, when he visited America in the 1830s. In *Democracy in America*, Tocqueville wrote, "There is no man who cannot reasonably expect to attain the amenities of life, for each knows that, given love of work, his future is certain. . . . No one is fully contented with his present fortune, all are perpetually striving, in a thousand ways, to improve it. Consider one of them at any period of his life and he will be found engaged with some new project for the purpose of increasing what he has."

If you go back even further, to Thomas Jefferson in 1776, you'll find these words written into the Declaration of Independence: "We hold these truths to be self-evident, that all men are created equal, that they are endowed by their Creator with certain unalienable Rights, that among these are Life, Liberty and the pursuit of Happiness."

There it is, perhaps the earliest definition of The American Dream: the unalienable right to the *pursuit* of happiness. It was exactly the same message that James Truslow Adams would encapsulate (and name) more than 150 years later.

POLLING THE DREAM

Today, the American Dream is seemingly whatever a politician or activist wants it to be. It's no longer rooted in the Declaration or in our founding principle of equality of opportunity; it's an amoeba that shape-shifts to fit whatever agenda is attempting to harness it.

When unions and far-left activists decided they wanted to form a countermovement to the Tea Party, they got together at the 2011 "Take Back the American Dream" conference. The agenda included sessions with titles like "The American Dream Movement," "Starving the Dream," "Stop Outsourcing the Dream," "Jobs, Justice and the

The Pursuit of Happyness

In 2006 Will Smith starred in a movie called *The Pursuit of Happyness*, a great film that I think was really about not being guaranteed anything by "the American Dream." It's about a man who loses just about everything—his job, his savings, his wife, his home—and ends up in homeless shelters and sleeping with his five-year-old on a restroom floor. Despite it all he retains his self-respect. He doesn't give up. He keeps working. He keeps trying. And it all pays off. He's now the CEO of a brokerage firm that bears his name.

I know Chris Gardner, the real-life man featured in the film, and have spoken with him many times over the years. I can tell you, without a doubt, that this is one story Hollywood did not have to embellish much.

American Dream," "Paying for the Dream: Progressive Tax Reform and Social Justice" (naturally the dream is expensive), and, my personal favorite, "How Hip Hop, Superheroes and Digital Shorts Can Hyper-Charge the American Dream Movement."

Defining the Dream: 1978

"More than a third of U.S. families interviewed in a study . . . said they had lost faith in the American dream because of economic problems."
—ASSOCIATED PRESS

Sounds like a great conference—I'm sorry I missed it. I think it would've been fascinating to hear exactly *what* the American Dream is that we're "starving" and "outsourcing" and need all of this extra money to pay for. I naïvely thought that ideas and dreams were free.

Obviously, those running a conference like that have a different definition of the Dream than our Founders did—but the only question that's really relevant is whom most Americans now relate to. After all, maybe those of us who think that the Dream is about opportunity are actually in the minority these days.

Jack Chambless, an economics professor at Valencia College, had 180 students in his sophomore class write essays on what they thought the American Dream meant. The results were not pretty: only around 10 percent thought that government should stay out of the way, have low tax rates, and deregulate to allow people to fulfill the dream. *Ten percent.* Over 80 percent thought that the American Dream meant a job, a house, retirement funds, vacations, and other material things. Eighty percent wanted the government to provide "free" health care, tuition, a down payment on their first home, and "a job." Oh, and to pay for it all, they wanted the government to tax the wealthy.

Defining the Dream: 1982

"Owning a home is one part of the American Dream that, for many people, is becoming just that—a dream."
—ASSOCIATED PRESS

Defining the Dream: 1984

"American Dream Is Still Strong: A recent survey of 1,324 college students around the nation reveals that most of them dream of owning a home that is larger and more expensive than the home in which they grew up."
—SPARTANBURG (SC) HERALD JOURNAL

Defining the Dream: 1988

"One grim general conclusion was shared by two studies of the U.S. economy this Labor Day: The American Dream is fading for many people, especially young couples, as the rich get richer and the poor get poorer."
—UNITED PRESS INTERNATIONAL

Those results are especially frightening when you consider that these sophomores are one day going to be parents. If they teach their kids that the Dream is about a free trip to the doctor's office or a low-interest government mortgage, then what hope do we have?

If you talk to older Americans, including immigrants, you get very different answers than what those sophomores came up with. When Xavier University surveyed over a thousand U.S. adults in 2011 they found that "only 6 percent of Americans ranked 'wealth' as their first or second definition of the American dream. Forty-five percent named 'a good life for my family,' while 34 percent put 'financial security'—material comfort that is not necessarily synonymous with Bill Gates–like riches—on top."

Even better: "Thirty-two percent of our respondents pointed to 'freedom' as their dream; 29 percent to 'opportunity'; and 21 percent to the 'pursuit of happiness.' A fat bank account can be a means to these ends, but only a small minority believe that money is a worthy end in itself."

That's great, and it makes me more optimistic—but why is that sentiment almost the exact opposite of everything we hear in the media and from most activist groups? Could it be that maybe the traditional version of the Dream doesn't rate on TV or bring enough people into conferences?

> **Taking It for Granted?**
> Here's one eye-opening result from Xavier's survey: "48% of immigrants rate the dream in 'good condition' compared to only 31% of the population overall."
>   Could it be that those of us who've been here for a while have become a little bit jaded on just how good things are and just how much opportunity there really still is in America compared to the rest of the world?

DON'T DEFINE IT, LIVE IT

Hatred of the American Dream is as old as the Dream itself. There always have been, and always will be, people who innately believe that America is evil. These are usually the "intellectual" or, really, the "pseudo-intellectual" elites who spend most of their time feeling guilty for being born here. But you know something? The "American Dream" has never been for elite snobs. They've never figured it out. They never will. The "American Dream" is for the rest of us—the people who get up every day and work hard in order to create a better life for ourselves and our families.

The American Dream is also just that: uniquely *American*. We should be proud of the fact that most other countries *don't even understand the concept of a Dream*. For example, in 1959 IBM set up a large computer at an exhibit called the "American National Exhibition" in Moscow. The idea was to allow Russians to ask the computer questions about America and life over here.

After receiving nearly ten thousand inquiries from curious Russians, two stood out as being asked more than any other: What is "the price of a pack of American cigarettes and [what is] the meaning of the 'American dream'?"

Imagine that—of all the questions you could ask about America, these Russians wanted to know what "the Dream" was. Not how to get it, or how many had achieved it, or how they could get it—no, even that was too advanced—they *didn't even understand the concept of a Dream*.

(By the way, the IBM computer answered them like this: "That all men shall be free to seek a better life with free worship, thought, assembly, expression of belief and universal suffrage and education.")

We all know that America has changed, and sometimes it's easy to fall into the trap of feeling that things are somehow different than they ever have been before; that no other generation of Americans endured a terrible economy, a terrible job market, an enormous price tag for education, and a declining view of their future, all at once. But that's just not true—every generation has its battles, many of which seem insurmountable at the time. And while they always *feel* unique, the truth is that life is a series of ups and downs. If we tossed aside the Dream every time there was a down period, then it would never have made it out of the 1700s.

Here's a column from John Cunniff that I think proves my point:

Defining the Dream: 1993

"The American dream that we were all raised on is a simple but powerful one—if you work hard and play by the rules you should be given a chance to go as far as your God-given ability will take you."

—PRESIDENT BILL CLINTON

Defining the Dream: Celebrity Edition

In 2007, Forbes asked a number of celebrities and politicians, "What is the American Dream?"

Former Speaker of the House Nancy Pelosi answered that "[t]he American Dream is the hope for a better future with equal opportunity for all to participate in the prosperity and success of our great nation." That's a pretty good answer; you'll have to excuse me for not believing that it's what she really believes.

Writer P. J. O'Rourke answered that the "Pursuit of happiness is the distinctly American Dream, proclaimed front and center in our Declaration of Independence. You'll find no such aspiration announced in the credo of any other nation, state, society or people."

But leave it to a nonpolitician, non-elite to deliver the best answer. Olympics figure skater Sasha Cohen hit it out of the park when she said: "To me, the American Dream is something deep inside that drives you to be who you are."

The American Dream, like real dreams, can't be defined or explained by anyone but you.

What seems to be missing from the lives of many Americans is the dream—the vision that tomorrow could only be better, the soul-deep conviction that they would participate in the future.

Like a kite flying out ahead, the dream tugged the dreamer into a new material reality: a new house, more money, education, a second car, a color TV set.

All through the last decade families found that it paid to dream because there was an excellent chance of turning dreams into reality. America was always on the verge of something exciting.

The credit suppliers realized that money was needed to translate the dream, and so they made the down payment smaller, the terms easier. Buy now, pay later.

The stock market was like an elevator, lifting many people to new financial achievements. Everyone was playing the game.

Do you think that was written this year? Or maybe in 2010?

Nope, it was written in 1974.

The Dream survived the 1970s and all the pessimism that op-ed captured. It survived—and, at times, flourished, in the 1980s and '90s. The turn of the century brought us a collapse, a recovery, and another collapse. And so here we are again, another crossroads in time; another chance to fall for the seductive rhetoric of those like Van Jones who say that the Dream is turning into "the American nightmare." With each downturn in the economy, there are seemingly fewer and fewer who are willing to stand up, dig in their heels, and remind everyone that the Dream is not something that can be owned. It can't be bought or sold, reclaimed or refurbished. You can't give it away, take it back, tear it to shreds, or outsource it.

> ## Defining the Dream: 2011
>
> "[W]e should have no doubt about the American dream. For four centuries, it has rested on the idea that government should do all it can to narrow the divide between those at the top and those at the bottom of society."
>
> —NICOLAUS MILLS, PROFESSOR OF AMERICAN STUDIES, SARAH LAWRENCE COLLEGE

You can't do any of those things because the American Dream that is packaged up and served to us by the press and our politicians is a lie.

The truth is that there is only one thing that you *can* do with whatever you define your American Dream to be: *live it.* 🐓

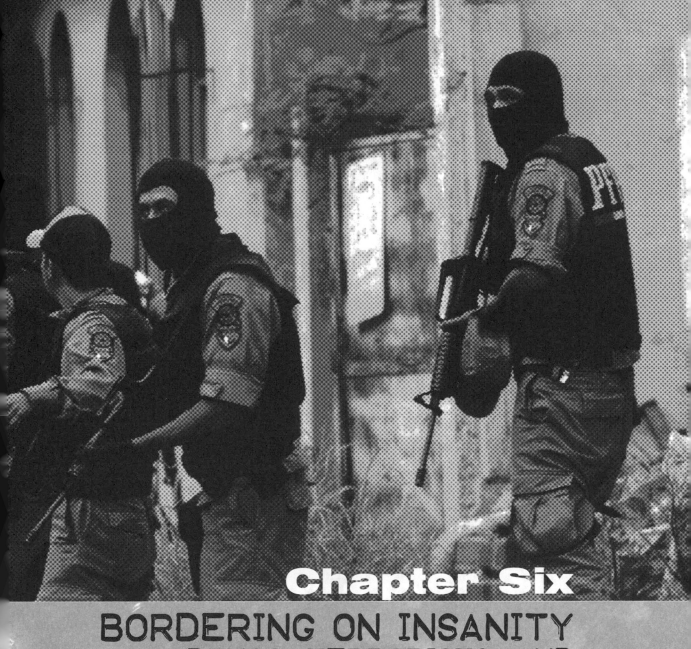

Chapter Six

BORDERING ON INSANITY
DRUGS, TERRORISTS, AND MURDER IN OUR BACKYARD

> **" So today I say to the cartels:** Don't even think about bringing your **violence** and tactics across this **border.** You will be met by an **overwhelming** response. **"**

—Janet Napolitano, U.S. Homeland Security Secretary, January 2012

THE DECADES we've spent arguing about

immigration reform and border security have resulted in a

lot of accusations of hate and racism—but very little prog-

ress. Unfortunately, while we've been yelling and screaming

at each other we've created a vacuum—and you know how

the old saying goes: "Mexican drug cartels abhor a vacuum."

There is a national emergency brewing on our side of the border. A war, actually. It's already in full swing just to our south, where at least 34,000 people have died in the last five years—15,000 last year alone (though, let's be honest, it's hard to count the dead accurately when bodies are burned or put into buckets of quick-lime so that they are impossible to identify). Despite all of that, along with the obvious national security implications for America, our only strategy seems to be to issue stern warnings to the cartels about how serious we'll get if the violence crosses some imaginary line in the sand.

It's time for a new strategy. This is not about stopping illegal immigration or coming up with that elusive "comprehensive immigration reform" bill—it's about stopping the culture of drugs and violence that has become almost routine. And it all starts by doing what the media and most politicians would prefer not to: telling Americans the truth about what is really going on along our southern border.

A BAD TRIP DOWN MEMORY LANE

What do thousands of Chinese immigrants, a Mexican woman, and heroin have in common? No, this isn't a "so-and-so walks into a bar" joke. The truth is that, together, they formed the foundation of drug trafficking in Mexico, dominating its history for almost seventy years.

Back in the 1860s, the Chinese started to arrive in Mexico in droves to serve as railroad and agricultural workers. No one knew it at the time, but these workers would change the course of Mexico's history by bringing with them a seemingly innocuous crop: the opium poppy. It turns out that poppies grow remarkably well in Mexico's Sierra Madre mountain range, and particularly well in the state of Sinaloa, where the Chinese population exploded at the turn of the century.

As you might imagine, the success of the poppy meant that Chinese traffickers soon became major players in the opium trade. Fast-forward a few decades and their role expanded even more when the U.S. government started ordering huge quantities of morphine for soldiers returning from World War II.

The landscape of drug trafficking in Mexico was dramatically altered again during the "hippie era" of the 1960s. As it just so happens, marijuana *also* grows extremely well in many parts of Mexico. As American demand for marijuana exploded, the drug trade evolved into a Mexican family business.

The next two decades turned into the golden era as powerful drug lords with nicknames like "the Godfather" and "the Lord of the Skies" emerged, living like kings in some Mexican version of the Don Corleone saga. This new breed of drug lords started out dealing in heroin and marijuana because cocaine isn't produced in Mexico. (And, not incidentally, also because cocaine was under the purview of the legendary Pablo Escobar and his buddies in Colombia—a group that didn't exactly have a reputation for tolerance when it came to competition.)

Things were going along fine for everyone in the trade when suddenly, in the 1980s, a funny thing happened: the U.S. Drug Enforcement Administration's ef-

Girl Gone Wild

All of this success didn't go unnoticed by the locals. In the 1920s, a Mexican woman by the name of Ignacia Jasso La Viuda de González (thankfully she went by the shorter nickname of "La Nacha") entered the drug trade with her husband in Ciudad Juárez, directly across the border from El Paso, Texas. After he died, she continued to sell drugs from her home, supplying El Paso and other U.S. cities for decades. La Nacha controlled much of the Juárez heroin, morphine, and marijuana trade until her death (as a free woman) in the 1980s.

forts against the Colombian cartels actually began to work. Trafficking routes from Colombia to the United States across the Florida straits into Miami were virtually shut down, leaving cocaine exporters in a jam: How could they continue to supply John Belushi without access to the United States?

Fortunately for the Colombians, Mexican "logisticians" were ready to step in and help. They began to develop a cocaine "trampoline" by which they would bring cocaine in from Colombia and transport it through Mexico and across the border into the States. Mexican traffickers became so adept at this trampoline so quickly that *they* began to dictate terms to the Colombians instead of the other way around.

And that is how the modern Mexican drug trade was born.

Juan Is the Loneliest Number

Oddly enough, the man who developed this method of bouncing Colombian cocaine off of Mexico and into the United States wasn't Mexican or Colombian; he was Honduran. His name is Juan Matta Ballesteros and, these days, he's pretty easy to find: he's living in the supermax prison in Colorado, where he's serving three consecutive life terms for drug and kidnapping charges.

THE GOOD OLD BAD OLD DAYS

It may be hard to believe given all of the modern-day violence, but Mexican drug traffickers actually got along (more or less) in the 1980s. There were no such things as "cartels" back then (a term that is actually a misnomer since traffickers don't conspire to set drug prices), and traffickers never referred to themselves as such. No, back in the good old bad old days, one man pretty much ran the whole show: Miguel Ángel Félix Gallardo, aka "the Godfather."

Things went smoothly for Félix Gallardo for a while, but then, in 1985, he made a big mistake: he became involved in the kidnapping and murder of DEA agent Enrique "Kiki" Camarena.

Feeling the increasing heat from U.S. and Mexican authorities, Félix Gallardo decided to hold a narco powwow in the resort city of Acapulco. It was there that he made the historic decision to divide up his drug empire into five pieces, placing trusted and lesser-known (at least to the DEA) bosses in charge of each drug corridor.

Those five pieces lived and worked under the same unwritten and unspoken code as the Italian Mafia here in the United States: business is business, settle accounts professionally, and stay away from the wives and children. Alliances and partnerships between the cartels came and went, girlfriends and wives caused tempers to flare, but, for the most part, there was relative peace.

Then democracy came to Mexico, and everything went to hell.

It sounds like a strange thing to say, but Mexican politics had *everything* to do with transforming the fairly benign drug "trade" into the daily carnage we see today. From 1929 until 2000 there was one political party in power—the Institutional Revolutionary Party (PRI). During that time it ruled Mexico with a very tight grip, and it had a nasty reputation for extreme corruption. It was an open secret that the PRI was in bed with the cartels, ignoring their illicit activities in exchange for having their bread buttered under the table with narco dollars.

But *this* is the crucial detail that people need to understand: the Mexican government had ultimate control over the cartels. If the drug lords or their underlings got out of hand and let things get too ugly, the government would immediately step in, make some arrests, or "disappear" some key people. The bad guys would step back into line, and everyone went back about their day in peace and harmony.

But in 2000 everything changed. The PRI got the boot, and Vicente Fox of the National Action Party (PAN) was elected president. With Fox's win it wasn't just the PRI's total dominance of Mexican affairs that went out the window; so did the implicit agreement between the Mexican government and the cartels. As a result, the *Pax Mafiosa* was officially over.

Now the *cartels* were in charge.

THE GAME CHANGER

In the mid-1990s, Osiel Cárdenas Guillén—then the head of the Gulf cartel—decided that he needed to raise his own private army to defend his territory and operations along the Texas border in northeast Mexico. To ensure he had the best of the best in his army, he turned to Mexican Special Forces troops and made them offers they couldn't refuse: *Leave the army, come work for me, and I'll make you rich beyond your wildest dreams.* It was not a difficult sell.

Real-Life Hunger Games
There were originally thirty-one Zetas recruited by Cárdenas Guillén. Authorities believe that only three of them are still alive today.

And, with that, Los Zetas—the most fearsome, ruthless, brutal, and bloodthirsty killing machine that Mexico has ever seen—was born.

Now, fast-forward to 2006. Vicente Fox's term was coming to end, and while he had taken down the full leadership of the Tijuana cartel and the head of the Gulf cartel, he never did stage a dramatic fight against the cartels. Outside of a few skirmishes, there was no major escalation in violence.

Things, however, were about to change.

That year, the PAN continued its winning streak with the election of Felipe Calderón. Calderón hadn't run on an antidrug or antiviolence platform, but it didn't take long for him to make the drug war the focus of his administration. He adopted a strategy of "hit 'em hard" and "give them no quarter," dispatching tens of thousands of army soldiers to various narco hot spots throughout Mexico. Calderón felt (with very good reason) that he couldn't rely on the extremely corrupt state and local police to take care of business.

Needless to say, the cartels weren't exactly thrilled with his decision. It was bad enough that the government was no longer ignoring their activities or accepting their hush money; they were now actively *fighting* them. If the cartels wanted to keep the drug profits rolling in (and, believe me, they did), then they only had one choice: fight back, and fight back hard.

So that's exactly what they did.

The U.S. government once called Los Zetas "the most technologically advanced, sophisticated and dangerous cartel operating in Mexico." I think that's a massive understatement. The Zetas had an *insane* amount of urban and guerrilla warfare training, knowledge of surveillance and countersurveillance techniques, and expertise with weapons and explosives.

But they also had something else: no soul.

Around 2004, Los Zetas introduced a tactic into the fight that soon became the hallmark of drug war violence: decapitation. While the number of murders in Nuevo Laredo, a Mexican city across the Rio Grande from Laredo, Texas, during that time wasn't as high as it is now in places like Ciudad Juárez, Los Zetas made up for it with the sheer viciousness of their kills. The rules of the game had changed.

From that point on, it became a ruthless cartel game of keeping up with the Joneses. It was almost as if they were following the script from *The Untouchables:* "They pull a knife, you pull a gun. He sends one of yours to the

What's in a Name?
The "Zetas" name was derived from their founding member: Arturo Guzmán Decena, whose military call sign was "Z1." Over the last fifteen years, the older members have passed down their skills to younger members, although many of them lack the extensive training and discipline of older members.

hospital, you send one of his to the morgue." If Los Zetas cut off someone's head and hung the body from a bridge, their competitors had to do the same thing (or worse) to show they were just as fearless and intimidating. Of course, as time went on, and Calderón continued to pour fuel on the fire that democracy had started, the violent acts got continually worse.

- In 2006, a new cartel called La Familia Michoacana emerged. Their "coming out" party consisted of rolling five severed heads onto the dance floor of a nightclub in the city of Uruapan.
- In January 2010, a cartel murdered and dismembered a thirty-six-year-old man, putting his body parts into a few containers and leaving them in different places across the city of Los Mochis. Upping the ante even more, they sent a memorable message by separating the man's face from his skull and sewing it onto a soccer ball.
- In September 2011, members of the Sinaloa Federation posted a video on YouTube of two men—accused of being snitches—being decapitated with a chain saw. While they were still alive.

THE CARTELS GET CREATIVE

All of the violence is, of course, only about one thing: money. More specifically, the billions of dollars American drug users spend every year on the four drugs that Mexican cartels specialize in: marijuana, cocaine, heroin, and methamphetamine. The United Nations estimates they're raking in anywhere from 8 to 30 *billion* dollars annually on these drugs, although this is just a mildly educated guess; it's not like PricewaterhouseCoopers is doing their books. As with any black market activity, we can only make educated ballpark estimates.

In 2010, U.S. Customs and Border Protection (CBP) seized more than 784 tons of marijuana, heroin, cocaine, and methamphetamine along the southwest border. For comparison, that's the typical weight of a loaded Ariane 5 rocket, or four standard locomotive trains. Worse, the consensus among law enforcement agencies is that they're only catching about 10 percent of the drugs that are actually coming across the border. In other words, for every four train cars full of drugs that we're catching, thirty-six more make their way in without a hitch.

Much of those drugs come across our border in the "traditional" way—in the trunks or hidden compartments of cars and trucks at the ports of entry, on the backs of human mules traversing the desert in between the checkpoints, etc. Smugglers still use *Miami Vice*–style boats and planes, but they are much less common these days. What are becoming *more* common, however, are border tunnels, drug submarines, and ultralight planes.

If necessity is the mother of invention then drug cartels are modern-day Benjamin Franklins.

The Tunnels

More than one hundred cross-border tunnels have been discovered in the past decade, including seven major tunnels along the San Diego border with Mexico in the past five years alone, according to U.S. Immigration and Customs Enforcement (ICE). Some of these tunnels are engineering wonders, with concrete-reinforced walls, ventilation systems, wired-in lighting, and track systems for transporting drugs quickly. Other tunnels are more like rabbit holes, where one person can barely squeeze through on his belly with a rope tied to his ankle and several bales of dope. But no matter their size or complexity, these tunnels can be extremely difficult to detect. Human intelligence is crucial, but some Border Patrol agents will tell you that the best way to find a border tunnel is to run over it with your truck.

Diversifying Their Portfolio

The cartels' business portfolios don't end with drug smuggling. Believe it or not, Mexican and U.S. enforcement efforts are actually having an impact on drug trafficking, so some cartels—most notably Los Zetas and La Familia Michoacana—have diversified into other fun extracurricular activities, like kidnapping and ransom, extortion, fuel theft, piracy of DVDs, CDs, and software.

According to the Motion Picture Association of America, movie piracy in Mexico costs Hollywood at least $590 million *annually*. Within the countries that make up the Organisation for Economic Co-operation and Development, Mexico has the third-highest rate of pirated software at 60 percent, after Chile and Turkey. Microsoft's associate general counsel for antipiracy, David Finn, wrote that La Familia alone could have as many as 180,000 points of sale, with profits reaching $2.2 million *a day*.

Another profitable expansion of their business has been cattle rusting. Yes, drug traffickers are now stealing Mexican cows.

Livestock organizations in eleven Mexican states have said that cattle rustling has significantly increased in the last three years. Why? Why else: money. It seems that cattle rustling can raise a decent chunk of change. A bull can sell for $10,000, a cow for $12,000, a horse for up to $30,000, and a calf for up to $20,000.

The Drug Subs

Drug subs, which are more formally known as "self-propelled semi-submersible vessels" (see why they just call them "drug subs"?), because they don't fully submerge, can be total marvels of construction—multimillion-dollar affairs built by Russian engineers in the Colombian jungle that look like they were just pulled out of the *Finding Nemo* ride at Disneyland. Others . . . not so much. The cheaper versions appear to have been cobbled together with cardboard, PVC pipe, and a few rolls of duct tape. But all of the drug subs have one thing in common: an enormous capacity for holding illegal narcotics. Many can haul up to six tons at a time and, if intercepted, can be completely scuttled in less than two minutes.

Working on one of these things is not exactly like spending a week on the *Queen Mary 2*. Drug subs are almost always bare-bones deals, with no midnight buffet or rock-climbing wall. The navigators have to endure a one-to-two-week journey with no air-conditioning, no showers, minimal food and water, and no functioning toilet. But they get the job done. And they're paid handsomely for their sacrifice.

The Ultralights

Depending on the model, an ultralight can carry one person and roughly 250 pounds of drug cargo. They fly below the radar, so they're very difficult to detect, but occasionally they have the pesky problem of running into power lines. Some pilots land in the United States to drop off their load with a courier, then take off again and head home. Others are getting better at releasing their drug loads while in flight, although this can mean disaster if they're dropped unevenly. Ultralight pilots who aren't trained properly can easily meet a grisly fate in some Arizona lettuce field.

There is nothing quite like drugs and money to bring out maximum creativity in criminals. For example, there was the load of Jesus statues in one woman's trunk, which were made of a plaster and cocaine mixture (yes, that cocaine-doll-dissolved-in-water scene in the movie *Traffic* is entirely realistic). Then there was the shipment of frozen sharks that had been hollowed out and filled with packages of cocaine. And there are plenty of people who are happy to use their own bodies as vehicles, swallowing dozens of little drug-filled balloons until their insides are close to bursting. Of course, what goes in must come out, and I'd hate to be the smuggler or CBP agent on the receiving end of that delivery.

This drug tunnel connected Tijuana and San Diego. It was 600 yards long and was equipped with lighting and ventilation.

YES, IN YOUR BACKYARD

To really understand the nature of Mexico's drug war today, it's important to know how new criminal entities like Los Zetas differ from the other "old school" cartels. Remember, Los Zetas didn't start out the way the other cartels did; they began as a private army for the Gulf cartel—essentially very well-trained professional killers. Their boss, Cárdenas Guillén, was arrested in 2003 and extradited to the United States in 2007. And, well, when the cat is away, the mice will play.

Los Zetas grew in confidence and drug trafficking expertise during this time. Finally, by 2008, they'd had enough of being under the Gulf cartel's control. They took advantage of Guillén's extradition to the States the prior year and officially broke away to become their own cartel.

If you take a look at an organizational chart for a Fortune 500 company, you're likely to see many similarities with a chart for the Tijuana or Juárez cartels. There is a CEO at the top, several layers of top managers underneath, and so forth, with each level of management reporting directly to the layer above.

But Los Zetas is run more like a franchise. They do have a boss at the top, but each Zetas cell more or less operates independently and gets to make its own decisions. Unfortunately, those decisions usually involve various ways to kill people.

In August 2010, seventy-three migrants from Central and South America were making their way north through Mexico when members of Los Zetas intercepted them roughly 120 miles from the Texas border. They were taken to a farmhouse in a remote area near the town of San Fernando, bound and blindfolded, and summarily executed. One man from Ecuador played dead until the Zetas left and then escaped, which is the only reason we know what happened.

What we still don't know is exactly *why* Los Zetas committed one of the largest atroci-

You Look Familiar

After Osiel Cárdenas Guillén was convicted for various drug-related crimes he was sentenced to serve twenty-five years and transferred to the top-security federal prison in Florence, Colorado. And how's this for irony? The original leader of the Gulf cartel that Osiel once controlled, Juan García Ábrego, is also serving multiple life sentences there.

ties ever recorded in the drug war against so many innocent people. Did they want to recruit the immigrants? Use them as drug mules? Or were they just feeling extra sociopathic that day? To make matters worse, the Mexican government kept many details surrounding the massacre to themselves. Gee, might the murder of seventy-two innocent people make Calderón and his drug-war strategy look bad?

But the Zetas weren't done.

Almost one year later at least twelve men in several vehicles arrived at the luxury Casino Royale in Monterrey, Mexico. In less than three minutes, the men had set the entire casino on fire and left. There were varying reports that claimed the men started shooting, threw grenades, and yelled at people to leave. Even if the latter were true, many (if not all) of the emergency exits were locked, and fifty-two innocent people died—many from smoke inhalation in the bathrooms, where they had holed up trying to survive. Unlike the massacre of the seventy-two immigrants, we know why the perpetrators (believed to be Zetas) targeted the Casino Royale: the owner hadn't yet paid his monthly *cuota*, or "tax" to the cartel.

Between the chain-saw beheadings (remind anyone of Nicholas Berg's decapitation in Iraq?), the San Fernando massacre, the casino attack, and *many* other examples of innocents being targeted or killed, this whole mess is starting to sound a lot like . . . terrorism. In fact, President Calderón labeled the Casino Royale attack exactly that, calling it an "aberrant act of terror and barbarity." His national security spokesman, Alejandro Poiré Romero, put it even more bluntly, stating, "an act of terrorism has been committed."

Typical Politician

Unfortunately, after labeling this a terrorist act, Calderón kept talking, eventually going on to partly blame the United States for the attack, citing our insatiable drug demand and lax gun laws as contributing factors. I guess by that logic we should blame Mexico every time a Hollywood star overdoses.

HEZBOLLAH IS HERE

As a result of the Casino Royale attack there was a lot of debate about whether the U.S. government should label cartels as terrorist organizations. But who needs cartels to be terrorists when we have actual terrorists who are terrorists? Many experts are concerned that members of "traditional" terrorist groups, meaning Islamist fundamentalist groups like al-Qaeda, are entering the United States from Mexico in order to do bad things here. The group whose name has been popping up over and over again in that regard is Hezbollah.

In September 2010, the Tucson, Arizona, police department issued a confidential memo that became known to the public only when it was leaked by the hacker group LulzSec. The memo stated, ". . . obvious concerns have arisen concerning Hezbollah's presence in Mexico and possible ties to Mexican drug trafficking organizations [DTO's] operating along the US–Mexico border." While the report said that no official connection had been made, the author cited two specific incidents: the arrest of Jameel Nasr in Tijuana, who was alleged to be tasked with establishing the Hezbollah network in Mexico and throughout South America, and the arrest of Jamal Yousef in New York City. Yousef owned a pretty decent weapons cache, including 100 M-16 assault rifles, 100 AR-15 rifles, 2,500 hand grenades, C4 explosives, and antitank munitions. He told police that the weapons, which were being stored in Mexico, had been stolen from Iraq with the help of his cousin, who was a member of Hezbollah.

In another incident, from May 2011, a local news station in San Diego interviewed a former U.S. intelligence agent (his name and agency were never mentioned) who said, "We are looking at 15 or 20 years that Hezbollah has been setting up shop in Mexico." He also told the news station that Hezbollah is partnering with unidentified drug organizations, and that the group receives cartel cash and protection in exchange for Hezbollah expertise, "from money laundering to firearms training and explosives training."

That is certainly alarming, but many people may have overlooked another part of the statement: "If they really wanted to start blowing stuff up, they could do it . . . but the organization [Hezbollah] sees the U.S. as their 'cash cow,' with illegal drug and immigration operations . . . The money they are sending back to Lebanon is too important right now to jeopardize those operations."

That, to me, is a really important point to consider: cartels don't have a religious or political ideology unless you consider power and money to be religion. Terrorists, on the other hand, generally *only* have a religious or political ideology. To mix those two groups together is not as easy as it might seem given that cartels are interested in keeping Americans alive (and using their product), not killing millions of them or doing something that might force the border to be sealed off.

Here's a fun little fact that may surprise you: thousands of people associated in some way with Hezbollah are living here in the United States right now, and have been for quite some time.

What?!? How is that possible??? How can the FBI not know about this, or not have warned us in some way? Why haven't all the major news outlets been telling us about this terrorist threat?

Wait . . . it gets even better.

We are willingly giving these terrorists our money, which they are then sending back to their terrorist buddies in the Middle East. And when I say "our money,"

I'm not talking about government funding (although that wouldn't be out of the realm of possibility), I'm talking about the money of normal, everyday Americans.

You know all those fake designer-label purses, hats, and shoes you see being sold on sidewalks and out of street carts in major U.S. cities? There's a good chance that the proceeds from those items are going to Hezbollah. In an April 2008 raid on a Queens, New York, warehouse—the largest such raid in New York City history—police confiscated 75,000 pairs of fake Nike sneakers, 75,000 knock-off handbags, and 5,000 pieces of fake name-brand clothing. The street value of these products was estimated at $4.5 million. New York authorities strongly believed the proceeds from the sale of these goods were headed to Middle Eastern terrorist organizations.

So, we have strong evidence that Hezbollah has a significant number of members and associates in Mexico. We also have strong evidence that members and associates of Hezbollah (and perhaps other Islamist terrorist groups) have entered the United States from Mexico, either on their own or by using human smugglers who specialize in moving other-than-Mexicans, or "OTMs," across the border. None of that is good news, but it's important to remember that there's a big difference between members of terrorist groups who come here to raise money and members who come here to blow things up.

First, let's state the obvious: the acceptable number of terrorists who should be able to slip through the (often wide) border (in both our north and south), or be allowed to go undetected in our communities is *zero*. I am not at all trying to downplay the risk or pretend that it's not an issue. I'm simply trying to separate fact from conjecture and hyperbole so that we can focus on solving the actual problem. (You may have noticed that we haven't made much progress in that regard in a while.)

So, here is the truth: there is no evidence that an *operational* member of a terrorist group—meaning someone toting a bomb, or

WARNING: ADULT CONTENT

What do you think might happen if a nuclear weapon went off in a U.S. city and it became clear that the bomb was brought in over the Mexican border with the help of a drug cartel? Do you think maybe that our lack of border security might lead the news every night? Do you think the president might give an address to the nation in which he says something about how the "debate over our border has gone on too long, it's time for action" before he sends the military to shut it down? Do you think a border fence might magically be erected in a year?

We've seen how this stuff works before: politicians generally don't act until Americans die or a close call is narrowly averted. Then, once they do, they *over*react, or put knee-jerk policies into place that do nothing to solve the actual problem (yes, I'm looking at you, TSA, and your stupid three-ounces-of-liquid rule).

actively planning to kill lots of Americans—has gotten into the United States via Mexico, yet. *And that is great news.* But, unlike a lot of politicians, I'm not someone who likes to wait until catastrophe strikes before deciding that something needs to be done. (I was playing bin Laden's words on my radio program years before 9/11, warning that we must take him seriously.) I know it's crazy, but I actually prefer to prepare for disaster and worst-case scenarios, rather than panic once they do occur.

A MATCH MADE IN HELL?

We know Hezbollah is working along our southern border. We know the drug cartels are working there as well. So, that begs the question: Are they working together?

Anything's possible, but at least so far, the evidence is just not there to support it. And, as I said earlier, the cartels and terrorists keeping their distance from each other actually makes a lot of sense.

In October 2011 the weirdest assassination plot in years came to light and started a minor international crisis. Iranian officials were accused of plotting to assassinate the Saudi Arabian ambassador to the United States at a Washington, D.C., restaurant. Sounds typical enough for Iran, but the odd part was that they reportedly intended to use a Mexican drug cartel to pull it off.

The two men spearheading this plot were an Iranian-American used car salesmen and a reported member of the elite Iranian Quds Force. They thought they were meeting with a man in Mexico who was a member of a violent cartel (widely reported to be Los Zetas, but that was never confirmed by U.S. authorities) willing to accept $1.5 million for the job: to blow up the D.C. restaurant where the ambassador would be dining.

U.S. and Iranian officials immediately went into an uproar when the plot was publicly revealed, hurling accusations at each other at a record pace. But analysts and observers of both Iran and Mexico were left scratching their heads, and with very good reason. First of all, the two Iranian plotters never met with a real cartel member. They were actually dealing with a DEA informant who convinced them that he worked for a cartel. At no time did any real cartel members know anything about this plot, or have any involvement whatsoever. Then there's the matter of the sum offered. Remember, drug cartels are raking in *billions of dollars* every year. One and a half million dollars is literally pocket change to these guys:

the equivalent of one lost drug load, or the monthly payment to bribe a handful of police officers. There is no way that any cartel in its right mind would risk that kind of exposure for what amounts to pennies in the drug trade. Ultimately, there was no true link between the Iranians and Los Zetas—or to any other Mexican cartel.

When we talk about a potential relationship between terrorists and cartels, we need to remember that, first and foremost, cartels are profit-maximizing businesses. They aim to minimize expenses and reduce risk as much as possible. They know that nothing would bring the wrath and full might of the U.S. government—including law enforcement and possibly the U.S. military—down on them faster and harder than aiding and abetting terrorists. Neither the cartels, nor the Mexican government for that matter, can afford the consequences that such an association would likely bring.

Of course, none of that changes the fact that our open border is responsible for clear cases of death and despair here in the United States. After all, the people who *do* have operational intentions and who *have* crossed the border in droves (and whom, for whatever idiotic reason, we don't seem to be too worried about) are the thousands of violent cartel members and human smugglers living and working in every corner of the United States.

Our Own Worst Enemy

I recently spoke to Kent Lundgren, chairman of the National Association of Former Border Patrol Officers, and he made a great point: No one person or group (terrorist or not) who comes across our border poses an existential threat to America's future. Instead, that threat comes from the inside, from the complacency and corruption of those of us who are already here. Lundgren said:

"The real threat that we should fear, one that can destroy the America we know, is corruption. Corruption is what makes possible drug trafficking on the scope we see in Mexico. When we think 'corruption' we tend to think of an officer accepting money to let a load of drugs go, or stealing money that he has seized or getting sexual favors in return for turning a blind eye to criminal activity.

"It is all that, of course—but we must expand our thought horizons. What of the politician who accepts campaign money to introduce a bill that makes things easier for the bad guys? Or a reporter who blows off a story? Or a prosecutor's secretary who misses a critical filing deadline in a case that forces it be dismissed? The list of vulnerabilities is long, and the cartels know each item on it.

"To a degree remarkable among the nations of the world, America operates on trust. Trust of each other and of our institutions. Erode and destroy that trust and we become no better than Mexico or Egypt. And that's exactly what the drug cartels and terror groups are counting on . . .

ONE NATION, UNDER SIEGE

One huge obstacle to examining the drug war clearly is the idea that it's all a "southwest border problem." There's a pretty good chance that most people in Montana, or Rhode Island, or Nebraska really aren't that concerned about what's happening in Mexico or along the border, or about the thousands of people being slaughtered in the name of illegal drugs every year.

Unfortunately, that just seems to be the new American way. If something isn't in our own little bubble, or in the bubbles of our friends and family members, we just don't have the time to really deal with it. And why should we? We work hard every day, get our kids to school on time, shop for groceries, get gas, and try to get some sleep. The problems in our orbits are our coworkers, traffic, food prices, gas prices and, of course, not getting enough sleep. What we *don't* spend much time worrying about is getting caught in machine-gun crossfire on our way to work, seeing decapitated bodies at the door to our kids' school, or having to avoid certain restaurants because cartel members on someone's hit list might be eating there that night.

But guess what: many people do have to worry about those things because of cartels. Right here, in America.

According to the Justice Department's National Drug Intelligence Center, Mexican drug cartels have a presence—either direct or by proxy, in *over one thousand U.S. cities.* Ninety percent of the illegal drugs consumed in this country come from our neighbor to the south. In 2009 (the latest year for which this data is available), drug overdoses and brain damage linked to long-term drug abuse killed an estimated 37,485 Americans. Meanwhile, cartels are co-opting thousands of gang members in our cities and communities to sell those same drugs on our streets. They're even making or growing those drugs well within our borders.

The precursor chemicals used to make methamphetamine were either outlawed or restricted in 2004 (which is why you have to go through everything but a body cavity search to buy a decongestant at a pharmacy these days), but the cartels don't follow our rules. They're able to get the raw chemicals from Asia and South America, and either make the meth in

Yeah, But Is It Organic?

As a recovering alcoholic, I guess I shouldn't be that surprised about what people are willing to put in their bodies, but methamphetamine is really nasty stuff. The fundamental ingredient is ephedrine, which is found in some cold medicines (and is the reason why many kinds are now restricted). The ephedrine is mixed, or "cooked," with other ingredients like battery acid, drain cleaner, lantern fuel, and antifreeze. The process of heating this mixture is very dangerous (as you know if you've ever seen the show *Breaking Bad*), as the chemicals are volatile and can cause the entire lab—often an apartment or trailer—to explode. It also leaves behind a toxic mess: the production of one pound of meth creates five pounds of toxic waste.

Mexican "superlabs" before bringing it across the border—or make it right here. One of the largest meth labs ever discovered in the United States was in Gwinnett County, Georgia—just outside Atlanta—and it was run by La Familia Michoacana.

Then there's the marijuana. Would it surprise you to know that Mexican drug cartels are growing marijuana plants in our taxpayer-funded national parks and forests? And out of the top ten states where they're doing it, only one (California) is along the southwest border. Marijuana "grows," as the plantations are called, have been discovered in North Carolina, Tennessee, Colorado, and Michigan, to name just a few states.

In February 2012, three Mexican nationals were each sentenced to ten years in federal prison for a marijuana-growing operation based in the sprawling, thickly wooded Chequamegon-Nicolet National Forest in northern Wisconsin. Typically, these grows contain thousands of plants, each one worth between $1,000 and $3,000, and the men working and guarding them are always armed, usually with automatic weapons. Sheriffs' deputies, hikers, and hunters have been shot at— and some deputies seriously wounded—in the process of searching for or stumbling upon these grows in the more remote areas of parks and forests.

If you were still in search of a reason to be personally outraged, there it is. Parks are where we take our families to go camping and hiking, and now we have to worry about finding pot plants and getting shot at? Why don't we hear more about this? More important, why isn't our government doing more to find these grows and put them out of business?

WHAT HAPPENS IN MEXICO DOESN'T STAY IN MEXICO

Sometimes it's hard for people to get too worked up about something like marijuana grows, but actual bloodshed here on our streets is another matter entirely. So let's pull out the trump card: cartel members are killing and kidnapping people on U.S. soil.

This violence is usually referred to as "border violence spillover" and, like most things that have been given politically correct terms, it's controversial. How can violence be controversial? Well, because spillover violence is kind of like an image of Jesus on a grilled cheese sandwich. You'll find a lot of people who will say you're crazy if you can't clearly see the image burned into the toast and you'll find just as many people who won't think twice before chowing down on the sand-

" There is a **perception** that the border is worse now than it ever has been. **That is wrong.** The border is better now than it ever has been. "

—Janet Napolitano, Secretary of Homeland Security

wich, thinking the other group off their collective rocker.

The truth is that border spillover violence is a war of statistics versus anecdotal evidence, and, since no one can agree on whether or not it exists, no progress is being made on how to address violence in the United States related to the drug war. Can you believe there isn't even a standard definition of spillover violence? Here's the one that Homeland Security (alone) is currently using:

WARNING: ADULT CONTENT

What other act is defined in a similar manner? You got it, terrorism. Yet the U.S. government, at least so far, doesn't agree with calling Mexican cartels terrorist organizations.

> [S]pillover violence entails deliberate, planned attacks by the cartels on U.S. assets, including civilian, military, or law enforcement officials, innocent U.S. citizens, or physical institutions such as government buildings, consulates, or businesses. This definition does not include trafficker on trafficker violence, whether perpetrated in Mexico or the U.S.

With some exceptions, the primary type of violence happening in Mexico right now is criminal-on-criminal. So wouldn't logic tell us that spillover violence would likely entail criminal-on-criminal violence happening here in the United States as well? Of course, but the Department of Homeland Security clearly says, *This definition does not include trafficker-on-trafficker violence.* In other words, if a drug cartel member beheads five rival drug cartel members in the middle of Dallas, DHS would not consider that to be "spillover violence." That only makes sense in Washington.

What about the official crime statistics instead; maybe they can shed some light on this.

One of the biggest fans of using violent crime statistics is DHS secretary Janet Napolitano. In fact, she used the ones found in the FBI's Uniform Crime Reports (UCR) database as justification for her oft-repeated statement that "the border is better now than it's ever been." She also says that overall violent crime is down across the southwest border

A Database with No Data

A Congressional Research Service report on spillover violence acknowledged that the government doesn't have exact stats on violence between cartel members in the United States. Seriously? So when cartel members kill each other we just mark it down as "jaywalking" and call it a day? I mean, honestly, what good is a violent-crime database when we can't even use it to give us stats on an important type of violent crime?

by 30 percent. The problem with using the UCR database is that it's the classic example of "statistics don't lie, but liars use statistics." There are literally hundreds of ways in which statistics can be pulled: by city, by city population, by county, etc. If you look only at big border city crime statistics then Napolitano is right. Places like San Diego, El Paso, and Nogales (Arizona, not Mexico) are some of the safest places in the country. Mayors and some border sheriffs have no problem telling the media that reports about spillover are exaggerated. *There's nothing to see here . . . move along.*

So what's all the fuss about? Well, perhaps it's about looking past the crime stats to the cartel member who was beheaded in his Chandler, Arizona, apartment for telling his drug bosses his drug load was seized, when in fact he had sold it and kept the money. Or the six-year-old boy who was kidnapped from his Las Vegas home at gunpoint because his grandfather owed a cartel more than one million dollars. Maybe it's about the five men who were tortured and then killed by having their throats slit in northern Alabama by men working for the Gulf cartel. Or the Hidalgo County sheriff's deputy in Texas who was shot three times while responding to a cartel-related kidnapping call. Could it be the shoot-out between Gulf cartel members that happened on a McAllen, Texas, highway? Or maybe it was the dismembered corpse discovered on a rural Tucson highway, and the possible link to another dismembered body found two weeks earlier in Southern California near the Hollywood sign.

The bad news is that those incidents are just a drop in the bucket compared to all the violent activities that cartel members are involved with on U.S. soil—particularly in south Texas. What else do we expect? They own homes here and often run businesses as front companies to launder drug money here. Many of them are legal residents or U.S. citizens, and can cross the border at will. How many of these incidents have to happen before our government wakes up and acknowledges that we have a huge problem, even if some properly sorted database does not?

Bullets Don't Need Passports

In early 2012, a forty-eight-year-old mother was pushing a child in a stroller down the street in El Paso when a bullet came seemingly out of nowhere and went right through her leg.

That bullet, it turns out, came from a shoot-out between police and carjackers in Juarez, Mexico. It's the third time (at least that we know about) that actual gunfire has reached El Paso (ironically enough, one hit City Hall, the other struck a building at the University of Texas at El Paso).

"It's always concerning," El Paso mayor John Cook said, "when you're living so close to the violence on the other side of the border." I guess Mayor Cook didn't get the memo: it's not concerning if you just ignore it.

It terrifies me that we still haven't crossed some kind of violence threshold in the eyes of our government. There should be no question that cartel violence, and therefore "spillover" (no matter how you want to define it), is happening in the United States. Any time that individuals associated with Mexican cartels engage in violent criminal activity against *anyone* on U.S. soil, *that* needs to be documented—and more important, publicly acknowledged—as border violence spillover.

EASY TARGETS

I know that keeping our borders open is supposed to be the "compassionate" thing to do, but has anyone ever stopped to think about how vulnerable that leaves the illegal immigrants who try to come here? They are literally targets—where is the compassion for them?

One of the more tragic trends we're seeing in Mexico, and one that is definitely spilling over into the United States, is acts of violence against illegal immigrants. They make very easy targets for cartels—mostly Los Zetas—because one of their primary travel routes runs directly through Zetas territory along the Gulf Coast. They're often tired and weak, unarmed, and usually have family members in the United States who can round up some ransom money. But violence against immigrants doesn't stop once they successfully make it across the border.

Human smugglers paid to bring people illegally into the States are called coyotes, or *polleros*—chicken herders. They are paid anywhere from $1,500 to $3,000 per person (sometimes more), and it's always up front. If they're unsuccessful, there are no refunds or do-overs. More often than not, human smugglers have some sort of relationship with drug cartels. Either the cartels are directly involved, actually running the smuggling rings, or they demand payment from human smugglers—kind of like a toll or tax—for using their routes into the United States.

Coyotes only care about getting paid; human life has very little value to them. They'll sometimes abandon their *pollos,* or "chickens," at the first sign of trouble. They'll tell migrants that, once they cross the border, it's only a one- or two-day walk to Chicago, or Denver, or whatever U.S. city they want to go to. Border Patrol agents or U.S. ranchers often come across migrants who are close to death (or already dead) because they were completely unprepared for the unforgiving journey.

And then there are the "rape trees."

Few things in the southern Arizona desert are more horrific than the sight of a rape tree. These are places where cartel members and coyotes rape female border crossers and hang their clothes, specifically their undergarments, from the branches to mark their conquests. The United Nations estimates that 70 percent of women and young girls who cross the border without husbands or other family members are sexually abused in some way. No one knows how many of these rape trees exist, if they're only in Arizona (which sees half of all illegal immigrant crossings), or how many female migrants have been victimized in this way. Most of them have no recourse, and will never report the crime for fear of being deported.

Other migrants are frequently held in "safe" houses in U.S. border cities with very little food or water, waiting until their family members can pay the smugglers or cartels for their release. In June 2010, U.S. immigration officials raided a safe house in Phoenix holding fifty-one Guatemalan nationals, including six children. They were thirsty, but otherwise in good shape. In December 2011, authorities in Avondale, Arizona, discovered a drop house holding seventeen men and two women who were not quite as fortunate. The four suspects running the operation had beaten several of the victims with a curtain rod, wooden sticks, and pistols as punishment for not paying the extortion fee. Three victims were taken to a hospital with broken ribs, cuts, and bruises.

"Virtual kidnappings" are another phenomenon that many people don't know about. This happens when Mexican nationals living in the United States get phone calls from unknown individuals claiming they're holding a loved one hostage somewhere in Mexico. Sometimes they play a recording that could sound like the relative; it's not hard to convince someone who is in a panic at the thought of a kidnapped relative. The perpetrators then usually manage to suck several thousand dollars out of a family for a kidnapping that never happened. But real kidnappings for ransom happen this way, too, and, in most cases, they're never reported. Despite the fact that the victim's family is living in the

Victim or Accomplice?

Many people—often those in government or the media—confuse the terms "human smuggling" and "human trafficking." They're definitely not the same thing, and are very different issues that are approached in a variety of ways by law enforcement agencies. The critical difference is the nature of the person's participation in either activity. In human smuggling, a migrant *voluntarily* embarks on a journey to another country, and sometimes pays a guide—always willingly—to help them along that journey. Human trafficking involves the *involuntary* movement of people—more often women than men, and quite frequently children—across borders for the purpose of essentially selling them as laborers or sex slaves.

United States, they're afraid to call the police for fear the victim will be harmed, or they're living here illegally and are afraid of being deported.

I'm sure that some people will say that we should have no compassion for any of these people; that the women who are victimized made their choice when they decided to cross into the United States illegally. But is that really the kind of country we want to live in? Do we really believe that rape trees and violence are okay because these people committed the first crime? I don't. You know that I am as tough on the border as anyone—I want it sealed—but, in the meantime, let's not allow our politicians to turn us into uncompassionate robots. We need to hold all those who break our laws responsible, but let's not make the mistake of believing that all criminals are created equal.

INMATES RUNNING THE ASYLUM

The connection between illegal immigration and the drug war has grown even more complicated with the significant increase in the number of Mexican nationals requesting asylum in the United States. Mexico has become one of the top asylum-seeking countries. U.S. immigration courts and officials received 25,223 political asylum petitions from Mexican citizens in fiscal years 2006 through 2010. Only 822 were granted—or 3.3 percent.

You might be thinking that's good news—after all, we shouldn't be giving asylum to anyone who asks, right? Of course, but there's a much bigger issue here: current asylum law is old and outdated, better suited for cases emerging from the Cold War and communism. To obtain political asylum, a person must prove that there's a well-founded fear of persecution on account of the person's race, religion, nationality, political opinion, or membership in a particular social group. An individual must also show that he is being persecuted by his government, or that authorities in his country are unable or unwilling to protect the applicant from persecution by another group.

Most of these Mexican asylum cases are very tragic, involving people who have been kidnapped or directly threatened by cartels, or who have had immediate family members murdered by cartels in Mexico. Some have witnessed crimes committed by cartel members, or owned businesses that were being extorted. In several cases, it's obvious that the individuals petitioning for asylum will be kidnapped, tortured, or killed if they were to be deported back to Mexico. But, to many immigration judges, none of that matters because the organization doing the persecuting isn't the Mexican government. Never mind the fact that the cartels *are* the de facto government in many parts of Mexico, or that they own the state and local police, or that there's no such thing as a witness protection program in Mexico.

It's obvious that the entire asylum application system needs updating and reform. But is there any real motivation for the U.S. State Department to do so? And if the U.S. courts started granting asylum to every Mexican who feared being killed by a cartel, how many people would start clamoring to cross the border?

It's a legitimate question, but it doesn't change the fact that what's happening in Mexico is a humanitarian crisis. More than forty-seven thousand people have been killed as a result of the drug war, and an untold number of innocent people have been threatened, kidnapped, assaulted, and extorted. It's easy to try to dismiss it all and say that this just isn't our problem, but it's just as easy to look at a map and realize why you're wrong.

DEEDS, NOT WORDS

So, how do we stop sitting back and admiring the problem and instead get people to start thinking about solutions? Well, first of all, I think everyone involved in the debate needs to define exactly what "securing the border" really means. I've been on the border fence bandwagon for a long time now for a few reasons: first, because it would give us all some tangible evidence that the government is actually taking this seriously; and second, because I think that it will dissuade the vast majority of people from attempting to come here. But even given that support I'm still rational enough to realize that no fence is going to keep *everyone* out, especially not sophisticated cartels. I've seen the images of smugglers using catapults to launch drug loads over the existing fence. And those subs and ultralight planes we talked about before would still work just fine.

Assuming we can't stop everyone and everything, we have to prioritize our limited resources and the top priority needs to be stopping terrorists from entering the United States from Mexico. The next priority should be stopping violent criminals and drug traffickers from crossing the border.

But before any real changes can be made, our leaders need to demonstrate that they are willing to tell the truth about the drug war and *all* the people who are being victimized by the violence. I'm not saying they're not concerned, but they all obviously have a political agenda for not letting on that they're worried. For example, picture the impact on Americans' sense of security if Secretary Napolitano were to go on TV and offer the truth: "We can't really secure long stretches of our border and actually have no idea how many people are coming across it every day, let alone who those people are. Oh, and the cartels? They come across at will and we really can't stop the spillover violence. In fact, we can't even decide on the definition of it."

If politicians and elected leaders say anything less than what a great job is being done and how safe the border is, then it's equivalent to admitting failure in managing the border—and that, we all know, is not an option in politics.

Mexico's drug war isn't just a battle against faceless murderers who want top dollar for the illegal drugs they're peddling. It's a conflict between criminals who operate with impunity and a complete disregard for human life and a decent, moral, civilized society in which the rule of law still matters. It's a struggle for common ground between two nations that have viewed each other with suspicion for over a hundred years. But most of all, it's a fight to give back to everyone what we all deserve most: safety, security, and the freedom to live our lives as we choose. 🐦

Chapter Seven

THE NEW POLICE STATE
BIG BROTHER IS ALL GROWN UP

"Guard with jealous attention the public liberty. Suspect everyone who approaches that jewel. Unfortunately, nothing will preserve it but downright force. Whenever you give up that force, you are inevitably ruined."

—Patrick Henry

THE NEXT TIME you have the pleasure of having your crotch fondled by the latex-fingered heroes of the Transportation Security Administration, take a moment to reflect on this simple, infuriating fact: Osama bin Laden won.

What are you talking about, Glenn? How can you say that?! We shot him in the face!

Yes, SEAL Team Six won the battle for sure, but we've been steadily losing the war. When it comes to the fight to retain our civil liberties—the rights and privileges granted by the Constitution we're claiming to protect—America is losing ground at an alarming pace.

Now, I don't think that bin Laden was clever enough to anticipate that his surprise attack on 9/11 would cause us to tear ourselves apart over the ensuing decade, but that's exactly what we've been doing. It hurts to think that these terrorists didn't just bring down four planes and a few buildings; they may very well have helped to bring down America as well. Or, at least the America we want to live in.

If you're not paying attention, you should be. And if you are paying attention, you should be worried. Things have happened fast—and they aren't about to slow down. Those who crave a more powerful and totalitarian government, and even those who genuinely believe that we can purchase security with liberty, are not about to take their foot off the gas.

A SERIOUS CRISIS DID NOT GO TO WASTE

We know one thing for sure: politicians will *always* take advantage of crisis. Even as the rubble at Ground Zero was still smoldering, the United States government, in full panic mode, rushed to establish a brand-new, poorly thought-out security behemoth. They endowed it with the humble moniker "Department of Homeland Security."

Before anyone knew exactly what this new bureaucracy would be doing for (or to) us, the *Wall Street Journal*'s Peggy Noonan was quick to point out that the name itself was pretty creepy: "The name Homeland Security grates on a lot of people, understandably. Homeland isn't really an American word, it's not something we used to say or say now. It has a vaguely Teutonic ring—*Ve must help ze Fuehrer protect ze Homeland!*"

I Was for It Before I Was Against It—Coming Clean on the PATRIOT Act

In the wake of 9/11 most of us anticipated that another attack could come at any moment. We weren't thinking clearly. We were in shock. Though I had reservations about the PATRIOT Act, I thought it made sense at the time. The reservations I had—that it gave the chief executive way too many powers outside of the Constitution—were addressed by the "sunset" provisions, as well as the fact that I believed George W. Bush to be acting in the best interests of the country. In retrospect, it turned out to be a raw deal. I should have known better. The sunsets were dropped later on and the act has been renewed every time it came up. Not to mention the fact that the act has been misused on numerous occasions. I believe it can do more harm than good, especially in the wrong hands. And it's definitely in the wrong hands.

I'm not trying to work a Nazi reference into this book for my own amusement, I'm just trying to point out that one of the country's most enormous bureaucracies was cobbled together so quickly, and with such lack of foresight, that they didn't even devote enough time to thinking up a name that doesn't conjure up images of Adolf Hitler.

We can also credit bin Laden with helping to put a dramatic and immediate (if not extremely temporary) end to partisanship in Congress, as a panicked mob of politicians managed to put their differences aside just long enough to pass one of the most liberty-threatening pieces of legislation in a long time: the USA PATRIOT Act. The name alone would be funny if it weren't such a desperate attempt to make all of us believe that we hated America if we didn't support it.

But we can forgive human nature—we all remember those days; we were freaked out—and

I was no exception. We demanded that government do *something*. And at that point, with all of those lawmakers standing out on the Capitol steps and singing "God Bless America," most of us would have accepted almost anything if they promised it would keep us safe.

In retrospect, that was exactly the moment that those who've had police-state-type plans lying around in their desk drawers had been waiting for.

The good news is that the PATRIOT Act was a temporary measure. Many politicians held their nose and voted for it because the "sunset" provisions in the bill meant that it would likely go away in a few years. The bad news, of course, is that economist Milton Friedman hit the nail on the head when he said "Nothing is so permanent as a temporary government program." Most of the sunset provisions are long gone—dropped at the first opportunity. Each time the PATRIOT Act has come up for a vote (under administrations led by both political parties), it's been renewed with very little debate. Like Vladimir Putin, the PATRIOT doesn't want to go anywhere.

The Power of One

In 2011, the PATRIOT Act was extended for four more years. The vote totals were 72–23 in the Senate and 250–153 in the House. President Obama signed it "minutes before a midnight deadline" would have caused it to expire. But if you don't think that one vigilant politician can make a difference, consider this account from the Associated Press:

> *Congress bumped up against the deadline mainly because of the stubborn resistance from a single senator, Republican freshman Rand Paul of Kentucky, who saw the terrorist-hunting powers as an abuse of privacy rights. Paul held up the final vote for several days while he demanded a chance to change the bill to diminish the government's ability to monitor individual actions.*

DUMB: Developing Useless and Misnamed Bills

I wonder how many congressional aides it took to figure out something believable that PATRIOT could stand for. Because you know they must have started with *patriot* and then tried to back into the dumb phrase, not the other way around, right? Here goes:

PATRIOT: Provide Appropriate Tools Required to Intercept and Obstruct Terrorism

Maybe that'll help you win a trivia contest one day.

THE HOBGOBLINS

Our constitution was designed to keep the federal government off our backs—and, frankly, it's done an amazingly good job of it. For that, we should give ourselves credit.

There have, however, been moments throughout history when the resilience of the Constitution has been tested; moments when this country's leaders have been tested in their understanding of, and respect for, the law of the land. And in many of those moments, our leaders have failed.

All of these instances of governmental overreach have one thing in common: they were done under the guise of protecting us from some collective danger. In other words, in an effort to "keep us safe" from some threat, real or perceived, the government usually targets the one document that *actually* keeps us safe: the Constitution.

From the earliest days of our republic we've known that if our rights were going to be stolen from us, they would be stolen by our own government, and that the government would do it while telling us that it was in our own best interest.

In 1783, the British politician William Pitt said, "Necessity is the plea for every infringement of human freedom. It is the argument of tyrants; it is the creed of slaves." Nearly a century and a half later, the libertarian journalist H. L. Mencken proved that Pitt's sentiment hadn't changed much. He wrote, "The whole aim of practical politics is to keep the populace alarmed (and hence clamorous to be led to safety) by an endless series of hobgoblins, all of them imaginary."

Those hobgoblins have come in many forms over the years, but the government's reaction has invariably been the same: *Don't worry, we'll protect you!* The problem is that protection isn't free; it comes with a very heavy price: we buy security—or at least the belief that we're buying security—with our liberty.

After the Pearl Harbor attack on December 7, 1941, the new hobgoblin became the Japanese. Americans were in a panic and wanted to be sure they were safe from what had been labeled the "yellow menace" (things weren't quite so PC back then). The government was there to protect us, of course, but this time the price tag would be extraordinarily high. While most people would never feel the sting, a high price was paid by those Americans who happened to be of Japanese descent.

In 1942, a little over ten weeks after the Pearl Harbor attack, FDR signed Executive Order 9066, authorizing the internment of American citizens. Ten weeks is all it took for fear to usher in an atmosphere where the civil rights of 110,000 individuals could be shredded. Not because they were a threat to the nation, or because they practiced some seditious ideology, but because of their ethnicity. People who thought they lived in "the land of the free" found themselves on the outside looking in—or, in this case, on the inside of a barbed wire fence looking out.

It's really hard to even fathom how this happened. After all, this wasn't a decision made by some dictator; it was a decision made by America's chief executive—a hero to many on the left still today—with the full support of members of Congress who had been sending FDR memos like this:

It is my sincere belief that the Pacific coast should be declared a military area which will give authority to treat residents, either alien or citizens, as camp followers and put them under military law, permitting their removal, regardless of their citizenship rights, to internal and less dangerous areas. (Harley M. Kilgore, D-WV)

Columnists like Westbrook Pegler also fanned the flames, penning influential columns that stated "[they] should be under armed guard to the last man and woman right now, and to hell with habeas corpus. . . ."

It's amazing to think just how fast a freedom-loving country is willing to turn its back on the very document that formalized that freedom in the first place. Plenty of blood has been shed, and many people have died to secure and protect our Constitution, yet the mere threat of bloodshed or death now causes us to trample it.

AN OPEN-ENDED INVITATION TO TRAMPLE OUR RIGHTS

When we've sold out the Constitution in the past we've always eventually come to our senses once the "hobgoblin" has subsided. We've been like a guy waking up in the morning after a night of heavy drinking—and thinking, *What happened? What did I do last night?* And then we pledged that we'll never have another drink again.

A RAND Corporation study made the same point in a slightly more formal way: "Throughout U.S. history in times of national security crisis, civil liberties have been curtailed in exchange for perceived greater security, the balance between liberties and security generally being restored after each crisis."

FDR Wasn't Alone

Our history is littered with examples of our leaders shredding the Constitution in reaction to the threat of the day:

- When the United States was busy fighting France in the undeclared war in the late 1700s, President John Adams pushed for the passage of the Alien and Sedition Acts, which allowed him to criminalize political dissent.
- President Abraham Lincoln, who suspended the writ of habeas corpus during the Civil War, set up military tribunals for civilians.
- In 1916, before the United States entered World War I, Woodrow Wilson supported legislation to suppress disloyalty. He requested that Congress give the president complete authority to censor the press should America enter the war. He wanted to make it a federal crime to mail any material deemed "of a treasonable or anarchistic character." Wilson argued that this power was "absolutely necessary to the public safety."
- Could you trust any president or politician (outside of maybe George Washington) with the absolute authority to decide what thoughts and words should be allowed in a debate over war and peace—or anything else for that matter?

"The Japanese in California should be under armed guard to the last man and woman right now—and to hell with habeas corpus until the danger is over."

—Columnist Westbrook Pegler, 1942

The Japanese internment camps were shuttered. Habeas corpus was restored. Joseph McCarthy's communist witch hunt came to an end. But today it's different. That's because the War on Terror does not have an end. And that's a tremendous problem if you're someone like me who cares not just about the "spirit" of the Constitution, but the actual letters of it.

When you're fighting a war on an abstract concept, there's no way to determine when you've won. Terror isn't a country that can be conquered. It doesn't have the capacity to wave a white flag and surrender. You can't put terror in prison or execute it. If you're fighting an enemy that can't be conquered and can't surrender, you really have no exit strategy from your war.

The definition of terror and terrorism is amazingly broad *and it will continue to grow* as the government redefines what constitutes terror and who a terrorist is. Today it's Muslim extremists—as it absolutely should be—but tomorrow the definition could easily include other groups. Why aren't Mexican drug cartel members labeled "terrorists"? What about computer hackers? Or people who protest the government too much. Or gun owners. Or whistle-blowers. Or tax evaders. Or (gasp!) people who spend a lot of time criticizing politicians on radio and television.

If we're being honest with one another then we should drop the "War on Terror" moniker and call it what it really is: a "War on Freedom" that has killed lots of terrorists in the process.

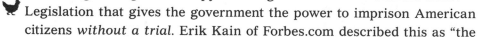

THE ENDURING CONSEQUENCES OF 9/11

A religious madman about seven thousand miles away in a dysfunctional, practically medieval country hatched an evil plot: Send a message to America by hijacking planes and flying them into famous symbols of American financial and military power. From conception to execution, 9/11 is estimated to have cost between $400,000 and $500,000—plus the expendable lives of the nineteen terrorists. For that investment, they got not only a day of terror and the lives of 3,500 innocent people, they also got:

 Legislation that reduces or eliminates judicial oversight in order to allow the intelligence agencies to spy on foreign nationals and citizens alike.

Legislation that gives the government the power to imprison American citizens *without a trial*. Erik Kain of Forbes.com described this as "the greatest threat to civil liberties Americans face." To soothe people's concerns, President Obama assured us verbally that he wouldn't use that power. Since he's lived up to all his other promises, we don't have to worry, right?

🐔 Assassination of American citizens abroad without judicial review. The government just has to declare that the target is a "terrorist" before targeting the individual.

🐔 Airport "security" that subjects travelers in the United States to a litany of indignities at the hands of a motley band of (mostly) ineffective, unskilled bumble-bots. Case after case has documented their harassment and humiliation of passengers, arbitrary enforcement of rules, flagrant violations of duties, and an overall contempt for the Fourth Amendment.

🐔 A security industry filled with government officials turned lobbyists. These individuals use their connections to sell their wares to the government at taxpayer expense. Michael Chertoff, former DHS chief turned lobbyist, made a fortune peddling invasive screening equipment to the TSA. As a bonus, this equipment has been banned in Europe because of cancer concerns.

🐔 An absolutely enormous security apparatus that numbers some 854,000 people in nearly 1,300 government organizations and 2,000 private companies dedicated to intelligence, counterterrorism, and homeland security that comes with an absolutely staggering price tag.

🐔 The National Security Agency, once tasked with monitoring communications abroad, which now focuses much of its effort domestically.

🐔 An increasingly militarized police force equipped with weaponry and vehicles once reserved for the country's armed forces. Machine guns, grenade launchers, battle-dress uniforms, military tactics, heavy use of SWAT teams, and an overall attitude that prompted one police chief to opine, "The police culture in our country has changed."

🐔 A wanton disregard of the First and Fourth Amendments by government officials and citizens alike.

Of course, those are just the changes that are glaringly obvious. Plenty of other items fall under the radar or simply have yet to be discovered. Did you know, for example, that the government now keeps track of all your pharmacy prescriptions? They do, thanks to a law passed in 2005. Enjoy that Xanax!

THIS IS STILL AMERICA, RIGHT?

Under the administration of George W. Bush, and continuing enthusiastically (and then some!) under Barack Obama, the United States has embarked on one of the most dangerous attacks on civil liberties in its history. Too many Republicans gave Bush a free pass when he started to trounce the Constitution. And today, too many Democrats are turning a blind eye as Obama does the same thing. This should not be a partisan issue. The only issue should be whether you want to live in a country that respects the Constitution and values liberty. If you do, then here are a few things to get outraged about:

Warrantless Wiretapping

Less than a month after 9/11, and under the express direction of George W. Bush, the FBI began unprecedented warrantless domestic surveillance. Spying on Americans with absolutely no judicial oversight made each incident of warrantless wiretapping a felony—or at least it *would* have been a felony if it had been prosecuted.

But when you're fighting a war on terror, all options are on the table. Concerns were met with reassurances that only suspected terrorists were going to be targeted. Nevertheless, with the floodgates open, and the Constitution drowning, it didn't take long before people who didn't fall into the "terrorist" category began to have their communications intercepted. At the time, then-senator Barack Obama rightly called the program illegal and demanded an investigation. But when he got the president gig he completely changed his mind. I guess it wasn't the warrantless wiretapping that bothered him, just that the Republicans were doing it.

Warrantless Cell Phone Tracking

Most of us know that a cell phone company can find your phone by figuring out which towers it is connecting with. But I doubt most people know that some police departments are asking phone companies to do that for routine calls, without a warrant, and with very little oversight.

A recent investigation into the practice by the A.C.L.U. yielded 5,500 pages of documents that were turned over to the *New York Times*. Among them was evidence that small towns were not only spending money on equipment to execute this tracking (Gilbert, Arizona, spent $244,000, for example), but that they were also purposefully keeping their activities secret from the public. The Iowa City Police Department, for example, told officers to keep the tracking out of police reports and to "[N]ot mention to the public or the media the use of cellphone technology or equipment used to locate the targeted subject."

After the *Times* called local police departments to ask about their use of cell phone tracking they reported that some "law enforcement officials said the legal questions were outweighed by real-life benefits."

Suspicionless Searches of Your Electronics

David House, a researcher at the Massachusetts Institute of Technology, was returning from a trip to Mexico when he was stopped by border agents who seized his laptop and mobile phone. He didn't get them back for forty-nine days. During that time the government had access to his emails, documents, photos, contacts, and everything else you'd expect to find on such devices.

House was presumably targeted by the border agents because he's involved with the Bradley Manning Support Network. Manning stands accused of leaking huge amounts of classified information to WikiLeaks (and if he's found guilty, I hope he spends some quality time in prison), but I don't know of any law that makes it illegal to be involved with the Bradley Manning Support Network.

In a similar incident, the head of the National Association of Criminal Defense Lawyers was also forced to surrender her computer at the border—which, as many attorneys know, is often referred to as a "Constitution-free zone" because the Supreme Court has ruled that the Fourth Amendment doesn't apply there.

But no matter what you think of criminal defense lawyers or Bradley Manning—this is not about them—it's about an overt attack on the Fourth Amendment. It's also a classic embodiment of the famous Martin Niemöller quote, "First they came . . ." You're next, Tea Party leaders, NRA members, or evangelicals who attend a certain church that the government doesn't like.

Better Rethink That Trip to Canada

Here's how two attorneys have described the government's powers at our borders: "Now, even without reasonable suspicion of any wrongdoing, the government can search, copy and seize travelers' laptops and other electronic devices at the border and can potentially continue to access personal and work data and information stored in the cloud, indefinitely and in an ongoing manner."

Targeted Assassination

Anwar al-Awlaki was a bad guy—there's no doubt about it. He railed against the United States and urged terrorist attacks on American and Western interests and civilians. He was a vile, fiery, angry jihadi loon. He was also an American citizen and, like it or not, American citizens are entitled to due process of law. Even the loud, smack-talking Islamist, murder-sanctioning ones. Unless, apparently, the government decides otherwise.

The government labeled Awlaki a terrorist and declared that he was connected to al-Qaeda. They didn't provide too many details on that, because what then-candidate Obama declared would be the most "transparent" administration in American history has actually become one of the least transparent administrations in American history. That's not just Glenn Beck bad-mouthing the president: it's a fact that has been bemoaned by plenty of Democrats.

While publicly declaring Awlaki a bad guy, the government was privately deciding his fate. With the approval of our Nobel Peace Prize–winning president, a meeting was held behind closed doors among people whose names we don't know (classified) where it was decided that Awlaki would die. There was no trial. We don't know what was said or how the decision was made (classified). We don't know what the criteria are that get you on a U.S. government kill list (classified). And, if you try to actually ask any of those questions, the answer of course, is "Sorry, that's classified."

Shortly after that meeting took place a Predator drone in Yemen blew Awlaki to atoms. A couple of weeks after that, his sixteen-year-old son (who was born in Colorado) was also blown up. Apparently he'd also made the kill list—for reasons we can't be told (classified). The government says that he was a terrorist, too. Maybe he was. But that's why Americans are given trials.

Attorney General Eric Holder held a news conference to answer criticisms that these extrajudicial killings of American citizens are illegal and unconstitutional. His response can be summed up as "No, we don't think so."

Legal scholars were appalled. You should be, too. Is America better off without these guys on the planet? Probably. But our Constitution most definitely is not.

Email Harvesting

You can now safely assume that a copy of every email you send and a log of every phone call you make will be kept in a secret facility somewhere. There's a really good chance it will someday sit in a $2 billion facility being built for the NSA in Utah, conveniently called the "First Intelligence Community Comprehensive National Cyber-security Initiative Data Center." At one million square feet, it's the size of five Capitol buildings.

The government hasn't come out and made any great proclamations about their amazing facilities, of course, but the evidence is there. Does that mean all of your emails will be read? Probably not, unless you have a habit of writing "bomb" and "Allah" a lot, but it does mean that, someday in the future, your emails could be used against you in some capacity by a hostile government. Just imagine what a field day President Nixon would have had if he'd lived in a time when he could have pulled up a copy of every single email sent by his rivals.

What gives the government the right to harvest our emails and intercept our telephone calls? National security, of course. *They're keeping us safe.* You see, a terrorist might send a message through email—so the safest thing to do is keep a copy of everything. *Don't worry, we won't look at it unless there's a good reason. Trust us!*

Good Luck Finding Anything

The Utah facility plans on holding so much information that they laugh at the word "gigabyte." They measure information in "yottabytes." What, you're not familiar with a yottabyte? Well, here's a reference: All of the data in the *entire* World Wide Web takes up approximately one yottabyte.

Perhaps we should all change our email signatures to "Sent by my iPhone, intercepted by the NSA."

Whistle-blower Prosecution

Speaking of the NSA, the agency's change in focus disturbed one agent so much that he decided he had no choice but to do something about it.

Thomas Drake reached out to Diane Roark, a staff member on the House Permanent Select Committee on Intelligence, and told her that he was concerned about the direction the agency was headed—in particular the dramatic change in policy from the strong protection of the privacy of Americans to the complete disregard for it.

The government's reaction was predictable and, once again, the differences between candidate Obama and President Obama are clear: While running for office, candidate Obama had heaped praise on the nation's whistle-blowers. Before assuming office, his website stated, "We need to empower federal employees as watchdogs of wrongdoing and partners in performance. Barack Obama will strengthen whistleblower laws to protect federal workers who expose waste, fraud, and abuse of authority in government."

But—and I'm sure you'll be surprised—President Obama has earned a reputation as one of the most aggressive prosecutors of whistle-blowers in recent history. What Obama once hailed as a noble act can now ruin your life. Thomas

Drake knows this all too well. The government came after him with full fury, charging him with violating the Espionage Act and intent on putting him behind bars for decades. They ultimately failed (Drake never passed along any classified information, only unclassified, though embarrassing, information about fraud and abuse), but they made their opinion of whistle-blowers crystal clear in the process. As Drake told journalist Matthew Harwood:

> [I consider Obama] [w]orse than Bush. I have to say that. I actually voted for Obama. It's all rhetoric for me now. As Americans we were hood-winked. He's expanding the secrecy regime far beyond what Bush even intended, interestingly enough. I think Bush is probably like, Whoa.

THE DISLIKE BUTTON

The technological advancements we've made in the last couple of decades are staggering. Smartphones and the Internet and iPads and all the amazing electronics

Translation: Too Many to Count

When Senators Ron Wyden and Mark Udall asked the U.S. government just how many law-abiding citizens had had their calls or emails monitored by a federal agency, the Obama administration couldn't come up with a number. The national intelligence office answered the senators that it was "not reasonably possible to identify the number."

at our disposal have made our lives easier, more fun, more interesting. There is also no denying that they've made our lives less private.

Social networking shares our thoughts, feelings, likes, and dislikes with friends, coworkers, and complete strangers. Our phones and cars know our location. Internet search engines reveal our interests. Cameras mounted outdoors, along roads, and inside buildings capture our movements from the moment we leave the house until the moment we return. The comments we leave around the Web reveal who we are as individuals. We express ourselves with emails and texts. We can easily record video or take photographs and send them around the world. It's wonderful. It's exciting. It's entertaining. It's frightening.

It's now easier for a hostile government to take advantage of that technology and turn it against its people than at any other time in history. In 2009, during the massive protests against the fraudulent election of Mahmoud Ahmadinejad, the regime in Iran used Facebook and Twitter to prosecute the opposition. Authorities tracked down protesters by identifying them in photos and videos that had been uploaded to the Internet—exposing them to prison, torture, and even death.

In Iran, family members of expats who were supporting the revolt and criticizing the regime from abroad were threatened or arrested.

Despotic Arab governments also used technology as a weapon during the Arab Spring. They pinpointed dissidents' locations, determined their next meeting points, and identified their friends and accomplices. Here in the United States, authorities haven't hidden the fact that they also monitor social media.

The lesson is clear: when necessary, governments will take advantage of all the technology at their disposal and use it against the enemy of the moment. If you don't think they'd use it against you, you're just fooling yourself. A former NSA official, holding his thumb and forefinger close together, told NSA expert James Bamford, "We are that far from a turnkey totalitarian state."

BUT AT LEAST WE'RE SAFER!

Maybe you're thinking things are a little disconcerting and we've bruised the Constitution a bit. But, you say, that's the price we pay for security. Right? Well, not really.

I hope you're acquainted with this perfectly appropriate quote from Benjamin Franklin, or perhaps you've heard some variation of it. If not, then it's my pleasure to introduce you to it: "They that can give up essential liberty to obtain a little temporary safety deserve neither liberty nor safety."

Man, I love that guy. He had more smarts in his thumb than 80 percent of Congress has in their heads. And he's right, too. We deserve neither, and that's exactly what we're getting. Neither. We're losing our liberty *and* we're not safer.

Let's not forget that the 9/11 plot succeeded in part *because* the FBI, CIA, and NSA failed. There were lots of indicators that something was up; red flags were all over the place as our intelligence folks missed one opportunity after another to put the pieces together. The government let Americans down, big-time, and a lot of people died as a result.

So, naturally, the answer to that problem is more people and more government, right? More organizations, more agencies, more acronyms, more centralized power. A gigantic homeland security apparatus is the perfect antidote to a failed gigantic homeland security apparatus.

> **Franklin 2:0**
> The 9/11 Commission argued that trading liberty for security was a "false choice" that we shouldn't have to make. Glad they thought enough of themselves to go ahead and trump Ben Franklin.

Obviously when you add 854,000 people to the payroll in a security capacity you're going to get some kind of uptick in "security." But you're also going to get nearly a million people whose jobs now depend on their ability to keep us "safe" in this War on Terror. With that many people you also get tremendous amounts of redundancy—agencies and bureaus and individuals doing the same things that another agency, bureau, or individual is already doing. That's a lot of folks gathering copious amounts of intelligence, writing report after report, working hard to justify their jobs.

It's amazing that we employ all of those people, and have a nearly unlimited budget, yet a guy who was being monitored by our government still managed to board a plane with explosive underpants. Our million-man State Security army didn't pick up on it. Fortunately the guy sitting next to him on the plane did.

Fun Future Fact!
Electronics maker Hitachi has announced a new surveillance system that will be able to scan 36 million faces a second. According to *Gizmodo*, "finding a face in the crowd in hours and days of recordings is a simple database search."

On a Monday morning in December 2012, police in the United Kingdom arrested a dozen terror suspects in a sweep in England and Wales. At 4 P.M. that same day journalist Diane Sawyer asked James Clapper, director of national intelligence, "First of all, London. How serious is it? Any implication that it was coming here?"

Clapper, who looked like a deer caught in headlights, took a long pause and replied, "London?"

That a man in his position had absolutely no idea of major terror sweeps in London is incredible—and very telling. *Everyone near a TV, radio, computer, smartphone, or newspaper knew about London!* Everyone, apparently, except the guy at the helm of the national security leviathan we created.

This massive security operation sucks up tremendous amounts of information, yet can't even come close to processing it all. Hunting terrorists was already like looking for the proverbial needle in a haystack. Now that haystack is the size of a small city.

THE WAR ON US

You and I know how difficult it is to pry power out of the hands of the government once they've taken it. You and I also know that when you have a government complex that employs nearly a million individuals and has countless corporate interests, they will do what it takes to justify their existence—even to the detriment of the country they insist they want to protect.

That's why it's not at all insane to worry about the direction we're headed and harbor fears of a future Orwellian nightmare state. The technology to empower it already exists. The will to disregard the Constitution already exists. The "War on Terror" that the government uses to justify its power grab continues without any end in sight. And our track record of trading liberty for "security" has not been a positive one at all.

A massive governmental and corporate security apparatus now operates in the shadows, outside of the law and at tremendous expense to the United States taxpayer. The casual surveillance of innocent American citizens was once unthinkable. Now it's absolutely routine.

It's become so routine, in fact, that the police state mentality trickles down to the citizens: A Minnesota girl is suing her school district after administrators pressured her to give up her Facebook password so that they could access her account. Colleges and employers have asked applicants for their passwords as well. In one instance, job applicants at the Maryland Department of Corrections were asked to log into their Facebook accounts so that the interviewer could browse their wall posts, photos, and anything else of interest. Some colleges are requiring student-athletes to "friend" coaches or compliance officers so that their online behavior can be monitored.

The America we live in today is remarkably different than the America we lived in on the morning of September 11, 2001. I worry that the children we're now raising will grow up to think that having their emails monitored, phone calls intercepted, whereabouts tracked, bags searched, and bodies groped by "security" personnel is perfectly normal. That being detained indefinitely or assassinated without due process is somehow okay.

It's not normal. *It's not okay.*

We have to constantly remind ourselves of that. And we have to constantly remind ourselves of what has happened since that moment when we all looked up to see a plane fly into the World Trade Center. We've changed. A lot.

And that is the true legacy of Osama bin Laden: The birth of the American police state. When I say that "bin Laden won" I'm not being flippant. I'm being honest. Destruction of buildings and planes is shocking and horrific and can damage a country for years; but the destruction of our Constitution will damage us forever. 🐔

Chapter Eight

JIM WALLIS AND THE ATTEMPTED HIJACKING OF RELIGION

> "You change **society** by changing the wind. **Change** the wind, transform the debate, recast the discussion, alter the context in which **political discussions** are being made, and you **will change** the outcomes.... You will be surprised at how fast the **politicians adjust** to the change in the **wind**."

—Jim Wallis

IT'S AN AMAZING TIME to be an American. We are standing on the edge. To one side is a course that leads us back to maximum freedom and minimum government; and on the other is a path that virtually every other country in the history of the world has walked.

The battle over which way we fall is being fought in a lot of different places. Obviously there are the voting booths, but there are also our classrooms, our television sets, and, of course, our churches.

Our churches?

Unfortunately, yes. Many of us like to pretend it's not the case or, even if we do see it happening, that we are personally strong enough to ignore those parts of the sermon—but there is no doubt that our churches are now a battleground for political ideology.

In fact, it's been this way for quite some time. It's just that now those of us who understand both scripture *and* the Constitution are finally beginning to put our hands up to say, *Hey, wait a second, those two things, both of which are sacred to us, are not mutually exclusive—in fact, it's just the opposite: they must be read together.*

Entire books have been written about the role of faith and God in America's founding, and I don't intend to rehash it here, but suffice it to say that America's earliest settlers fled oppressive governments in Europe that dominated every aspect of civil society, including religion. As a result, most Americans since then have embraced a religious faith that demands personal liberty and limited government—the very principles that are reflected in our Constitution.

But there's a big problem with that kind of faith: it leaves no room for progressivism. How can the government grow and expand its power if, every Sunday, Americans are being reminded that their faith favors exactly the opposite?

The truth is that it can't—and so something had to change. But before we get to *how* the change happened, it's important to first understand *why* we got to this place and who's responsible. So, let's start with a quick refresher on religion in America and exactly why big-government progressives were left shopping for a new home.

THE LEFT FINDS RELIGION

The percentage of Americans who attend and belong to a church has remained constant for over seventy years. But predominantly liberal mainline Protestant denominations have lost members for almost fifty years—with no end in sight for their spiral. Their membership losses range from about 20 to 50 percent, even while the U.S. population has increased by 50 percent.

Why?

Know Your Mainline

The "seven sisters" of mainline Protestantism are the United Methodist Church, Evangelical Lutheran Church in America, Presbyterian Church (USA), Episcopal Church, American Baptist Church, United Church of Christ, and Christian Church (Disciples of Christ).

I don't think it's a coincidence that these once great denominations have been rotted from the inside out by their elites' rejection of traditional beliefs and embrace of the Social Gospel's notion of "social justice." And, not coincidentally, that shift leftward started right around the time the Progressive era was getting into full swing.

In 1907, at a meeting in Washington, D.C., among leading Methodists, including then U.S. vice president Charles Fairbanks, the Methodist Federation for Social Service (MFSS) arose. MFSS, led by Harry Ward (who would later gain infamy as a pro-Soviet apologist during the reign of Soviet dictator Joseph Stalin), drafted a "Social Creed" focused on "equal rights and complete justice for all men in all stations of life," protections from occupational hazards, abolition of child labor, safeguards for women, reduced working hours, and the highest "wage that

The Original Social Network

Walter Rauschenbusch, a liberal Baptist minister from upstate New York, helped found the "Social Gospel" movement, which asserted that Christianity was not so much about personal redemption as social reform—especially combating poverty and militarism. The Protestant Social Gospel of the early twentieth century sometimes merged with much more mainstream nineteenth-century Roman Catholic notions about "social justice."

Original Catholic ideas about social justice affirmed their church's core teachings about God and salvation, but in the twentieth century, liberal Protestants and Catholics often joined together under the "social justice" banner to advocate big government while minimizing traditional Christian teachings about human sin that warn against centralized power.

each industry can afford." The initial version of the Creed was very modest, especially by modern-day standards.

In 1908, MFSS persuaded the Methodist Episcopal Church, then America's largest Protestant church, to adopt the Creed. It was the first time a major denomination had endorsed a social creed. The Methodists enthusiastically declared: "We believe that in the teachings of the New Testament will be found the ultimate solution of all the problems of our social order. . . . When the spirit of Christ shall pervade the hearts of individuals and when his law of love to God and man shall dominate human society, then the evils which vex our civilization shall disappear."

Full of confidence about the anticipated coming age of social justice, peace, and prosperity, the Methodists sang "The Battle Hymn of the Republic" and "America" at their convention. In 1908, Methodist bishops warned against trying to create utopia via class warfare, citing "reckless anarchists." They celebrated America's private philanthropy, noting that "nowhere in the world does wealth manifest its obligation to contribute to the public welfare as in the United States." They added that education, religion, and philanthropy all benefit from the "munificence" of "rich men of America."

Unfortunately, those warnings would soon be forgotten. Like all progressive policy, the first version is just a test balloon, something to make the public think you are reasonable, even mainstream. Only once people have decided that the policy is harmless do progressives begin to shift it toward their real agenda.

The Federal Council of Churches, encompassing thirty-two major denominations, soon endorsed an expanded version of Methodism's Social Creed, adding support for old-age pensions and the "abatement of poverty." As a result, nearly all of mainline Protestantism, which included most of America's most influential churches, was now tied to the Social Gospel and its emphasis on a perverted version of social justice. Other groups, like the Young Women's Christian Association (YWCA), also went on to endorse the creed, giving it even more mainstream appeal.

Given their success, Social Gospel's enthusiasts quickly became more ambitious in their goals and began to switch their focus from labor rights to assail the "profit motive," that is to say, capitalism. A few even provocatively praised the Bolshevik Revolution in Russia. In the early 1920s, for example, Lewis O. Hartman, a prominent editor of a Methodist magazine, visited the Soviet Union. Upon his return to the United States he declared that Marxism was very similar to Christianity in "ideals of social justice and fair play." Having met Leon Trotsky and reviewed Soviet troops in Red Square, he announced: "The Soviet regime . . . is essentially a struggle for human freedom, and the Communist leaders with all their mistakes are sincere, honest men working for what they conceive to be the good of humanity."

In the 1920s, Social Gospel liberals solidified their control over mainline Protestantism's seminaries and agencies. Kirby Page, a prominent Disciples of Christ minister and activist, exulted, "Among all the trades, occupations, and professions in this country, few can produce as high a percentage of Socialists as can the ministry."

He was right. The Federal Council of Churches soon amended and expanded its Social Creed to urge "subordination for speculation and the profit motive to the creative and cooperative spirit." And it urged "social planning and control of the credit and monetary systems and the economic processes for the common good."

Many senior churchmen complained the New Deal did not go far enough. For example, in 1933 the Episcopal Church's House of Bishops insisted that "Christ demands a new order . . . which shall substitute the motive of service for the motive of gain." Episcopal bishop Edward Parsons went even further: "We are living in the twilight of the gods of capitalism."

The following year, northern Presbyterians urged "new motives besides those of money-making and self-interest" to create an "economic system more consistent with Christian ideals." They also denounced "competition" as the "major controlling principle of our economic life" and instead urged "secure rational planning." And, in 1935, New York Methodist clergy opined that the New Deal failed its own "high-sounding prophecies of the economic temple cleansers" and instead "blindly" upheld capitalism's "exploitation."

Those views continued to deepen over the ensuing decades. By the 1960s, Liberation Theology, which claimed that the church's role was not to preach salvation, but to help overthrow unjust (that is, capitalist) economic and political systems (even aligning with violent revolution if necessary), began to gain notoriety. It began among Latin American leftist Catholics like Peruvian theologian and Dominican priest Gustavo Gutierrez, who credited Marxism for focusing on a "transformation of the world." By the 1980s, mainline Protestant officials in the United States were impressed enough to launch pilgrimages to the Sandinista promised land to learn more. One Methodist bishop denounced attacks on Liberation Theology as "an act of blasphemy."

Throughout the 1970s and 1980s, before the Soviet bloc fell, mainline Protestant officials, along with their missions and lobby agencies and groups like the National and World Councils of Churches, enthusiastically supported communist revolutions around the world. Sandinista strongman Daniel Ortega preached from a Methodist pulpit in New York to a gushing congregation, which hailed him as "Brother Ortega." And officials from the National Council of Churches, along with clergy from sixteen Protestant denominations and two Catholic orders, enthusiastically met with Fidel Castro at the Cuban mission to the United Nations in New York in 1995.

By the end of the twentieth century, mainline churches had become sidelined. Liberal politics and theology, which deemphasized personal faith and evangelism, fueled a membership exodus that is now in its sixth decade. In the early 1960s, one in five Americans belonged to one of the seven largest mainline Protestant churches.

By 2012, it was less than one in fifteen.

Even worse, the Religious Left may have captured the imaginations of mainline Protestant church bureaucracies and elites, but they never fully captured the hearts or minds of most church *members*. In spite of their efforts, the rank-and-file Protestants who remained still tended to vote Republican.

THE RISE OF THE RELIGIOUS RIGHT

While the mainline denominations were fading, another group was growing rapidly: evangelicals.

Evangelical churches began to surge in the 1960s and 1970s, just as the mainline churches were turning to the Social Gospel. The 2001 *World Christian Encyclopedia* estimated that U.S. evangelicals numbered about 45 million in 1970, comprising about 22 percent of the U.S. population. By 2000, the number had exploded to nearly 100 million, or 35 percent of the population. Southern Baptists surged beyond once dominant United Methodists. The Assemblies of God, a Pentecostal denomination, swept past the once prestigious Episcopal Church.

Evangelicals are now the country's largest religious demographic. And they are overwhelmingly conservative.

Like America's founders, evangelicals tend to believe in liberty, limited government, and entrepreneurship. A majority of the Tea Party is evangelical. Small business owners also are disproportionately evangelical. Evangelicals were central to Republican electoral victories in 2004 and 2010.

Sensing the shifting tides, the mainstream media stopped putting political pronouncements from groups like the National Council of Churches on their front pages and instead focused—not always happily—on the rise of the Religious Right, embodied by groups such as the Reverend Jerry Falwell's Moral Majority and later, Pat Robertson's Christian Coalition. Policy makers followed suit (don't they always?) and began to ignore pronouncements from the old Religious Left.

But if you thought progressives would sit back and allow this to happen, you don't know them very well. Smart leftist philanthropies, including those run by George Soros, knew that electoral victories required evangelical votes. And once strident street radicals like longtime Religious Left activist Jim Wallis recognized that the old techniques of angry protest no longer worked, they needed a new strategy, something that could be used to co-opt suburban evangelicals and show the media and policy makers that they were still relevant.

And, with that, the Evangelical Left was born.

Targeting evangelicals with their causes like environmentalism, welfare expansion, disarming America, and ending our special relationship with Israel, leftist activists and philanthropies have, especially since the 2004 election, attempted to shift evangelicals away from their concerns about abortion and traditional marriage.

Meanwhile, the Left's social gospel advocates have been working to capture evangelical elites, especially academics, students, ministry workers, and some larger church pastors who aspire for approval from urban secular elites. Strategists understand that peeling even a small minority of evangelical voters away could dramatically change things in their favor. And, just as important for anyone trying to influence the political system: winning over evangelical elites who claim to speak for large evangelical institutions can provide powerful images and sound bites for the media.

But, despite these campaigns, rank-and-file evangelicals remain strongly conservative—over 70 percent voted Republican in the 2010 midterm elections. Does that mean the Evangelical Left has failed? Unfortunately, no; just the opposite: it means they are just getting started.

But, if that's the case, then this cause, this relentless push by the Evangelical Left toward, essentially, socialism in the name of Jesus, needs a leader; someone with enough street cred and experience to take a radical approach and make it look mainstream. Someone who might even have access to the president himself.

America, I'd like to introduce you to the evangelical pastor Jim Wallis.

WHAT WOULD JESUS CUT?

Organized religion is a funny thing. People can claim to "speak for" large swaths of followers when, in reality, they have absolutely no standing to do so. I guess in that way it's a lot like politics. A politician can go on a Sunday morning talk show and pretend to speak for an entire party even though the actual voters in that party may have very different ideas.

Of course, the media doesn't care. Trot out someone with a fancy title and they're more than happy to give that person a microphone. The Left knows how to play this game very well.

For example, remember the recent crisis over the statutory limit on our national debt? Congress was deadlocked over tax increases and spending limits on welfare and entitlement and it was all serving to put President Obama between a rock and a hard place. How, given America's exploding national debt, could he possibly be seen as reckless enough to allow the spending party to continue? But, on the other side, he had another election to worry about. Caving to Republicans would put him in a terrible spot. How could he get out of this mess?

Enter longtime Religious Left activist Jim Wallis.

Wallis led an ecumenical delegation into the White House to offer their spiritual solidarity with the president. Claiming to speak for most of America's Christians, Wallis's spiritual photo op with President Obama included representatives of the National Association of Evangelicals, the National Council of Churches, the Salvation Army, and the U.S. Catholic Conference of Bishops. The group's rhetorical appeal to the country was "What Would Jesus Cut?" as they announced that they would stand as a "Circle of Protection" around federal antipoverty programs.

These religious elites collectively represented over 120 million American church members—at least on paper. In reality? Who knows. And, honestly, if you're the media, who cares? The photo op and sound bites (like this one from Wallis: "If you're going to come after the poor, you have to go through us first") were all the Left needed. Ultimately Congress and the president agreed to theoret-

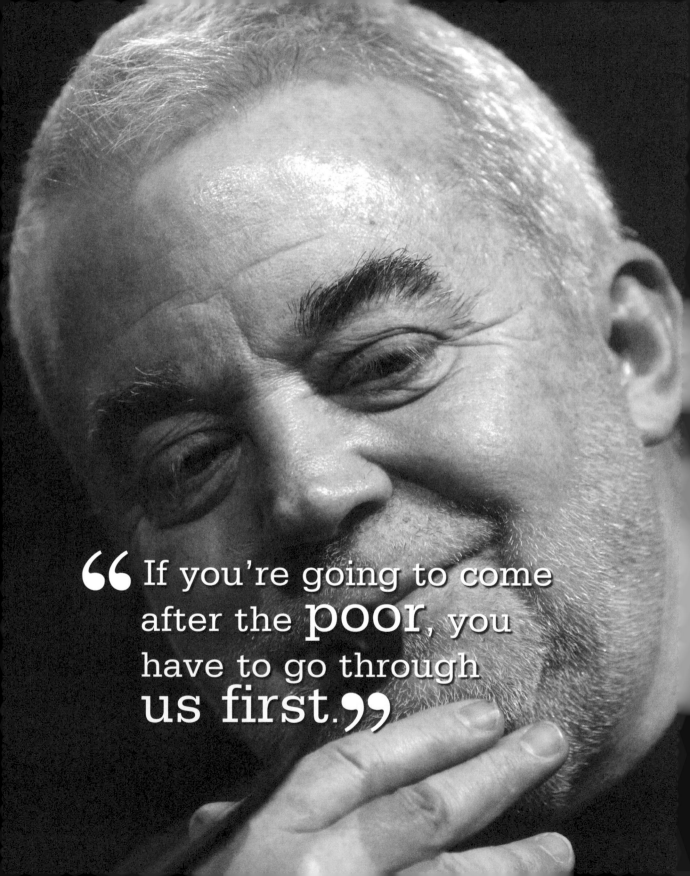

"If you're going to come after the poor, you have to go through us first."

ical "cuts" of perhaps $2.5 trillion over ten years. "It appears that the voice of the faith community was at least heard and made some difference in the outcome of the default debate," Wallis announced, commending the White House for having "protected low-income entitlement programs" and Medicaid. He complained that the deal's "most glaring problem" was no tax increases. But, whether the deal met his approval or not, Wallis had made himself the most prominent face in the Circle of Protection's coalition.

And, with that, Jim Wallis, a man who'd spent his life toiling in obscurity and craving mainstream appeal, had become the face of the Evangelical Left.

OBAMA'S LEFT-HAND MAN

Pastor Wallis is an interesting choice for a leader. Raised in a small evangelical church called the Plymouth Brethren, Wallis himself has rarely, if ever, publicly detailed his own personal faith beliefs. He typically defines himself as "evangelical," though he represents no church, except for a small circle of leftist activists who sometimes meet for prayer in his Washington, D.C., office. He has also led a liberal activist group called "Sojourners" for over thirty years and publishes a magazine by the same name.

Over the years, Wallis has turned into one of America's most politically prominent religious voices, representing the new, more polished brand of Religious Leftists who now appeal not to post-Woodstock hippies in Volkswagen vans, but to minivan-driving suburbanites who worship at megachurches. The pinnacle of his mainstream success came in 2009 when he was tapped by President Obama to be part of a handful of spiritual advisers who, according to the *New York Times*, he would consult with "for private prayer sessions on the telephone and for discussions on the role of religion in politics."

Hanoi Jim?

Sojourners is the successor to Wallis's journal that he originally founded in 1971, titled the *Post American*, which celebrated the ostensible end of American dominance. "To be Christian in this time is to be post-American," it rejoiced, while trumpeting Wallis's anti-American opinions and siding with global Marxist revolutionary "liberation" movements throughout the 1970s. "I don't know how else to express the quiet emotion that rushed through me when the news reports showed that the United States had finally been defeated in Vietnam," Wallis characteristically gushed after North Vietnamese tanks rolled into conquered South Vietnam, solidifying police state communism over Indochina. "There was an overwhelming sense of relief and thankfulness that the American intruders had finally been thrown out and that the desire of the U.S. government to control the destiny of Indochina had been thwarted."

If you were concerned that Wallis and the other advisers might be radical Leftists who would try to push Obama even more toward Marxism, you can relax. It turns out that Obama doesn't need the push: "These are all centrist, social justice guys," said the Reverend Eugene F. Rivers about the group of advisers. "Obama genuinely comes out of the social justice wing of the church. That's real. The community organizing stuff is real."

Jim Wallis might not have been mainstream enough for the White House had he not experienced success four years earlier with the release of his bestselling (and presumptuously titled) book *God's Politics: Why the Right Gets It Wrong and the Left Doesn't Get It*. The book audaciously aligned Christianity with big-government liberalism, even as Wallis himself professed nonpartisanship.

Wallis's orchestrated political theater at the White House may have been his greatest public stunt, but it wasn't his only one. Earlier that year he deftly exploited the Christian season of Lent, which is traditionally focused on quiet self-denial, by embarking on a very public Lenten fast to protest "cuts" in the 2011 federal budget by sinister congressional Republicans.

He was joined by over two dozen spiritually awakened U.S. House Democrats, along with the radical left group MoveOn.org, which is not typically known for its religious devotion. MoveOn's executive director, Justin Ruben, solemnly announced that he and other "progressive" groups were joining religious leaders to "protest the brutal and unjust budget cuts being debated in Washington."

In case Wallis himself had omitted any of the White House's talking points, Ruben melodramatically explained: "All week long I've been looking into the eyes of my 2-year-old daughter, and thinking about the hundreds of thousands of kids who will get kicked out of preschool, who will lose access to health care, who will go to bed hungry each night if these cuts pass." Metaphorically opening up his Bible, Ruben then quoted the Prophet Isaiah about fasting, claiming: "I joined because, according to my faith and my conscience, letting children starve while giving handouts to giant corporations is wrong, plain and simple."

Other endorsers of Wallis's fast were United Methodist Church agencies, the some-

You Can Judge a Book by Its (Back) Cover

The back cover of *God's Politics* is a sight to behold. Right under the heading "God Is Not a Republican . . . Or a Democrat" are five endorsements that, I guess, are supposed to prove how nonpartisan the book is, but instead read like the guest list to a Rachel Maddow cocktail party: Bono, of the rock band U2; Bill Moyers; E. J. Dionne, the liberal columnist from the *Washington Post*; and Cornel West, an honorary chair of the Democratic Socialists of America.

Facts Are More Stubborn than Rhetoric

Explaining the fast on his blog, Wallis said that he felt compelled to do this "Because those of us who are Christians are bound by Jesus' command to protect the least of these. So people of faith ask, 'What Would Jesus Cut?' The extreme budget cuts proposed to critical programs that save the lives, dignity, and future of poor and vulnerable people have crossed a moral line." He offered nine other reasons that all gave a similar rationale: the poor's safety net is being targeted so that we can declare more wars or make sure millionaires keep more of their money.

There's only one problem: his logic is completely wrong—at least if you want to rely on actual numbers instead of a progressive activist's blog post. I don't want to turn this into an economics chapter, but Brian Riedl, the Heritage Foundation's budget expert, and someone I know and trust, had this analysis in 2011, right around the time of the Wallis fast:

> The nonpartisan Congressional Budget Office reports that the richest 20 percent of taxpayers now shoulder a record 86 percent of the federal income tax burden. This is substantially higher than when Ronald Reagan took office (64 percent) and even higher than when George W. Bush took office (81 percent).
>
> The flip side of the "tax cuts for the rich" mantra has been "spending cuts for the

> poor." Again, the official government data flatly contradict the conventional wisdom.
>
> According to the White House's Office of Management and Budget, federal anti-poverty spending has soared from $190 billion in 1990 to $348 billion in 2000, and to a staggering $638 billion this year (all adjusted for inflation). The growth since 2000 has been particularly remarkable in the Children's Health Insurance Program (470 percent), food stamps (229 percent), energy assistance (163 percent), child care assistance (89 percent) and Medicaid (80 percent).
>
> These expansions have been bipartisan: Mr. Bush—unfairly derided as bad for poor people—became the first president to spend more than 3 percent of the nation's income on anti-poverty programs. President Obama then pushed it above 4 percent. In fact, since 1990, anti-poverty spending as a share of national income has expanded as fast as Social Security, Medicare, defense, and education—combined.
>
> So why the perceived "spending cuts for the poor"? Because anti-poverty spending increases (as large as $60 billion annually) occur automatically, and therefore go largely unnoticed. Yet any lawmaker proposing to shave even $1 billion off that growth is loudly attacked for "declaring war" on the safety net.

times radical Islamic Society of North America (named by the U.S. Justice Department as an unindicted co-conspirator in the 2007 Holy Land Foundation terrorist financing case—see the chapter on Islamists for more), and the evangelical relief group World Vision, along with trade union groups like SEIU, the aforementioned MoveOn.org, and former Ohio Democratic congressman Tony Hall. Hall, himself a liberal evangelical and frequent Wallis cohort, likened this fast to President Lincoln's call for national fasting during the Civil War. "On Easter Sunday I will start eating again," Hall brazenly intoned at a press conference with Wallis. "But millions of people here in America and around the world will not have the same luxury; they will continue to go hungry."

For Wallis, every aspect of sacred faith often becomes just another prop for ideological battle for big government. And for him, even a holy season is the right time for harsh name-calling. Wallis denounced Republican budget cutters as "bullies," "corrupt," and "hypocrites."

Wallis and other committed Religious Leftists believe that justice for the poor is impossible without endlessly expanding

Your Music Is "Incredibly Offensive"

MoveOn.org later posted a video from the musician Moby, who solemnly explained to Americans that he found it "incredibly offensive" that "Republicans have a budget that gives tax breaks to huge corporations and . . . to millionaires but yet it hurts veterans and the elderly and the children and women's rights."

centralized state power at the expense of individual liberty. Remember, the 2011 federal-budget and debt-ceiling controversies were over limits on future *growth* of federal programs—there were virtually no actual proposed "cuts" in most spending programs. But even that couldn't be tolerated because this is not really about the poor, it's about ideology.

Wallis coyly likes to pitch his political appeals by citing Jesus to evangelicals, who are supposed to obligingly shout "Amen!" But he never explains whether Jesus would engulf America in spiraling debt, or suffocate Americans under a mountain of taxes. Never during his spiritual defenses of the Welfare State does Wallis ever ponder whether Jesus would permanently entrap multiple generations of the poor into welfare dependency. When he does talk about the overall deficit he says that we should get our spending under control—but only if we cut the things he's okay with.

"The president and Congress are engaged in an intense debate over the national budget," Wallis announced after his pilgrimage to the White House, "with an upcoming vote on raising our national debt ceiling being used as a tool in a political and ideological battle. Programs for the poor and vulnerable are caught in the middle. But risking our social safety net for political advantage isn't just irresponsible—it's immoral."

Practice What You Preach

Just four months before calling Republicans "bullies" and "corrupt," Wallis coauthored an op-ed titled "Conviction and Civility." He wrote: "[W]e, as leaders in the faith community, affirm with one voice our principled commitment to civil discourse in our nation's public life."

I hope his fast lasted longer than his affirmation.

It's amazing how that word *immoral* keeps popping up, isn't it? Religious Leftists typically don't ever like to be judgmental or denounce "immorality" except, of course, when condemning those who don't believe that the Welfare State is the answer.

Wallis and his religious allies at the White House profess to speak for "real people who are struggling, some of whom are poor; families, children, and the elderly." But for the materialistic Religious Left, only government entitlements and taxes seem to qualify as true Christian charity. Religious Leftists don't usually fret over working families oppressed by high taxes, entrepreneurs fighting to navigate waves of regulations to create new businesses, or the chronically unemployed who prefer jobs over welfare. Americans of any economic bracket who believe in personal liberty and responsibility evidently don't qualify for Wallis's "Circle of Protection."

THE CIRCLE MEETS THE OVAL

In July 2011, prior to a meeting with lawmakers about the budget, President Obama spent forty minutes meeting with a group of "Christian leaders" to, as one paper put it, "seek their advice and ask them to pray for him." Those leaders were, of course, the Leftist "Circle of Protection" group headed by Jim Wallis.

After the meeting with Obama, Galen Carey, of the National Association of Evangelicals (NAE), gushed about the president to reporters, saying, "He agrees with us that the 'least of these' and the most vulnerable citizens should not have to sacrifice for the well-being of our country." Obama must have appreciated the support from envoys claiming to represent tens of millions of American Christians. But how many churchgoers actually believe their churches should always bless an unlimited Welfare State?

Wallis's White House religious summit recalled a strikingly similar political photo op by the once important National Council of Churches (NCC) with President Clinton in 1995. Back then, churchmen and women joined hands with Clinton in the Oval Office and prayed he would be "strong for the task" of resisting the newly elected Republican Congress and their evil cutting ways. Foreshadowing Wallis sixteen years later, the NCC even touted Holy Week protest "fasts" between Palm Sunday and Easter.

There is, however, one big difference between the 1995 and 2011 White House stunts. Back in the 1990s evangelical groups like the NAE abstained from the NCC's embarrassing political exploitation of the passion and resurrection of Jesus Christ. But now, thanks in large part to persuasion by Wallis and others, many evangelical elites now want to follow old, discredited Religious Left groups like the NCC into eventual irrelevance by confusing God's Kingdom with the Welfare and Regulatory State.

Other Christian leaders (who were not invited to the White House during the debt ceiling crisis) weren't all that happy that Wallis and his "Circle of Protection" were claiming to speak for all Christians. The group Christians for a Sustainable Economy (CASE), which includes prominent evangelicals such as Chuck Colson of Prison Fellowship and Southern Baptist leader Richard Land, countered Wallis in their own letter to President Obama.

"Just as we should not balance the budget 'on the backs of the poor,'" they wrote, "so we should not balance the budget on the backs of our children and grandchildren." Warning against the evils of "stagnant economy and the enslaving power of debt," and clearly taking a shot directly at Wallis, they declared, "To the question, 'What would Jesus cut?' we add the question, 'Whom would Jesus indebt?' The Good Samaritan did not use a government credit card."

Cut Spending . . . Except the Stuff I Like

Carey also told reporters that government officials have a "spiritual and moral" responsibility to reel in government spending. "I talked about the importance of fiscal responsibility, which the president articulated very clearly, so we're with him on that," he said.

Just three months earlier, the Circle of Protection had issued its own statement that echoed those tones. "As Christian leaders," the statement read, "we are committed to fiscal responsibility and shared sacrifice."

So, let's get this straight: According to the Religious Left (or "Christian leaders," if you want to play their word games), which is now somehow running our budget and dictating our morality, we need to be "fiscally responsible" but we can't really cut any social programs. So that leaves tax increases (on the wealthy only, obviously) and, let me take a wild guess: cuts in defense spending? If so, the "Circle of Protection" sounds like they have a lot in common with run-of-the-mill progressives. They should get together sometime.

PAST IS PROLOGUE?

Jim Wallis does not have the kind of past that you might expect from someone who considers himself to be a mainstream religious leader. In the 1960s he had been a strident agitator in Students for a Democratic Society. In the 1970s he gushed over the Viet Cong and the Sandinistas and saluted the accomplishments of Fidel Castro. In the 1980s, under the dreaded President Ronald Reagan, he urged neutrality between America and the Soviet Union, explaining: "We must refuse to take sides in this horrible and deadly hypocrisy," since a "totalitarian spirit fuels the engines of both Wall Street and the Kremlin."

By the mid-1990s Wallis had founded "Call to Renewal," an annual interfaith jamboree for liberal activists. It professed a "third-way" transcending ideology but, more predictably, it bashed America, capitalism, and religious conservatives while equating true faith with old-style class warfare.

The "Call" originally featured politically inconsequential, old Religious Left fixtures like the Episcopal Church's presiding bishop and officials of the National Council of Churches, along with aging "Social Gospel" Catholics. One early stunt was a protest of "Call" activists inside the U.S. Capitol Rotunda to protest Republicans' "Contract with America." But nothing seemed to be breaking through. The "morning zoo" type stunts were doing nothing to reach the mainstream of America, and without those voters, his real agenda had no shot.

So, he changed tactics.

Wallis realized that more softly appealing to churchgoers, especially suburban evangelicals, was much more politically viable. That shift in strategy was pretty evident in his actions. When denouncing President Clinton's endorsement of welfare reform in 1996 as a "great national sin," Wallis, in an obvious precursor to the "What Would Jesus Cut?" campaign of 2011, said that Jesus would be demonstrating outside the White House against welfare reform. He complained that "[b]y sacrificing hundreds of thousands of poor children to his bid for reelection, Bill Clinton failed the most serious test of his presidency. . . . We're now about to experience a hurricane of human suffering."

It was vintage Wallis—a direct plea to yuppies and middle-class families on behalf of America's most vulnerable.

The problem for his message was that the hurricane never came. Soup kitchens were not deluged, Depression-era bread lines did not return. Welfare reform, in fact, was widely considered to be a success.

When challenged on his old rhetoric and stances, Wallis is careful. In a 2010 debate with American Enterprise Institute president Arthur Brooks at evangelical Wheaton College, Wallis somewhat sheepishly insisted that the welfare reform of 1996 was "inadequate" but was helped by the "good economy" of the 1990s. "So I still don't think that welfare reform, though the right direction, had in it . . . things that really would have helped people move out of poverty, and not just off the welfare rolls."

Whether Wallis admits it or not, the success of welfare reform (backed by a Democrat,

According to Jim

"The truth is that most of the important movements for social change in America have been fueled by religion—progressive religion. . . . As the religious Right loses influence, nothing could be better for the health of both church and society than a return of the moral center that anchors our nation in a common humanity."

no less) ultimately persuaded Wallis by the late 1990s that he had to shift to the center, at least in imagery and rhetoric. So, when George W. Bush took the Oval Office, Wallis was initially half friendly to the new president. He embraced Bush's faith-based initiatives and featured that program's first chief, John Dilulio, to speak at a Call rally. In a 2001 interview, Wallis said he found it "encouraging" that the Bush administration was listening to the "faith community" about poverty. "My hope is that we will have a partnership," he said.

It wasn't long after the inauguration that Wallis was part of a clergy group that met with Bush to talk about inner-city ministry, an issue that fit neatly with Bush's "compassionate conservatism." With his typical flair for self-promotion, Wallis reported his Bush meeting in seemingly any newspaper that would publish him. In a 2001 *Washington Post* op-ed, he proclaimed that he was pleased the new president was "reaching well beyond his base of conservative Evangelicals." In a *New York Times* op-ed, he wrote, "I didn't vote for President Bush, but I welcome the new White House office that will coordinate 'faith-based and community initiatives.'" In a *Washington Times* column, he opined: "I think many of us in the churches are inclined to give Mr. Bush a chance."

In 2001, Wallis contrasted the Bush administration with the Clinton administration, which he said was "very solicitous" of religious groups like Sojourners and the Call but failed to offer "much content." Both Clintons had sent Wallis notes and invited him to White House prayer breakfasts, he recalled, but he wanted more than photo ops. Bill Clinton "had no space for critical dialogue" and "no moral compass," Wallis lamented, saying the White House circulated an internal memo cutting him off from further contact after he had publicly condemned welfare reform.

In 2010, *World* magazine revealed that George Soros, himself indifferent to religion but a key player in the rise of the Evangelical Left, had funded Wallis with $200,000 in 2004, $25,000 in 2006, $100,000 in 2007, and $150,000 in 2011 through his foundation. While it's probably unfair to exclusively credit the Soros funding, Wallis's soft heart for the Bush administration did not last.

Initially restrained about the U.S. military response after 9/11, Wallis, a pacifist (despite his enthusiasm in earlier years for Marxist revolution in Southeast Asia and Central America), became more critical while still trying to avoid the hard-left rhetoric of his earlier days. He also began to urge white evangelicals, nearly 80 percent of whom voted for Bush in 2004, to make issues like poverty,

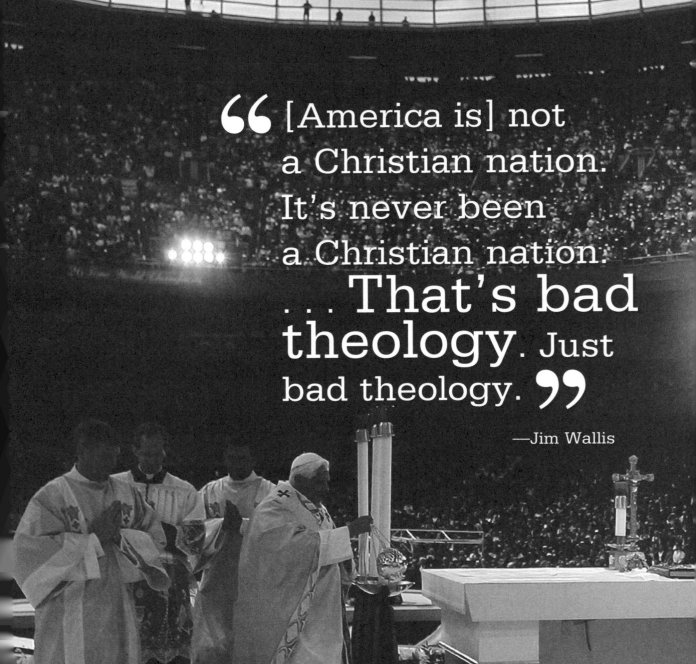

> "[America is] not a Christian nation. It's never been a Christian nation. . . . That's bad theology. Just bad theology."

—Jim Wallis

the environment, and peace their priority over things like abortion and same-sex marriage—a shift that would obviously push them toward the left.

Despite Wallis's efforts, white evangelicals still voted overwhelmingly for John McCain in 2008—but a larger minority of younger evangelicals did vote Democratic. And Wallis's activism coincided with a growing Evangelical Left elite on Christian college and seminary campuses.

By 2009, everything had changed. Not just for the country, but for Wallis himself. "My prayers for decades have been answered in this minute," Wallis breathlessly announced after Obama's 2009 inauguration, boasting of his multiyear friendship with the president. "We've been talking faith and politics for a long time."

Wallis seemed to have access to the administration right from the start. "This White House wants our advice," he rejoiced in early 2009. "Leaders from the faith community have been virtually inhabiting the offices of the Transition Team over the last weeks, with our advice being sought on global and domestic poverty, human rights, criminal justice, torture, faith-based offices, foreign policy, Gaza and the Middle East. A staffer joked one day, 'We should have just gotten all of you bunks here.'"

The imagery of Wallis's devoted corps of progressive liberal activists populating and guiding Obama's White House transition team must have delighted the onetime radical outsider, who forty years earlier was likelier to have been arrested outside the White House.

In return for the access, Wallis has rushed to support Obama whenever he's needed it. When Obamacare faced political turbulence, for example, Wallis helped host a 2009 conference call to energize religious support. "I'm going to need the help of all of you," Obama said on the call. "I'm going to need you to spread the facts and speak the truth," he continued, complaining that "our religious faith" is inconsistent with America's current health-care system.

When Obama claimed that his plan would not fund abortion or facilitate "death panels," Wallis supportively interjected: "We are in danger of losing the moral core of the health care debate." When the Roman Catholic bishops and many evangelicals opposed Obamacare's facilitation of abortion funding through insurance exchanges, Wallis obligingly stumped for the administration's claims to have compromised on abortion. He helped organize liberal evangelicals to back the last-minute maneuver, giving some religious cover to pro-life Democrats who had caved, and ensuring Obamacare's passage.

GOING MAINSTREAM

Despite his clear alignment with Obama, Wallis's claims to be a post-ideological, nonpartisan evangelical have continued to gain him entrée into new, traditionally conservative circles. In 2010, he addressed the annual "Lifest" evangelical festival in Oshkosh, Wisconsin, which typically attracts seventy thousand people. One Christian radio station very publicly canceled its support, protesting Wallis's proposed "unholy alliance between the Church and Government," but the event's organizer still introduced Wallis enthusiastically. "I've read his books," the organizer announced, "I've studied with him, I've been on retreats with him. This is my brother in Christ. I believe he has a message from God for the church today."

On the podium in Wisconsin, Wallis responded with self-deprecating humor and a rare reference to his radical, sometimes pro-Marxist past. "I heard somebody around here thought I was an avowed Marxist. Well, I'm not. But I was reading them when I was a student—Karl Marx, Ho Chi Minh, Che Guevara. But then I began to read the Gospel of Matthew, where Jesus said, 'Repent, for the king-

> **According to Jim**
> "**W**e are accountable to God's purposes and God's principles but there's no special covenant with America here. It doesn't exist and to say so is really, well, it's a heresy. American exceptionalism, theologically, is a heresy."

dom of heaven is at hand!'" Citing Jesus's command to care for the "least of these," Wallis explained: "That's how He knows whether we love Him or not. That was more radical than Karl Marx and Che Guevara and Ho Chi Minh. And I signed up to be a follower of Jesus."

The mostly young audience responded enthusiastically. They were probably never taught about the Sandinistas or other Marxist groups that once inspired a more openly radical Wallis in previous decades.

Wallis had achieved another evangelical breakthrough and now, with growing confidence, he's been actively engaging and targeting conservatives. In his 2010 debate with the American Enterprise Institute's Arthur Brooks at evangelical Wheaton College, he reasoned that a "new generation is tired" of the "argument between big government and small government" and the emphasis should now be on "what is smart and effective government." Wallis insisted he is not reflexively a "government person," proudly citing his twenty-two arrests over the decades. Instead, he is more a "movement person" supposedly akin to Martin Luther King Jr.

In 2011, Wallis debated conservative commentator and Kings College president Dinesh D'Souza over American "exceptionalism." Wallis extolled "God bless the world" over "God bless America," warning that many Americans advocate a "kind of exceptionalism" that creates "self-delusion" and "disasters." He professed love for America's "values" but lamented "I don't love when we violate those values . . . acting like an empire."

D'Souza exuberantly countered that "We should be jubilant, [as] American foreign policy has made the world much better." In response, Wallis simply changed the subject back to his ongoing fast in protest of proposed budget cuts.

Later in 2011, as Occupy Wall Street gained steam, Wallis could not help himself. Despite his carefully crafted new moderate image for the twenty-first century, he could not avoid publicly admiring the Occupiers. "When they stand with the poor, they stand with Jesus," he rejoiced. "When they talk about holding banks and corporations accountable, they sound like Jesus and the biblical prophets before him who all spoke about holding the wealthy and powerful accountable."

In early 2012, Wallis was initially concerned over the Obamacare mandate that religious charities, schools, and hospitals were not exempt from paying for insurance covering contraceptives, abortifacients, and sterilization. He rightly saw it as a threat to his coalition. But, when forced to choose, he naturally sided with Obama and against religious liberty protections. "We applaud the Obama administration's decision to respond to the concerns of many in the faith community around respecting religious liberty," his Sojourners group declared of the "compromise" forcing insurance companies to provide "free" contraceptives to employees of religious institutions. "This compromise respects the conscience concerns of those persons and institutions opposed to the use of contraception while still allowing greater access to those services for women who seek it."

FOLLOW THE MONEY

Behind all of this very public lobbying and support under the guise of religion, there's a lot of very private money. In the mid-2000s, new Evangelical Left advocacy groups, funded by George Soros or the Tides Foundation, among others, began to arise. They touted liberal stances on "creation care," immigration, federal budget policies, national security, and policies toward detained terrorists, all coated in evangelical language.

These groups would often claim that "Jesus" has specific political stances— always aligned with the Left—but in reality they were merely repeating the "Social Gospel" themes that the old Religious Left had originated decades earlier. In other words, this was purely a political ploy. The same old message was simply repackaged and targeted toward a new audience.

This financial alliance between the typical progressive foundations like Tides and an allegedly "religious" organization like Wallis's Sojourners was not something that was meant for public consumption. When *World* magazine editor Marvin Olasky confronted Wallis about the funding he'd received from Soros, he brought up Wallis's own quote from 2005: "I know of no connections to those liberal funds and groups that are as direct as the Religious Right's ties to right-wing funders."

Wallis responded by likening the *World* editor to someone you may have heard of: "It's not hyperbole or overstatement to say that Glenn Beck lies for a living." He added: "I'm sad to see Marvin Olasky doing the same thing. No, we don't receive money from Soros. Given the financial crisis of nonprofits, maybe Marvin should call Soros and ask him to send us money. . . . So, no, we don't receive money from George Soros. Our books are totally open, always have been. Our money comes from Christians who support us and who read *Sojourners*. . . . [T]ell Marvin he should check his facts, and not imitate Glenn Beck."

After proof of the Soros grants appeared online (despite the Soros-funded Open Society Institute's having removed the original links), Wallis had his public relations staffer release a reluctant confession: "I should have declined to comment until I was able to review the blog post in question and consulted with our staff on the details of our funding over the past several years," he explained. "Instead, I answered in the spirit of the accusation and did not recall the details of our funding over the decade in question."

Wallis denied that Sojourners is "beholden to funders on the political left," while he insisted it promotes nonideological "biblical social justice." But he'd tacitly admitted that the "allegation" concerning three Open Society Institute grants

According to Jim

"The Bible has no objection, in my view, to making the wealthy pay their fair share, which is more than they're paying now."
—JIM WALLIS, 2011

I wonder if the Bible, in his view, tells us exactly who is wealthy and what their "fair share" should be. If not, I'm sure he'd just say it was an oversight on the part of the Bible's authors and he'd be happy to fill in the blanks.

was true. These funds "made up the tiniest fraction" of Sojourners budget, "so small that I hadn't remembered them," he claimed about grants that amount to hundreds of thousands of dollars.

Soros's support for Evangelical Left fixtures like Wallis proves that he, or at least his staff at the Open Society Institute, understands the importance of religion in American politics—even if the billionaire financier himself is an adamant nonbeliever. How evangelical recipients of Soros cash, claiming to be nonpartisan and nonideological, explain to their churchgoing constituents this support from a hyperpartisan atheist billionaire who touts abortion, same-sex marriage, and legalized prostitution may be more complicated.

A REAWAKENING

Very few of the evangelicals who now follow Leftists like Jim Wallis realize that the technique of exploiting the churches for progressive policies has been tried before. And it failed miserably. Their fixation on a fictitious version of social justice that promotes big government almost killed once-dominant mainline Protestant churches—will evangelicals now succumb to the same fate?

Not necessarily.

The good news is that it's not too late to wake up our congregations, especially if people understand what is really going on behind the scenes. Church members need to ask whether their congregation belongs to the NAE. They need to research whether the relief and missions groups they support make leftist political pronouncements. They should ask who is teaching at the religious schools where they send their children and exactly what is being taught there.

People should be leery of political causes being broadcast in their local churches. The verbiage is often benign (for example, "creation care" for environmentalism, "caring for the sojourner" instead of amnesty for illegal immigrants, "Christian peacemaking" for absolute pacifism and isolationism), but the underlying political agenda often is not. Church members need to find solid, sensible policy alternatives to the Religious Left's proposals. Groups like the Acton Institute, Cornwall Alliance, and Institute on Religion and Democracy specialize in helping church members counter big-government politics that are disguised as Christian compassion. They are also great resources.

Most important, church members must hold their congregations to a focus on God and scripture—not on their pastor's personal political views or answers to rhetorical questions like "What would Jesus cut?" When we stand up for the basic tenets of our faith—morality and freedom—we stand up for the tenets of America by default. Religious Left activists like Jim Wallis may claim to preach the word of God, but those words have been run through a filter of politics and ideology and are no longer recognizable.

And if all else fails, and you still cannot tell the difference between an authentic sermon and one that is straight from the pockets of George Soros, then take a page out of the activist playbook and ask yourself this: "Whom Would Jesus Listen To?" If your answer is a former radical who twists the gospel for political ends, who preaches bipartisanship as a cover for his Marxism, and who measures his success in book sales and television appearances, then Pastor Jim Wallis could not be a better fit.

Chapter Nine

CHANGE THE MEDIA, CHANGE THE WORLD

" The world is changing very fast. Big will not beat small anymore. It will be the fast beating the slow. "

—Rupert Murdoch, Chairman and CEO, News Corporation

NOVEMBER 23, 2004. The time had finally come for Dan Rather to step down. The pressure, ratcheted up by bloggers, had been building for months. His speech to the CBS newsroom on this day would not exactly put it that way—but everyone knew the truth. The ticking hand on the *60 Minutes* stopwatch was about to stop on Dan Rather for good.

What would happen over the next few minutes has largely been forgotten. You won't find it in any journalism textbooks. Even in blog lore, it probably hasn't gotten much play. It would be too strong to call it a "tipping point" moment, but, in some ways, it perfectly foreshadowed how the media landscape was about to change forever.

OLD ANCHOR MEETS NEW MEDIA

The main newsroom inside the CBS News complex on Manhattan's West Side had come to be known as "the Fishbowl." It was composed of a semicircle of offices that opened into a news gathering and broadcast floor where Dan Rather sat nightly to anchor *The CBS Evening News*. Today, however, Rather would enter the Fishbowl to speak to the staff. He wouldn't be resigning, per se—he wouldn't leave the company for a few months—but he would say, out loud, that the time had come, that he would be stepping aside.

Not everyone at CBS News could walk to the Fishbowl to watch this historic moment on West Fifty-seventh Street. No matter—an in-house closed-circuit television feed would carry his speech to the larger CBS News family. And that, in retrospect, changed everything.

As it turned out, one CBS News staffer in New York that day happened to be talking on his cell phone with a friend in another city. The friend, a journalist named Scott Baker, who now works for me as editor in chief of *The Blaze*, mentioned to him that it would be cool to listen to Rather's speech on the phone as it happened. "No problem," the staffer responded. "I'll just put my phone down next to the TV monitor—listen as long as you want to."

After realizing that he'd likely be hearing history in the making, Baker quickly sent an instant message from his laptop to someone he thought might be interested in a live transcription of Dan Rather's "resignation" speech. That message put into motion a series of events that would take Dan Rather's words on a unique path.

As Rather spoke in the Fishbowl, a camera carried his words live on that in-house feed. The words exited a TV monitor and entered a cell phone, where they ricocheted to a tower (and maybe a satellite or two) and then zipped to a distant city. Scott Baker, listening via headset, transcribed the words rapidly into an instant messaging window as he heard them.

Within a matter of moments, Dan Rather's words began to appear on the front page of the *Drudge Report*.

> *It's time to move on . . . I will continue to report to you . . . it has been . . . an honor to report to you. . . .*

By that time *Drudge* had already become a newsroom essential. Everyone monitored it. All day long. Even at CBS News.

One CBS News employee who was in the Fishbowl at the time of that speech would later recount his amazement as he listened to Rather speaking and saw his *Drudge*-tuned computer screen refresh with the very words he had heard spoken just moments before.

A key *Drudge* contributor had just one word for the moment: "Epic."

While no one in the Fishbowl that day wanted to admit it, the ground was shaking underneath the traditional media elites. But denial can't stop an earthquake. The fact that their boss had just resigned "live" on the Web, let alone that another news source had literally scooped CBS News on its own story, made it all the more clear: everything was about to change.

INSTA-JOURNALIST

There have been plenty of grassroots new-media success stories since that day, and plenty of reasons to be proud if you're a conservative or libertarian. But this is not a chapter about patting each other on the back; there is far more to be done. And you don't need me to tell you that the mainstream media outlets still let America down. We still have major, systemic problems in the media. There are so many stories of radical bias, so many instances of clear hatred and bigotry toward conservative thought, that it would almost be boring to keep recounting them all if the stakes weren't so high.

And that's why I'm here to tell you whom to blame for it all: Us. You and me. Conservatives, libertarians—anyone who feels like they've been manipulated or, at best, misunderstood, by the media is at fault. Why? Because, for far too long, we've been pretty much uninterested in doing the job of actual journalism ourselves.

Young conservatives who've aspired to jobs in the media usually wanted to be columnists or radio talk show hosts or the host of their own prime-time opinion show. That's where the money is, the fame, the power . . . the fun. O'Reilly, Rush, Hannity, Ingraham. They want to give perspective and point of view.

But getting to that point in a career is a long and difficult road. Believe me, I know from firsthand experience. While I may have taken an unorthodox route, I did enough Top 40 morning radio and local talk to last multiple lifetimes. The same is true of almost everyone else in the field who's "made it." Overnight sensations are usually far from it.

I've done a lot of job interviews with young conservatives over the years and it's struck me that few of them seemed to be very interested in doing the hard work that it takes to get a job in the mainstream media as a journalist. They don't dream (or even tolerate the thought) of covering a school board meeting on Tuesday night or being the beat reporter at the courthouse. But that's where the real action is. That's where you learn the ropes and put the necessary time in to build a career.

Fox News, while an invaluable resource and amazing success story, has not solved the problem. Despite their growth, we are still left with a media culture that is nearly always devoid of any nuanced conservative insight. Fox can beat the drum on a story all day, but when it's reported the opposite way on every nightly newscast and in every major newspaper, we still lose.

THE OUTSIDERS

Over the last few decades, conservatives have been rightly angered by a media that has mocked and marginalized their values and principles. For a long time, liberals in the media tried to deny that there was any kind of a bias problem. But that eventually became laughable. Study after study showed what we all knew instinctively to be true: in the Major Leagues of Media, liberals played all the positions.

But I'm here to let you in on a secret: While I have many horror stories from my

One of a Kind?

I was in the newsroom at CNN on the day that Tim Russert passed away and I remember a lot of the journalists and producers all having the same general reaction: *They just don't make them like that anymore.*

I also remember my reaction after hearing that: *Huh?*

What do you mean "they" don't make them like that anymore? The reason that Tim Russert was so beloved as a journalist was that viewers never really knew which side he was on. He'd ask someone a tough question and you'd cheer; and then a minute later he'd ask the guy you support an even tougher question and you'd get mad. That's exactly what fair and honest journalists are supposed to do!

Instead of saying "they don't make them like that anymore" we must become that ideal ourselves. We create our own destiny and live up to the standards we set. If we dismiss the guys like Russert as journalists of the past, then we're guaranteed a future of lazy, partisan journalism.

early days in cable news, there is no secret elevator at the CNN operation in the Time Warner Center. There's no unmarked door that takes you into a conference room where the media elites secretly gather to plot how to undermine and discredit all that is good and wholesome. There's no Batphone with a direct line to some unseen executive who matches up scripts to Democratic talking points.

The sad reality is that most of the people who work for these companies think they are being fair—they just don't have any idea what that really means.

I remember one instance at CNN when I spent hours on a conference call with people from Atlanta who were concerned that I was not fully explaining the motivations behind the terrorists in Afghanistan who were targeting and killing American troops. I couldn't believe that I had to have those conversations, but I realized later that this wasn't happening because of some political ideology; it was happening because these people really believed that if we just understood the terrorists we might be able to explain why they hate us so much.

A conservative I know who once interned at a network news operation says he saw a correspondent with a stopwatch in her hand declare that a story was fair because the conservative had been given seventeen seconds and the liberal had been given only fifteen seconds.

That is exactly what I mean when I say that the root cause of this bias is not always politically motivated. They think they can measure fairness with a stopwatch, but no stopwatch can ever provide real perspective when there is such a widespread and systemic lack of understanding about how real people, in real communities, live their lives.

Peggy Noonan has a great story about how this works in practice. You may know Peggy as a thoughtful newspaper columnist and commentator on television. You may even know that she once wrote speeches for Ronald Reagan. But one part of her résumé that many people don't know about is that she once worked at CBS News, where she wrote radio scripts for . . . Dan Rather.

In her book *What I Saw at the Revolution: A Political Life in the Reagan Era*, Noonan describes the culture at CBS News in the early 1980s:

> *My peers at the network, the writers and producers in their late twenties and thirties, thought of themselves as modern people trying to be fair.*
>
> *There are conservatives over here and wild lefties over there—and us, the sane people, in the middle. If you made up a list of political questions—should we raise taxes to narrow the deficit; should abortion be banned; should a morning prayer be allowed in the schools; should arms control be our first foreign-policy priority? Most of them would vote yes, no, no, yes.*
>
> *And they would see these not as liberal positions but as decent, intelligent positions. They also thought their views were utterly in line with those of the majority of Americans. In a way that's what's at the heart of our modern political disputes, a disagreement over where the mainstream is and what "normal" is, politically and culturally. I think a lot of the young people at the networks didn't really know what normal was in America, and I hold this view because after working six years in broadcasting and three in New York, I no longer knew what normal was.*
>
> *A small example. Once I wrote a radio script in which I led into a*

story by saying, "This Sunday morning you'll probably be home reading the papers or out at brunch with friends, but Joe Smith will be . . ." A middle-aged editor listened as he walked by the studio and approached me afterward. "Peggy, a small point but maybe not so insignificant: This Sunday morning most Americans will be at church."

He was, of course, correct. But I forgot. I wasn't at church on Sunday mornings, I was in a restaurant on Columbus Avenue eating mushroom omelets and reading the Arts and Leisure section of The New York Times.

I can relate to her story. After working in New York City for six years wasn't sure if I knew what normal was anymore, either. Is seventy-five dollars a day to park your car normal in America? What about constant honking and yelling in the streets? Is it normal to pay four thousand dollars a month in rent for a one-bedroom, 700-square-foot apartment? Is it normal to have gun laws so strict that it takes a year for a license just to get one in your home (and a permit to carry a handgun is virtually impossible)? Is it normal that everyone sends their kids to private schools and laughs at homeschoolers? Are organic markets on every corner normal? What about activists with petitions for every liberal cause known to man combing the streets each day looking for signatures—is that normal?

I think you get my point: it's really easy to become really jaded, really fast.

Thirty years have passed since Noonan's editor gently corrected her, but I'd submit that things aren't that much different in Manhattan newsrooms today.

The truth is that we shouldn't be all that surprised that the media gets the story wrong so much of the time. To be fair, if the circumstances were reversed, it would be tough for us, too. Imagine someone from the Heartland being dropped off in midtown Manhattan and told to report on New York City life. You might try your best to report accurately on what you're seeing, but you'll never succeed because you have no context. Is traffic on the George Washington Bridge really heavy that day, or is that how it always is? Would you describe a certain crime as "particularly gruesome" or is it just that you've never seen a murder victim before? Your life experience from growing up in the Heartland is completely different and there's simply no way to change that overnight.

That is exactly what has happened with the New York, Los Angeles, Washington, D.C.–based media. They simply don't have the context to understand the rest of the country. How can you fairly report on guns if you've never seen one in

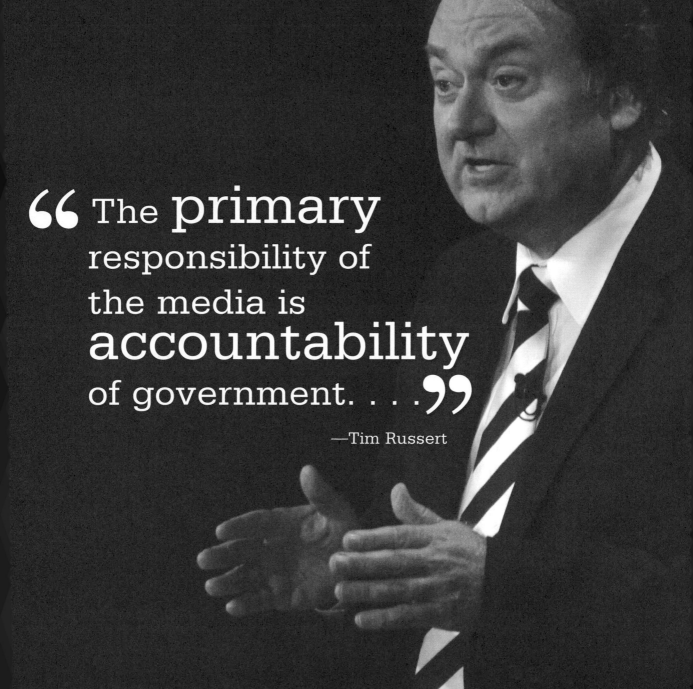

" The **primary** responsibility of the media is **accountability** of government. . . . "

—Tim Russert

person, or never fired one at a range, or if you live in a city like New York where you're banned from carrying one? How can you fairly report on issues of religion if you're an atheist? How can you fairly report on wars if you've never even known anyone who's served in the military?

A news anchor who worked at one of the big stations in Washington, D.C., in the early 1990s told me that he remembers what it was like reporting on the early days of the first Gulf War. It suddenly struck him like a slap to the forehead: in a large newsroom of maybe one hundred people, he was the only veteran. The people around him didn't even know where to start when talking about military operations.

Scott Baker, whom I mentioned earlier in the Dan Rather story, once worked at CBS News on a fellowship program right out of college. He told me that he remembers the little old ladies in his church being aghast at his decision to join the media. They thought maybe he should go to seminary to be a pastor. But working with . . . Dan Rather? They began to question his faith! It would have gone over easier had he defected to the Soviet Union.

When I first met Scott he described to me a strange encounter he'd had in a hallway a few weeks after he'd moved to Manhattan and started working.

A young man reached out to stop him in the hallway. "Hey, are you Scott Baker?"

Scott paused for a second and replied, "I think so, yes."

The young man seemed excited. "I heard about you—you're a Republican!"

Scott looked around the hallway to see who might be listening. He thought for a second. Maybe this was some kind of a rookie test.

He replied cautiously, "Well, I think Mr. Rather would rather see us defined as, er, objective brokers of information." He added that he had worked in Republican politics for years, but, after deciding to pursue a journalism career, he'd registered as an independent.

The young man wasn't deterred. "No, it's okay," he said, lowering his voice to almost a whisper. "I'm one, too." He explained that he worked in a research office down the hall.

Scott was sympathetic. "So, you're the only Republican in the research office—that must be tough."

"No, you don't get it," he said quickly. "I'm the only Republican *in the building*."

Scott told me that he was tempted to hug him. But he wasn't sure who might be watching.

Do you want a hundred more examples like this? I'm sure I could find them easily enough, but would it really make a difference? The fact is that the people who populate the majority of mainstream newsrooms don't have all that much in common with the majority of the people they broadcast that news to.

In a way, it's not so shocking that they don't understand us. It would almost be more shocking if they did. The bigger question is how newsrooms came to be this way in the first place. Why do so many journalists come from the same cities, same cultures, same colleges, and same sensibilities? And what has happened to all of the conservatives along the way?

Where Are the Conservative Media Heroes?

There is nothing wrong with wanting to be a talk show host. There is nothing wrong with wanting to argue with passion. To persuade. To evangelize. We need more conservative/libertarian voices, not fewer. We need more people of deep conviction willing to speak up. But we also need more people willing to do the hard work of finding facts and connecting the dots; more people willing to cover that local school board or town council meeting on a random Tuesday night.

Weekly Standard editor Fred Barnes once spoke to a group of young conservatives at the Leadership Institute in Arlington, Virginia. He told them that he was always amazed at how many young writers he encountered who graduated from college with the sense that they nearly had a "constitutional right to their own newspaper column."

Barnes relayed to them the story of longtime columnist Robert Novak. Novak never wrote a column that did not contain some piece of original information. Barnes noted that, long before Novak even became a columnist, he was a beat reporter in Nebraska, Illinois, and Indiana. When he finally got a break and went to Washington, D.C., he covered the House Ways and Means Committee— when it was closed to the press! Novak learned to develop sources, to make phone calls, to show up in person to find out what was really going on.

That's a good model to follow.

Many successful conservative pundits first spent years as working reporters. Fred Barnes, for example, was at a newspaper in South Carolina. Cal Thomas spent a while as a correspondent for NBC News. Brit Hume spent years as a print reporter before eventually turning to television.

Michael Goldfarb, a *Weekly Standard* contributing editor, told the *Huffington Post* that "a lot of conservatives, they want to be involved in journalism, but our heroes are all pundits. They want to be Rush Limbaugh. They want to be Bill Kristol. They want to be Charles Krauthammer. The model is not Woodward and Bernstein on our side."

He's right, and while there is absolutely nothing wrong with wanting to do opinion—those who do opinion best root their monologues in fact and logic anyway—we must have people willing to fill all of the roles in the media, not *just* the ones focused on opinion.

GET RICH NEVER

It's easy to complain about media bias, but it's important to understand how difficult it can be to get one of the cherished jobs inside a major national news operation. Not because of any bias—on the application they don't ask whom you voted for—but because of something that we conservatives hold dear: capitalism. Supply and demand. The free market.

The truth is that launching a successful journalism career (one that takes you to the highest reaches of American media) is hard—and living the life of the working journalist can be even harder. At the beginning, the numbers are stacked against you. Schools are full of journalism students. After graduation, jobs are scarce. The professors might not tell students this when they first enroll, but very few of those who study journalism in college will ever end up in a job that actually requires reporting on the news.

Those who do graduate and land a job in journalism probably aren't making a great salary—especially compared with their friends in New York who go to work on Wall Street. As fans of the free market, we can hardly complain about that. If there are few jobs and lots of people willing to do them, then starting salaries are low. The hours and quality of life are usually terrible as well. This is not a nine-to-five job with three weeks of vacation kind of deal. You might work weekends. Or overnight. Or start your morning at 4 A.M., every single miserable day.

The 99% Reports on the 1%

Just 1 in 62 newspaper writers and editors are in the top 1 percent of American wage earners. Only 2.7 percent of those who majored in journalism make it into that income group.

The early years of a media career aren't exactly stable, or stationary. Young journalists are the first ones fired when the inevitable restructuring happens, and if you're lucky enough to work for a national company, then you'll likely be awarded with assignments in places not found on anyone's bucket list. I started in radio when I was a teenager. By the time I was thirty I had worked in cities all over the country—from New Haven to Baltimore to Houston to Phoenix.

I've talked to young people who've tried careers in journalism and didn't last long. One took a job in corporate communications. Why? He'd been working weekends at a newspaper and hadn't been to church in a year. Another young woman who'd been an assignment editor at a California TV station quit after a year because she didn't think she could handle the job after the birth of her first child. Can't really blame either of them.

" We're always **wired.** Never static. And we're completely freed from slow-moving, **obsolete** corporate media **restraints** and biases against 'non-traditional' sources of news.**"**

—Michelle Malkin, leading new media entrepreneur and founder of HotAir.com and Twitchy.com

Think about it: if you are a talented college senior with aspirations of landing the kind of job that comes with a healthy salary potential—maybe an annual bonus or stock options—and a great work/life balance, would you really pick journalism as a career?

I know I'm painting a grim picture here. Can a person pursue journalism only if they are a hard-living drinker who detests church and would rather look at a laptop than their own family? It's not quite that bad, but, in all honesty, it's not *that* far off. The "good people" are often chewed up and spit out by the machinery of the media before they even get their feet wet. There are, of course, exceptions to the rule—good people with good families do make it to the top—but they are just that: exceptions.

INFORMATION > DISTRIBUTION

The good news is that everything is changing. Fast. The days of having to choose between a journalism career and a good life are over—conservatives can finally have both. New media, and all of its forms of distribution, from the Web to cell phones to tablets, has created the single best opportunity for conservatives and libertarians to spread their message since Gutenberg invented the printing press.

I've jumped headfirst into the revolution, first starting a news and information website called *The Blaze* (I named it that because the biblical Burning Bush consumes everything but the truth) and then launching GBTV, the first ever streaming television news and entertainment network.

If you've never seen a show on GBTV, the best way I can describe it is that it's television on the Internet, not Internet TV. Why the distinction? Well, because when most people hear "streaming network" they think of a guy in his basement with a webcam. I wanted to show people that it doesn't have to be that way. Yes, I spent an absolute fortune on it, but I believe that the way you present yourself to the online world is a major factor in how you will be regarded. A blogger writing opinion columns is not about to compete with the *New York Times*, and me setting up a few webcams with a white sheet for a backdrop is not about to scare CNN.

Of course, that's not to say that bloggers and webcams don't have their place—they absolutely do. But if you want to compete in the major leagues of media then it's going to take major-league resources. Both properties have their own newsrooms, studios, salespeople, and support staffs. I am treating them as mainstream media properties because that's exactly who I'm going after. I have total confidence that both *The Blaze* and GBTV will show the world that digital doesn't mean sacrificing first-class journalism and top-notch production values.

The Blaze Is Born

The Blaze was created with the conviction that the truth has no agenda. We knew we wouldn't be the first conservative news site—plenty of terrific, talented journalists and bloggers came before us (Michelle Malkin and Jonah Goldberg come to mind), and there is a long history of thoughtful conservative magazines, from *National Review* and the *American Spectator* to *Townhall* and *Newsmax*. And I've already mentioned the tremendous reach and influence of the *Drudge Report*.

Still, we felt there might just be room for a new site that would focus on more than just politics and government. It would go deep into all kinds of stories, from faith and religion to technology and science. We put our heads together and, in less than two months, we built TheBlaze.com.

I'll be honest: I wasn't totally sure at first if people would like it. I believed we were filling a void, but as we got close to launch I started to worry that I was the only one seeing that void. We didn't do focus groups, or test audiences. I was worried that people would think I was throwing up a website just to make money, when, in reality, I was going to take a bath on it.

It turns out that we didn't need to worry much. Scott Baker's internal prediction of 2–4 million page views for the first month was about as accurate as my jump shot. TheBlaze.com did not do two million page views in the first month . . . it did two million page views the first day. And the traffic hasn't stopped since. By the time TheBlaze.com reached the eighteen-month mark, we had topped one billion page views. Nearly 60 million people had been to the site at least once.

The goal from the beginning was for *The Blaze* to be more than a website. More than anything, I wanted *The Blaze* to *stand for something*. A commitment to finding and telling stories that matter to an underserved audience; an audience that the mainstream media can never reach effectively, because they simply don't understand them.

But while new media presents us with huge opportunities, it also has huge consequences if we fail. If conservatives use these platforms to simply do more opinion pieces or ideological attacks then we will lose the battle for this medium as well. The distribution platform is, after all, simply the way that this information reaches people; it's still the *information itself* that matters. And that means we have to focus on real journalism, real investigations, real sourcing and fact-checking and research. We don't "win" simply because we can build slicker websites. We only win if we can literally change the way reporting is done; if we can take it from the hands of the coastal elites and deposit it back into the Heartland.

The GBTV Studios in Dallas, Texas

That, by the way, is one reason that I moved part of my operations from New York City to Dallas recently. I knew that if I was going to talk the talk about bringing media back to the center of the country then I'd have to walk the walk.

IN WITH THE NEW, BUT KEEP THE OLD

We are truly at a pivot point in the history of media—especially conservative media. And it's because we are finally taking responsibility. We are not waiting for the establishment to change, or for entry-level journalism salaries to skyrocket so that more young conservatives will take those jobs. We've decided to tell the stories ourselves. Stories that matter. Truths that last.

But many Americans, perhaps *most* Americans, will still get the bulk of their news from "mainstream" outlets. It's kind of ironic, actually: most young people, when asked, say they prefer to get their news online—yet most of those same people would prefer to go work for one of the legacy mainstream media companies.

It would be a huge mistake for conservatives to abandon those platforms. We need people who not only understand our way of thinking, *but also live it themselves*—at the highest levels in all fields of media. We need to encourage our journalism-minded young people to aspire to those jobs. I fear that one downside of "new media" is that so many of our best will jump to it that we'll have abandoned "old media" completely. That would be a huge, dangerous mistake.

For those conservatives who do take jobs in the mainstream media, let me offer this advice: Bring your background to the table. Don't have a chip on your shoulder and don't come with an agenda. Have an open mind, but don't balk away from the inevitable discussions and de-

Still the Gold Standard

Roy Greenslade, a journalism professor at City University London and former editor of the *Daily Mirror*, recently asked his class a simple question: what is your primary news source? Here's what happened:

"Newspapers? *No more than 20 hands went up.* Radio? *About the same.* Television? *Maybe 30.* Internet? *A forest of hands.*

Interestingly, many of the people taking the newspaper course—people hoping to get jobs on papers—admitted to not reading printed editions.

Given that part of the lecture was devoted to entrepreneurial journalism, I also asked: how many of you are hoping to get jobs in traditional "big media" outlets?

Virtually the whole room put up their hands. They may be digital natives, but their ambition is to work for others rather than themselves. They know the risks. They have been told there will be few job openings. They know that they will be expected to work for weeks, maybe months, for nothing. But they are undaunted. Mainstream media remains a lure."

bates you'll be thrown into the first time there's a story about a racially motivated murder, a homeowner's association that wants to ban someone from flying their American flag, or a school board that wants to eliminate "God" from the Pledge of Allegiance.

You will need to hold everyone you work with to a higher standard. The esteemed conservative social scientist James Q. Wilson had a good sense of this. Arthur Brooks, president of the American Enterprise Institute, recently wrote about the advice Wilson once had for him:

> *At one point in my academic career, I called Jim for advice about how best to navigate the waters of liberal academia when one is openly conservative. "Simple," he told me lightheartedly. "Be twice as productive and four times as nice as your colleagues." It was a formula he himself had followed.*

You may see those you work with get away with all kinds of ideological ills. Don't get sucked in. Don't duplicate sins you might see on the left with equivalent sins on the right. This business is not about an eye for an eye; it's about heart and brains and soul.

No matter what happens, what medium you find yourself working in, or whether you're working the beat at the local police station for the *Cheshire Herald* or the Department of Justice for the *New York Times*, always hold yourself and others to a higher standard—a standard where the truth has no agenda. 🐔

The Califate in 750

Conquests of the Arabs (Saracens) up to the death of Mohammed, 632

" " " under the first three Califs, 632-656

" " " Ommiad Califs, 661-750

Boundary of the Califate

Chapter Ten

THE ISLAMIST AGENDA
FACTS OVER FEAR

"Jihad for Allah is not limited to the specific region of the Islamic countries, since the Muslim homeland is one and is not divided, and the banner of Jihad has already been raised in some of its parts, and shall continue to be raised, with the help of Allah, until every inch of the land of Islam will be liberated, and the State of Islam established."

—Mustafa Mashhur, leader of Muslim Brotherhood in Egypt 1996–2002

JUNE 2009 The Muslim woman sat in the courtroom waiting for the judge. This was it, the day when her misery would finally end. Her life had been filled with pain and humiliation. Her husband had repeatedly raped her over a period of months as she cried and pleaded with him to stop. Today, she was seeking a court order that would finally end the abuse.

After what seemed like an eternity, the judge entered the courtroom. You could cut the tension with a knife. The abused woman hoped this would be the last day that she would ever have to live in fear of this man. A simple restraining order was all she needed.

Silence fell over the court as Judge Joseph Charles began to speak.

A few minutes later, the judge had finished with his ruling. Silence once again overtook the courtroom, but this time it was because the spectators had been left in shock.

According to Judge Charles, the preponderance of the evidence clearly demonstrated that the defendant had harassed and assaulted his wife, but there was more. The judge also ruled that the husband had done so with no criminal intent. In fact, the judge said, "The Court believes that (the defendant) was operating under his belief that it is, as the husband, his desire to have sex when and whether he wanted to, was something that was consistent with his practices and that was not prohibited."

You can understand why the spectators might have been confused. How could harassing and abusing your wife not be prohibited? How could a man's desire for sex trump his wife's right to not consent to it?

The answer is as simple as it is outrageous: It's because this Muslim man lives according to Islamic law—known as shariah. This law allows him to beat and rape his wife, especially when she resists his sexual advances. Since he was operating under the teachings of his faith he had every right to act as he did.

Sanity Ruled in the End

So that you're not left totally outraged, our legal system did work . . . eventually. An appellate court overturned Judge Charles's ruling and issued the restraining order, giving the woman the protection she was seeking.

What is most incredible about this story is that it did not occur in Iran or Morocco. It happened in a New Jersey family court.

This specific kind of court case is (thankfully) relatively rare, but it serves to illustrate how our democracy can, without vigilance, incubate "a state within a state." The legal system of the Islamic state can live and breathe within our supposedly secular democracy.

Despite the thundering silence from the mainstream media, the truth is that a small but increasing number of American Muslims are slowly, almost silently, being allowed to live by their own shariah law. Whether it's misguided allegiance to political correctness, or just pure incompetence, that is preventing this reality from being discussed openly, I do not know. But I do know this: if we continue to pretend that it is not happening, that those who practice shariah would love nothing more than for it to be widely accepted as the supreme law for U.S. Muslims, then it most certainly will.

ISLAMIC LAW 101

Since the concept of Islamic law is new to many Americans, it's helpful to first take a step back and understand exactly where it comes from.

Shariah is an Arabic word meaning "The Straight Path" (Quran 45:18). Another translation is "the path to the watering hole." To the Muslims who practice this version of Islam strictly, shariah is a codification of the rules of the lifestyle (or "deen") ordained by God (or "Allah"). In other words, shariah can govern and dictate every aspect of life. It's considered by many Muslims to be the perfect expression of divine will and justice and is therefore considered to be the supreme law that governs all aspects of Muslims' lives—irrespective of where they live.

Shariah is derived from four principal sources: the Quran, the Sunna or Hadith, Ijma, and Qiyas.

The Quran: The central, sacred text of Islam. Muslims believe that it was revealed by God to the Prophet Muhammad through the Angel Gabriel during twenty-three years of the Prophet's life at Mecca and Medina.

The Sunna or *Hadith*: Sunna is the example and practice of the Prophet's life as gleaned from the Hadith, which are a broad range of oral traditions of the Prophet Muhammad. These have been collected by variably reliable sources that chronicle what Muhammad's contemporaries noted that he did, said, or personally observed others to have done during his lifetime.

Ijma: This can be loosely translated as "consensus" of the Muslim community, especially of Muslim scholars (*ulemaa*). It is one of the main sources of law and ethics in Islam.

Qiyas: The process of reasoning by analogy, during which the teachings of the Sunna and Hadith are compared with those of the Quran. This is used primarily when Islamic law comes in conflict with the laws of other societies or religions.

The most comprehensive English language translation of shariah can be found in a book titled *Reliance of the Traveller*. This book has been authenticated by the Fiqh Council of North America, a group that advises its members on how to apply shariah within the "North American environment," and has been "approved" by scholars under the jurisdiction of Saudi Arabia.

All of that is a long-winded way of saying

Can You Rely on *Reliance?*

Reliance of the Traveller is an authoritative summary of Shafii—one of the four schools of thought in Sunni jurisprudence. Shafii is considered to be the most stringent of the four, but it's also widely accepted around the world. The book itself is one of the best sellers at the Islamic Society of North America website and is endorsed by preeminent leaders, such as Dr. Taha Jabir al-Alwani of the International Institute of Islamic Thought, who said, "There is no doubt that this translation is a valuable and important work, whether as a textbook for teaching Islamic jurisprudence to English speakers, or as a legal reference for use by scholars, educated laymen, and students in this language." *Reliance of the Traveller* has also been endorsed by al-Azhar University in Cairo, the preeminent institute of Islamic learning, which stated, "We certify that this translation corresponds to the Arabic original and conforms to the practice and faith of the orthodox Sunni community (Ahl al-Sunnah wa al-Jama'a)."

that this book was not written by someone with an axe to grind against Islam; it is considered by many scholars to be a legitimate and fair translation. Knowing that, most Americans who read *Reliance of the Traveller* will be (or at least *should* be) struck by how brutal and cruel shariah can be. And yet this book is sold by major Islamic outlets in America as a primary source of Islamic law for ortho- dox Sunni Muslims. Some argue that few Muslims actually follow its guidance. Thankfully, that is true, especially in the United States. Yet how many Muslims in the West have even attempted to deconstruct it or marginalize it? How many Muslims stand up and unequivocally say "That is not the Islam we follow!"?

Shariah classifies women as inferior beings and it provides them with con- siderably fewer privileges than a man. For example, in the Islamic Republic of Iran, a female may be punished beginning at age nine; a boy not until age fifteen. Beating and raping one's wife is authorized and, by some interpretations, even encouraged. A woman's testimony in court is valued at half that of a man.

Shariah calls for the amputation of a thief's right hand. (The right is used for eating, while the left hand is used for personal hygiene. Eating with one's left hand is, therefore, considered unclean.) If the thief commits a second offense, his left foot is amputated. A third offense means his left hand, and if he steals again, he loses his right foot.

Shariah is in direct conflict with the First Amendment of the U.S. Constitu- tion because it mandates the denial of free speech and freedom of religion. In 2006, a Muslim posted a question to the Assembly of Muslim Jurists in America asking how he should respond to questions about the punishment for apostates (those who leave Islam). The answer, according to Sheikh Mohammed Al-Hajj Aly, was that "it is the punishment of killing for the man . . . as the prophet, prayers and peace of Allah be upon him, said: 'Whoever a Muslim changes his/ her religion, kill him/her.'"

Muslim supremacy is a constant theme of shariah, and Holy War (jihad) against nonbelievers is required of all adherents. The shariah texts like *Reli- ance of the Traveller* confirm this death sentence mandate for apostates. Youcef Nadarkhani, a Christian pastor in Iran, was ordered to be executed not only be- cause he left Islam, but because he refused to recant his faith in Christianity. Unfortunately, this is not uncommon. To say that shariah can be repressive and cruel is an understatement.

An Islamic republic is a nation in which shariah is the law of the land, but Muslims are expected to adhere to shariah regardless of where they reside. Countries like Iran, Sudan, Somalia, and Saudi Arabia rely on shariah as their legal system. Even when living in a Western nation, Muslims are expected to use shariah as their guide for how to live and worship.

That, of course, includes Muslims in America.

Although many Muslims who live in the United States reject Islamic law, Islamic jurists and scholars, as well as a large number of imams, still mandate that they live according to the provisions of the law. That is an enormous problem considering that many academics and Islamic scholars have repeatedly said that shariah and democracy are incompatible.

Imran Ahsan Khan Nyazee, a professor of Islamic law in Islamabad, Pakistan, articulates this point in his book *Theories of Islamic Law: The Methodology of Ijtihad.* "Islam, it is generally acknowledged, is a complete way of life," he wrote, "and at the core of the code, is

Secular Shariah?

It's counterintuitive, but there are some countries, like Somalia, where the government is secular, but shariah is still practiced. The Council on Foreign Relations quoted Abdullahi Ahmed An-Na'im, a professor of law at Emory University, with a possible explanation for this: "Enforcing a [shariah] through coercive power of the state negates its religious nature, because Muslims would be observing the law of the state and not freely performing their religious obligation as Muslims."

That's all well and good for enlightened, modern, reform-minded Muslims who rely on reason, but it's not going to help the abuse of human rights inherent in shariah. Separating mosque and state is irrelevant if the followers of shariah prioritize their religious obligations ahead of their obligations as a citizen of that country and the laws of the land.

the law of Islam. . . . No other sovereign or authority is acceptable to the Muslim, unless it guarantees the application of the laws (shariah) in their entirety. Any other legal system, howsoever attractive it may appear on the surface, is alien for Muslims and it is not likely to succeed in the solution of their problems: it would be doomed from the start."

After reading that quote, and understanding what shariah is all about, you may feel as though there is no middle ground, no way out. But that is the big lie. Americans must understand that Nyazee's Islam is *political* Islam—the Islam of Islamists, of those who believe in the dominance of the Islamic state. We make a mistake when we try to equate Islamism with all of Islam or all Muslims.

In most Muslim communities there is a struggle for power between Islamists and moderate Muslims. We can blame that struggle on everything from oil money, to the dominance of the Muslim Brotherhood movement around the world, or to a million other things, but the bottom line is that much of the Muslim leadership continue to peddle Islamism (political Islam) as Islam.

SETTING A BAD PRECEDENT

Despite the opinion of numerous scholars that many elements of shariah and democracy are not compatible, Islamic law continues to make its way into America. If you think that is just hyperbole or conspiracy theory, you're wrong. Here are the facts.

The Center for Security Policy recently reviewed fifty court cases from twenty-three states to determine if shariah had been used in deciding the outcomes. Their findings, detailed in the center's report "Shariah Law and American State Courts," might surprise you:

> The study's findings suggest that shariah law has entered into state court decisions, in conflict with the Constitution and state public policy. Some commentators have said there are no more than one or two cases of shariah law in U.S. state court cases; yet we found 50 significant cases just from the small sample of appellate published cases.
>
> Others have asserted with certainty that state court judges will always reject any foreign law, including shariah law, when it conflicts with the Constitution or state public policy; yet we found 15 Trial Court cases, and 12 Appellate Court cases, where shariah was found to be applicable in these particular cases. The facts are the facts: some judges are making decisions deferring to shariah law even when those decisions conflict with Constitutional protections.

The study, while eye-opening, is really only the tip of the iceberg. Abed Awad, an adjunct law professor at Rutgers University law school and a New York attorney who runs the site ShariaInAmerica.com, recently boasted that he had "handled as an expert, or consultant or attorney for, more than 100 cases (in the United States) with a component of Islamic Law or the laws of the Middle East in the past 11 years."

In February 2012, Pennsylvania state court judge Mark Martin dismissed an assault and harassment case against a Muslim man who attacked an atheist who was dressed in a "Zombie Muhammad" costume during a Halloween parade. The atheist man was pretending to walk among the dead and was joined by another individual dressed in a "Zombie Pope" costume.

From a U.S. legal perspective the assault case was pretty straightforward: the attacker allegedly admitted his guilt to a police officer. And while the act may have been offensive to some, the atheist was exercising his First Amendment right to express himself, along with his right to freedom of religion (or, in this case, no religion).

Judge Martin ruled that the atheist had offended the Muslim who assaulted him and that, according to Muslim belief, the man was compelled to defend his faith. In fact the judge dressed the victim down with a very harsh diatribe:

Before you start mocking someone else's religion you may want to find out a little bit more about it. That makes you look like a doofus. . . .

Islam is not just a religion. It's their culture, their culture. It's their very essence, their very being. . . . Then what you have done is you have completely trashed their essence, their being. They find it very, very, very offensive. . . . It is not proven to me beyond a reasonable doubt that this defendant is guilty of harassment. Therefore, I am going to dismiss the charge.

Stifling Debate

Abed Awad was also asked what he thought about the campaign to officially ban shariah law from the United States. I don't know about you, but I think he doth protest too much:

Other than the fact that such bans are unconstitutional . . . they are [also] a monumental waste of time. Our judges are equipped with the constitutional framework to refuse to recognize a foreign law or take into account religious law. In the end, our Constitution is the law of the land. The only explanation is that they appear to be driven by an agenda infused with hate, ignorance and Islamophobia intent on dehumanizing an entire religious community. The fringe right-wing minority in our country is trying to turn this into a national 2012 election issue. Are you with the Shariah or with the U.S. Constitution? It is absurd.

Actually, what's absurd is for someone to inject "hate" and "ignorance" and "Islamophobia" into a legitimate debate in an attempt to shut it down.

Some interpretations of shariah require Muslims to respond violently to any insult directed against the Prophet Muhammad. And now we have a judge supporting these arcane laws that conflict with the very freedoms provided by the U.S. Constitution.

Several states have recognized the problem and are trying to take action to protect their courts and arbitration systems from this encroachment. A Michigan lawmaker, for example, has proposed a bill that, according to the American Islamic Leadership Coalition, "is intended to bar Michigan courts from enforcing any foreign law, if doing so violates any rights guaranteed by the U.S. Constitution and/or the state of Michigan's constitution." I can't believe we actually need to pass a law for that to be clear (I was pretty sure the Constitution was the supreme law of the land), but if that's what it takes, then that's what we need to do.

The Michigan law does not mention the words *Islam* or *shariah,* a fact that makes it much harder for groups like the Council on American-Islamic Relations (CAIR) to complain that Muslims are being singled out. Other states (like Oklahoma) have attempted to pass laws targeted more specifically at Islamic law, but those attempts have generally been ruled unconstitutional.

Another tenet of Islamic law that makes it incompatible with our democracy is shariah-compliant finance (SCF). While this is not a concept that dates back to the days of the prophet Muhammad (as some Muslims would like us to believe), it is nonetheless an accepted part of Islamic law today. And it, too, has come to America.

Developed primarily by Sayyid Qutb, one of the early leaders of the Muslim Brotherhood in Cairo, SCF is a means of infiltrating financial markets and institutions for the purpose of integrating shariah into yet another element of society. While the general assumption is that an SCF transaction cannot include interest and cannot be associated with anything determined impure by Muslims, there is a far more sinister side to SCF transactions.

In order to be SCF compliant, a financial institution must have Islamic "advisers," or an advisory board that is deemed qualified to judge or issue "fatwas" (religious rulings) as to whether transactions are pure (halal) or impure (haram). This gives these advisers unprecedented insight into, and influence over, the activities of companies in America. In some cases, these advisers can advise who the companies deal with and how their transactions are accomplished. For example, they could object to a deal with an Israeli company on grounds that it is impure.

The idea that these transactions are without interest is also inaccurate. Zakat (a tithe or charitable donation) is one of the five pillars of Islam and is considered mandatory for every Muslim. Rather than charging interest on a loan, SCF lenders build in a healthy zakat up front. They also devise creative "lease-to-buy" schemes that mask interest as fees, all the while empowering Islamist clerics to control the finance system.

The charity component is also potentially troubling and deceptive. Among many areas of Islamic charity, shariah describes three categories of zakat that involve indirectly supporting jihad, and also explicitly providing support to Muslims who are fighting in the cause of Allah. Many, if not most, Muslims may be unaware of where the leadership of various charities in the faith community end up sending the money they put into the hands of these organizations. But that doesn't matter much when the leadership is driven by the ideology of Islamism,

"[Sharia law] seems **unavoidable** and indeed, as a matter of fact, certain provisions of Sharia are already recognized in our society and under our law; so it's not as if we're bringing in an alien and rival system. . . ."

—Dr. Rowan Williams, the Archbishop of Canterbury, when asked if Sharia was necessary for social cohesion in Britain which mandates that zakat monies go to the poor or to jihad, "those fighting for Allah." The Holy Land Foundation for Relief and Development (HLF), which was once the largest Muslim charity in America, was, in fact, shuttered and designated as a "Specially Designated National" by the U.S. Treasury for funneling funds to the terror organization Hamas under the guise of zakat.

THE BROTHERHOOD

In 2004, a Maryland Transportation Authority police officer performed a traffic stop on a car in which a Muslim woman in traditional Islamic dress was filming the support structure of the Chesapeake Bay Bridge out the window. The woman's husband, Ismail Elbarasse, who was driving the car, was arrested for an outstanding material witness warrant that had been issued in Chicago. The Elbarasses' home in Annandale, Virginia, was searched, and a hidden subbasement was located. The FBI discovered that the basement housed the archives of the Muslim Brotherhood in America.

According to the book *Shariah: The Threat to America*, these documents "confirmed what investigators and counterterrorism experts had suspected and contended about the myriad Muslim-American groups in the United States—namely, that the vast majority of them are controlled by the MB (Muslim Brotherhood) and, therefore, as their Shariah dictates, are hostile to this country, it's Constitution and freedoms. The documents make clear that the groups' sole objectives are to implement Islamic law in America in furtherance of the goal of re-establishing the global caliphate."

I know, I know, *caliphate* is a dirty, conspiracy-theory-laden word. Those who talk about it are craaaazy, or, in the words of our attorney friend Abed Awad, they're "infused with hate, ignorance and Islamophobia intent on dehumanizing an entire religious community." Or, maybe there's another explanation. Maybe it's those who want to pretend that this does not exist, or keep Americans in the dark about it, who are actually the ones filled with hate and ignorance. Maybe these documents about the global caliphate and the Brotherhood's plans are actually a sign of a deeper, far more pervasive problem among many Muslims: the supremacy of political Islam.

More on that later, but for now, back to those archives recovered from the Elbarasses' basement. Included in them was a five-phase plan for how the Muslim Brotherhood and its front groups plan to turn America into an Islamic country. I know, we all have plans, big deal. (I planned to be a magician when I was younger, so I get it: man plans, God laughs.) But there's a good reason to pay attention to these particular plans: there's already a road map for how this works. It's not quick, it's not easy—but it's definitely possible.

About a decade ago, most Europeans would have laughed in your face at the suggestion that Islam might one day find a home there. Yet, today, almost all of the experts, including Princeton's Bernard Lewis, the most renowned expert on Islam in the United States, are stating emphatically that by the end of this century "at the very latest," Europe will be predominantly Islamic.

The Europeans made the same mistakes that we are making right now: They did not take the idea seriously. They simply buried their heads in the sand and either bought the propaganda of the distractors or bought into the political correctness and decided to "mind their own business." They tried to appease the very groups that were out to take over their countries by allowing them to incrementally integrate shariah into European societies.

> **Quality, Not Quantity**
>
> It's not really the number or percentage of Muslims in any population that should concern people (just as no one worries about the "percentage of Catholics" in a country)—it's whether those Muslims follow a politicized version of Islam. Bassam Tibi, a prominent moderate Muslim in Germany, summed up the issue pretty well: "Either Islam gets Europeanized, or Europe gets Islamized. . . . The problem is not whether the majority of Europeans is Islamic, but rather which Islam—sharia Islam or Euro-Islam—is to dominate in Europe."

Soeren Kern, senior fellow at the Madrid-based Strategic Studies Group, recently wrote an article about the proliferation of private Muslim enclaves in Europe:

> *Islamic extremists are stepping up the creation of "no-go" areas in European cities that are off-limits to non-Muslims.*
>
> *Many of the "no-go" zones function as microstates governed by Islamic Shariah law. Host-country authorities effectively have lost control in these areas and in many instances are unable to provide even basic public aid such as police, fire fighting and ambulance services.*
>
> *The "no-go" areas are the by-product of decades of multicultural policies that have encouraged Muslim immigrants to create parallel societies and remain segregated rather than become integrated into their European host nations.*

This self-segregation has encouraged and strengthened Muslim groups in Britain. One group has initiated a program called the "Islamic Emirates Project" with the stated intent of modeling several cities all over Britain as areas for Islamic law. Many experts estimate that there are already eighty-five shariah courts in Britain operating outside British common law. The result is that Christian preachers, for example, have been accused of hate crimes for handing out Christian material in predominantly Muslim neighborhoods.

France is not faring much better. According to Kern, their "no-go" areas are made up of 751 so-called "Sensitive Urban Zones" (ZUS), encompassing five million Muslims. The French government has a website, complete with exact addresses and satellite maps so that non-Muslims can avoid these areas.

You'd be hard-pressed to find a part of Europe that has not been affected in some way by the growth of Islam:

Freedom Takes a Detour

Given France's history with riots, the government is very cautious in the way it handles these enclaves, for fear of inciting more of them. This kid-gloves approach is great until you consider how it affects the non-Muslim population. For example, in some areas Muslims are allowed to essentially take over streets and sidewalks for Friday prayers. There are plenty of YouTube videos showing what this looks like, and there's been plenty of outrage about it—yet nothing seems to be done. Why would any group of people—whether they've come together to pray, riot, or protest—be allowed to take over public walkways and streets at the exclusion of others?

 In some parts of Belgium police cruisers travel throughout "no-go" zones in pairs. The first squad goes about their business, and the second car looks out for the first.

 In Germany, the police commissioner was asked about these "no-go" areas and how they are patrolled. He responded:

> *"Every police commissioner and interior minister will deny it. But of course we know where we can go with the police car and where, even initially, only with the personnel carrier. The reason is that our colleagues can no longer feel safe there in pairs, and have to fear becoming the victim of a crime themselves. We know that these areas exist. Even worse: in these areas crimes no longer result in charges. They are left to police it 'among themselves.' Only in the worst cases do we in the police learn anything about it. The power of the state is completely out of the picture."*

Similar situations exist in Italy, Sweden, and the Netherlands, and Europe is now watching its nations being destroyed by the infiltration of shariah into every corner of society. Proponents call it "multiculturalism" and tolerance—but when a nation no longer has a common bond keeping it together, then tolerance and political correctness won't matter much.

THE BROTHERHOOD EXPLAINS THE CALIPHATE

With Europe setting the precedent for how shariah can be slowly integrated into society, let's turn our attention back to America.

Earlier in this chapter I mentioned the trouble that the Holy Land Foundation found itself in, but it's worth looking at that trial in more detail. Known as the "Holy Land Foundation Trial," the case concluded with five defendants being convicted of all (108) counts of raising funds in America to support Hamas, a State Department–listed terrorist organization and an arm of the Muslim Brotherhood, under the guise of charity.

One of the documents entered into evidence during the trial had been found in the Elbarasses' subbasement in 2004. It is the Muslim Brotherhood's strategic plan for North America, titled "An Explanatory Memorandum: On the General Strategic Goal for the Group." The author was Mohammad Akram (aka Mohammad Adlouni), a member of the board of directors for the Brotherhood in America and a senior leader in Hamas.

The document, which clearly establishes the mission of the Brotherhood in North America, was approved by the Brotherhood's Shura Council and Organizational Conference in 1987 and said, in part:

Understanding the Role of the Muslim Brotherhood in North America

The process of settlement is a "Civilization-Jihadist Process" with all the word means [sic]. The Ikwan (Brotherhood) must understand that their work in America is a kind of grand jihad in eliminating and destroying the western civilization from within and "sabotaging" it's [sic] miserable house by their (our) hands and the

Crazy Caliphate Conspiracy Critic: Bill Kristol

When Glenn Beck rants about the caliphate taking over the Middle East from Morocco to the Philippines, and lists (invents?) the connections between caliphate-promoters and the American left, he brings to mind no one so much as Robert Welch and the John Birch Society. He's marginalizing himself, just as his predecessors did back in the early 1960s.

—WILLIAM KRISTOL, EDITOR OF THE *WEEKLY STANDARD*

"[The Islamic State starts] by reforming the individual, followed by building the family, the society and the government, and then the rightly guided Caliphate, and finally [achieving] mastership of the world— a mastership of guidance, instruction, truth and justice."

—Mohammed Badie, General Guide of the Egyptian Muslim Brotherhood *hands of the believers (Muslims) so that it is eliminated and God's religion is made victorious over all other religions.*

The HLF trial resulted in a list of unindicted co-conspirators that numbered over 250 people and organizations, meaning that there was enough evidence to bring them to trial. (U.S. attorney general Holder has chosen not to proceed.) In essence, this demonstrated a web of networks that were either fronts for the Brotherhood or supporters of them.

While the vast majority of Islamic organizations in America were listed as unindicted co-conspirators, the Council on American-Islamic Relations (CAIR) and the Islamic Society of North America (ISNA), two of the largest American Muslim organizations, were right at the top of the list. Yet these groups, along with the rest of the co-conspirators, are still operating in America today. Worse, there is little to no mainstream critique of those groups and so they still enjoy tremendous influence with the U.S. government, the U.S. media, and among Muslims. This is in spite of the fact that, in 2009, the assistant director of the FBI specifically outlined in a letter to Senator Jon Kyl that "the FBI suspended all formal contacts between CAIR and the FBI" because of their connection to Hamas.

ARAB SPRING AND THE MEANING OF THE WORD "FREEDOM"

The Arab Spring has been celebrated by many as the fuse that will eventually ignite real freedom in the Middle East. The threat from Islamist groups like the Brotherhood in Egypt was generally discounted because the Brotherhood pledged that they would not seek the presidency—and why wouldn't we just take them at their word?

In what came as a surprise to no one who understands their true motivation, the Brotherhood eventually broke their pledge and nominated Khairat el-Shater, their chief strategist and financier (and the very person who'd made the pledge that the Brotherhood wouldn't seek the presidency), for president. In explaining the flip-flop, Mahamed el-Morsi, president of the Brotherhood's Freedom and Justice Party, said, "We decided that Egypt now needs a candidate from us to bear this responsibility [of combating 'threats to the revolution']. We have no desire at all to monopolize power." Well, that's a relief! And we should definitely believe him because, well, he promised.

Can't Make Up Their Minds

It's amazing how our own government can contradict itself. On the one hand you have the U.S. Justice Department writing in a response to a federal court brief that "from its founding by Muslim Brotherhood leaders, CAIR conspired with other affiliates of the Muslim Brotherhood to support terrorists." On the other hand, you have many government leaders across the country still actively meeting with these groups to make sure they are not offended by our tactics.

Government officials from New Jersey and New York City, along with Department of Homeland Security leaders, met with Islamist "grievance group" leaders from CAIR and other Islamist groups in March 2012 after the Left's unfounded attacks against the New York City Police Department's counterterrorism programs reached a crescendo. It's also been reported that FBI director Robert Mueller recently met with leaders from seven different ethnic or religious groups after it was revealed by *Wired* magazine that the FBI had used some training materials that contained Muslim stereotypes or were "anti-Muslim." *USA Today* has also reported that the head of the Detroit field office met with "about 50 Arab-American and Muslim leaders in October to address their concerns about anti-Muslim training. And U.S. Attorney Barbara McQuade of the Eastern District of Michigan worked on outreach, speaking on an Arab-American radio show to assuage concerns."

These meetings convey a message that the Islamist narrative of what is and what is not anti-Muslim is somehow approved by our government. This, in turn, allows the Islamists to insulate themselves from criticism.

Too few Americans understand how most Muslims in the Middle East view the Arab Spring events that continue to unfold. When viewed through the prism of Western logic and values it's easy to see a democracy movement taking shape. But many Islamists in the Middle East see it much differently. They recognize it as a necessary step toward the establishment of the global caliphate, something that many Muslims around the world and throughout Islamic history have strived for. Many consider the Organisation of Islamic Cooperation, a union of fifty-seven Islamic-majority nations that exerts inordinate control over the U.N., as the building block of a neo-caliphate. And for very good reasons: why else would these otherwise unrelated autocracies form a union?

The truth is that these Muslims have a very different concept of freedom than most of us. To them, the word *freedom* means freedom from man-made laws. Brigitte Gabriel, a Christian born in Lebanon, explains this concept in her book *They Must Be Stopped* by quoting Abu Abdullah, a senior member of the Hizb ut-Tahrir al-Islami (Islamic Party of Liberation), a group with membership in the hundreds of thousands: "We want to free all people from being slaves of men and make them slaves to Allah."

The group believes that this is a religious duty and an obligation that Allah has decreed for all Muslims and commanded them to fulfill. They warn Muslims of the punishment that awaits those who neglect this duty. Hizb ut-Tahrir is growing in numbers and influence, including in America, and they are convincing many followers that establishing the caliphate is their religious duty.

Historian and theologian Jim Murk explains the concept of the Islamic caliphate like this: "[D]edicated Islamists envision a military takeover of all nations of the world and restoration of a united Islamic super state—called a caliphate. This would be a theocracy with all men in subjugation to Allah and his Shariah Law. It is the primary goal and motivating force behind fundamentalist Islam."

Other scholars agree that the establishment of a global Islamic state or Ummah (Islamic community) is the primary goal of Islamic fundamentalists who believe that the Quran mandates it in the following translated passage:

> **Two Paths, Same Destination**
>
> **A**ll of these terms that are used to define various segments of Islam can get confusing since they're not all interchangeable. For example, "fundamentalist Islam," as Murk wrote, can really take two forms: militant and lawful. Militant Islamists use force to achieve their global vision of Islamist domination, while "lawful Islamists," as dubbed by Daniel Pipes, use democratic means to rise to power and then implement Islamist systems, states, and laws (shariah) in order to dominate nations and ultimately the world. The end goals might be the same, but the means are very different.

God has promised those of you who have attained to faith and do righteous deeds that, of a certainty, He will cause them to accede to power on earth, even as He caused [some of] those who lived before them to accede to it; and that, of a certainty, He will firmly establish for them the religion which He has been pleased to bestow on them; and that, of a certainty, He will cause their erstwhile state of fear to be replaced by a sense of security [seeing that] they worship Me [alone], not ascribing divine powers to aught beside Me. But all who, after [having understood] this, choose to deny the truth—it is they, they who are truly iniquitous!

Another well-known Islamic scholar, Mullah Muhammad Taqi Sabzevari, puts it this way: "Allah has promised that the day will come when the whole of mankind will be united under the banner of Islam, when the sign of the crescent, the symbol of Muhammad, will be supreme everywhere."

If you're not an Islamic fundamentalist, you may have been underwhelmed after you finished reading that Quran verse that provides the theological ammunition for the caliphate. You may be wondering how this obscure verse could really

Crazy Caliphate Conspiracy Critic: David Brooks

[T]here was an interesting split among the Glenn Beck types, really with delusional ravings about the caliphate coming back, and I would say the conservative establishment, which saw [the end of the Mubarak regime in Egypt] as a fulfillment of Ronald Reagan's democracy dream. . . . And Glenn Beck, and you—for the first real time, you began to see a lot of really serious conservatives taking on Beck and people like that, and saying, you know, your theories are just wacky.

—*NEW YORK TIMES* COLUMNIST DAVID BROOKS, APPEARING ON PBS

compel followers to want to conquer the world through jihad (holy war). I don't blame you; I had the same reaction. But what you need to understand is that it is all a matter of interpretation over the centuries. Renowned and influential jurists, imams, and scholars have written extensively about this subject with the same view: it is doctrinal that Muslims must bring the world into submission to Allah and establish the Islamic world community or caliphate.

Ayman al-Zawahiri, the current leader of al-Qaeda, wrote a letter in 2005 to the leader of al-Qaeda in Iraq confirming that the caliphate is an objective of the world's most notorious terror network: "The establishment of a caliphate in the manner of the prophet will not be achieved except through jihad against the apostate rulers and their removal."

THE CALIPHATE: PAST AND FUTURE

The final caliphate was the Ottoman Empire, which conquered most of North Africa and much of the northern Mediterranean, including vast areas of southern Europe, during a time when the Iberian Peninsula was under Arab rule. The Ottomans were the great hope of most of the Islamic world for establishing the global caliphate that would ultimately be the Mahdi's domain.

The hope of the Muslim world did not last. Mustafa Kemal Atatürk destroyed the Ottoman Empire in 1924 when, as part of his reforms, he constitutionally

Sunni versus Shia

Both Sunni and Shia Muslims believe in an Islamic messiah or "Mahdi" (promised one) but they differ somewhat on how the Mahdi will return and what the lineage of the Mahdi will be. The two sects split early in the history of Islam (632 A.D.) over the issue of who should succeed Muhammad after he died. Sunnis believed that a pious man must be chosen by the community, while Shias insisted that the leader be a blood relative of Muhammad. That divide, with a number of additional differences in the details of the traditions, still exists today, but both sects generally believe in the coming Mahdi. The caliphate will be the Mahdi's kingdom, over which he will rule and bring Islamic law.

abolished the institution of the caliphate. The Turkish Republic was then formed, and the dreams of many Islamists throughout the world were destroyed.

In 1928, an Islamic cleric's son in Cairo decided to resurrect that great hope by creating a new organization that would seek to bring about Islamic dominance across the world and ultimately unite the global community under a single legal system: shariah. Hassan al-Banna founded the International Muslim Brotherhood (IMB), also known by its Arabic title, "Ikhwan al-Muslimeen." Its express purpose was twofold: to implement shariah worldwide, and to reestablish the imperial Islamic state (caliphate). Their creed: "God is our objective; the Quran is our law; Jihad is our way; and death for the sake of Allah is the highest of our aspirations."

The Brotherhood has since become a global organization that has given birth to offshoot extremist groups like al-Qaeda, Hamas, and many others. The exact date that the Brotherhood came to America is not clear, but in 1963 they created their first American front organization at the University of Illinois, Urbana: the Muslim Student Association, which now has chapters at over a hundred colleges and universities throughout the United States and Canada.

While the Brotherhood has created other front organizations (many of which were listed as co-conspirators in the Holy Land Foundation trial), they have not changed their objectives; they are still determined to destroy America from within and make shariah the law of the land. And they are growing exponentially in virtually every part of the world. The nations experiencing the Arab Spring are in many cases, such as Egypt, seeing the Brotherhood surface as the dominant political power. This could ultimately turn many of those nations into Islamic republics.

If history is a window into the future, then we only need to reflect on the Islamic Revolution in Iran in the late 1970s for a template as to how this "Arab Spring" may go. The Ayatollah Khomeini used eloquent terms like "de-

I Guess He's a Conspiracy Theorist, Too?

Magnus Ranstorp is the director of the Center for Asymmetric Threat Studies at Sweden's National Defense College. In his work on "Preventing Violent Radicalization and Terrorism: The Case of Indonesia," he wrote:

"Our research demonstrates that the Caliph imagery is a strong motivator within Muslim discourse. Pious zealots are often swept into the political expression of Jihad while attending small study groups. . . . For some Muslims, the imagery of an Islam reflective of the golden era of Muhammad is a religious value worthy of pursuit in terms of life goals, finances, and personal sacrifice 'in the cause of Allah.' This ideological war for the 'hearts and minds' for Muslims is considered a war for a 'collective identity' and has no shortage of patriots willing to join the struggle."

mocracy" and "liberty" when writing to his supporters. He even made secret audiotapes that were smuggled into Iran with messages for the people. He promised that if the people of Iran would rid themselves of the hated shah, then he would return from exile in France and bring freedom to the Iranian people.

There was just one problem. His concept of "freedom" was much different than ours. He meant freedom from man-made laws.

The shah was deposed in January 1979. Within two months after returning to Iran, Khomeini declared the country to be an Islamic republic that would be ruled under Islamic law. The same thing is now happening in many of these "Arab Spring" countries.

Crazy Caliphate Conspiracy Critic: Jeffrey Goldberg

Of course, the conspiracy goes deeper than Beck has yet revealed. I'm hoping that, in coming days, if the Freemasons, working in concert with Hezbollah and the Washington Redskins, don't succeed in suppressing the truth, that Beck will reveal the identities of the most pernicious players in this grotesque campaign to subvert our way of life.

I can't reveal too much here. But I think it's fair to say that Beck will be paying a lot of attention in the coming weeks to the dastardly, pro-caliphate work of Joy Behar; the makers of Little Debbie snack cakes; the 1980s hair band Def Leppard; Omar Sharif; and the Automobile Association of America. And remember, you read it here first.

—JEFFREY GOLDBERG, WRITING IN THE *ATLANTIC*

THE WAY OUT

Dr. Zuhdi Jasser (full disclosure: he's a good friend of mine) is a devout Muslim whose family has helped build a number of mosques across the United States, including one he helped found in his current hometown in Arizona in 2001. The son of Syrian immigrants who fled Baathist oppression for American freedom, Dr. Jasser is a Wisconsin native who served eleven years in the U.S. Navy as a medical officer. He's also the founder of the American Islamic Forum for Democracy, a prodemocracy Muslim group that rejects Islamism and shariah in government, and he's written a great book, *The Battle for the Soul of Islam*, that I cannot recommend highly enough.

Dr. Jasser has dedicated his life to encouraging other Muslims to be bold and outspoken in their rejection of political Islam and its shariah, as defined by groups like the Muslim Brotherhood. His reward for his work on behalf of his fellow Muslims has been isolation and criticism from many Muslim communities and threats from radical Islamists in America and abroad.

Dr. Jasser believes that most Muslims in America enjoy the liberties offered here and reject the fundamentalist view of shariah, but that they are too intimidated to speak out. When radical Islamists encouraged Muslims in America not to speak to police, Dr. Jasser countered with encouragement to Muslims to help police and to engage and cooperate with law enforcement as an issue of civic duty. He has even testified multiple times at congressional hearings to be an example for other Muslims in America who reject shariah.

Dr. Jasser is not alone in his efforts. There are other groups in America who are working with Muslim communities to help them to have a voice in the U.S. dialogue on shariah. He has, in fact, brought many of them together in an emerging coalition called the American Islamic Leadership Coalition, a diverse group of over twenty anti–Muslim Brotherhood (anti-Islamist) American Muslim leaders. The problem is that most Muslims are still so frightened by the hard-core, radical Islamists that they are afraid to speak candidly for fear of retaliation by elements of the Muslim Brotherhood and its affiliates.

At nearly every level, politicians and the mainstream media go to great lengths to appease and mollify the groups who are trying to, at best, circumvent and, at worst, destroy, our Constitution. When U.S. government "outreach" programs focus on the radical Islamist elements of the Muslim community, it sends a very discouraging message to the likes of Dr. Jasser and his group. No one seems to be making a serious effort to find and engage those Muslims who reject the teachings of shariah.

Americans should be encouraging and supporting these people, and the media should not be ignoring them. We must help them find their voice. Then again, it's absolutely true that the squeaky wheel gets the grease—and there is no wheel making more noise in the world today than those who are passionately promoting their cause of worldwide Islamic law.

Muslims who support the U.S. Constitution and love their country are the natural allies of all free Americans, yet they remain relatively silent. They are discouraged by what they see in the American government and by the American media. We cannot turn our backs on them. 🐔

Chapter Eleven

EDUCATION
RADICAL IDEAS TO
DEFEAT THE RADICALS

"Osama Bin Laden is not going to come here and destroy America. Our education system is doing that just fine."

—Geoffrey Canada, President and CEO of Harlem Children's Zone

IT'S NO coincidence that America has been debating how to "improve" the quality of education for as long as the government's been involved in it. While we're one of the top nations in the world in terms of per capita education spending, we're nowhere near the top in terms of student performance. Out of 34 civilized countries, American kids rank 25th in math, 14th in reading, and 17th in science.

There's something wrong here. And somebody's making an awful lot of money off the status quo.

Ideas and proposals for reform have come and gone over the decades. Some, like "No Child Left Behind," have actually been implemented, only for the public to quickly realize that those kinds of programs often just make things worse. It's too bad that it takes failing federal regulations for people to realize that the federal government itself is the problem.

This may be painful to read, but I think it's important to be reminded of all the political rhetoric and broken promises over the years. If you're like me, you'll feel your blood start to boil as you read these quotes and think about all of the time we've wasted and all of the kids we've let down as a result.

Let's go back to President George H. W. Bush's administration. During his 1992 State of the Union address, Bush explained, "We must be the world's leader in education. And we must revolutionize America's schools. My America 2000 strategy will help us reach that goal."

Except, nothing really changed. By 1993, it was President Clinton's turn to echo that same message. "We'll push innovative education reform to improve learning, not just spend more money," he said.

The following year he took a page out of the Bush playbook: "Our Goals 2000 proposal will empower individual school districts to experiment with ideas like chartering their schools to be run by private corporations, or having more public school choice. . . ."

In 1995 he called for a government "that helps each and every one of us to get an education and to have the opportunity to renew our skills." And, three years later, he repeated virtually the exact same message. "We must make our public elementary and secondary schools the world's best. . . . I laid out a 10-point plan to move us forward and urged all of us to let politics stop at the schoolhouse door."

Five years after that, in his 2000 State of the Union address (by that point you really couldn't name things after the year 2000 anymore), Clinton explained, "First and foremost, we need a 21st century revolution in education, guided by our faith that every single child can learn."

But Clinton was a lame duck by this point, so now it was time for President George W. Bush to pick up the torch—or at least the rhetoric. Which he gladly did. In his 2002 State of the Union address, Bush said, "Good jobs begin with good schools, and here we've made a fine start. Republicans and Democrats worked together to achieve historic education reform so that no child is left behind."

Now no child would ever be left behind. They promised.

President Obama has also made education a top priority. In his 2009 State of the Union address, Obama explained, "We must address . . . the urgent need to expand the promise of education in America . . . our schools don't just need more resources. They need more reform."

In 2011, he declared, "The quality of our math and science education lags behind many other nations. . . . Instead of just pouring money into a system that's not working, we launched a competition called Race to the Top." He also pressed for more funding of college education.

As all of this has been going on, our children have been the ones suffering. In one 1992 study, American thirteen-year-olds ranked 13th out of 15 industrialized countries in science and 14th out of 15 in math. Despite the last two decades of rhetoric, it hasn't gotten any better.

In 1996, just 25 percent of our fourth graders, 28 percent of our eighth graders, and 34 percent of our high school seniors were proficient readers. Reading performance had not improved since the early 1970s. Today, just 33 percent of fourth graders, 32 percent of eighth graders, and 38 percent of high school seniors read at or above grade level. So our kids aren't doing much better now than they were doing *forty years ago*.

From 1965 to 2009, the federal government spent some $2 trillion on education. And we have almost nothing to show for it.

So, here we are at another crossroads in time. If we do nothing then I can assure you of two things: First, our politicians will continue to stand before the nation every January to offer ideas on how to "fix things"; and second, our kids will keep paying the price. With that in mind, I'm ready to offer a solution that, while admittedly impossible to ever get done, would actually help to radically alter this heart-wrenching game we're playing with our future. Ready? Here it is:

We should fire all 3.5 million public school teachers in America and shut down all of our publicly funded universities.

Calling that controversial might be the understatement of the century, but I'd argue that what we're doing now—which is basically fiddling while Rome burns (or, in some cases, pouring gasoline on the fire)—is actually the radical thing. What I am proposing is far less controversial when you consider that it has a chance to actually solve the problem.

THE REAL THIRD RAIL: EDUCATION REFORM

It's funny—people say that entitlement programs like Social Security are the "third rail" of American politics (talk about reforming them and your campaign dies), but I think

Save the Patient

Let's compare our education crisis to a health crisis. Instead of a massive epidemic of terrible test scores and failing teachers, let's instead pretend that we have a massive flu outbreak in schools across the country.

Under my proposal we'd shut down those schools immediately so that we could stop the spread of the disease, find the source of the problem, and come up with a clear way to kill it. On the other hand, what we're actually doing is letting the kids continue to show up to infected schools every day even though we know many will get sick and that, eventually, the flu will spread destruction throughout our entire society.

Given that analogy, which plan is really the radical one?

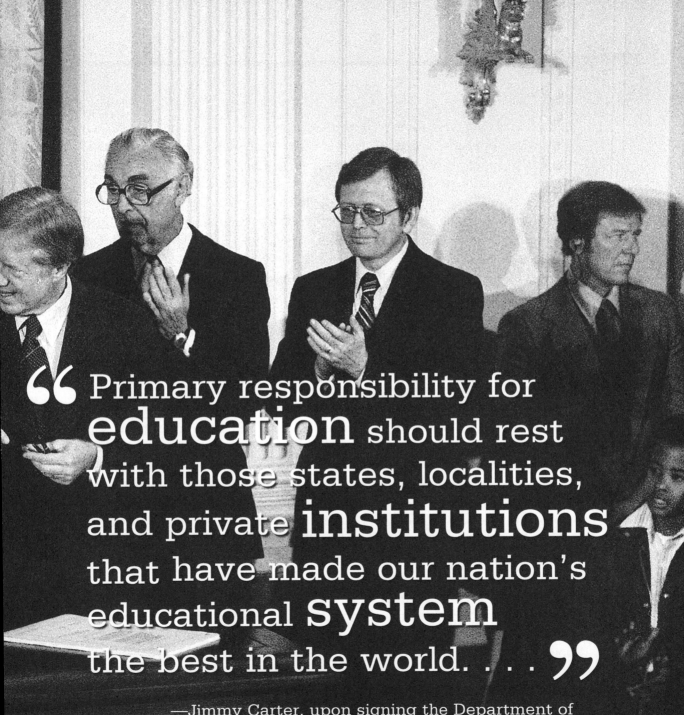

"Primary responsibility for **education** should rest with those states, localities, and private **institutions** that have made our nation's educational **system** the best in the world. . . ."

—Jimmy Carter, upon signing the Department of Education Organization Act in 1979 education is the real third rail. Think about it: when is the last time you've heard a politician offer a meaningful (translation: *radical*) idea to reset our education system? It hardly ever happens. Instead we continue to spend more and more money even as the results get worse and worse. It's the very definition of insanity.

Since apparently no politician has enough backbone to say it, I will: spending more money on public education is the same thing as flushing it down a toilet—except that flushing it down the toilet doesn't make your kids stupid. It's not "compassionate" to maintain the status quo and watch our kids keep falling behind the rest of the world. The compassionate thing would be to offer something new, something that has a real chance to reform the system.

The evidence is clearly on my side. America's educational performance has gone nowhere over the last four decades, even though we've tripled spending per student since 1970 in real dollars.

If the numbers don't persuade you, then maybe a moral argument will. By failing to act, we are proving to be delinquent not only as Americans, but as parents. This kind of neglect would be unacceptable in any other realm. If we fail our kids physically, by not providing food or clothes or shelter, the government comes knocking at the door to take them away. But when we fail them mentally, by not providing the teachers and facilities and equipment they need to compete in the world, the government pats itself on its back and gives itself more money.

Worst of all, *we let this happen.* It's easy to lay blame, and there's plenty of it to go around, but, ultimately, it's us—average American parents—who have allowed this to happen. We elect the politicians who pass these laws and who raise our taxes to pay for them. And even when it's clear they're failing, we agree to put those same people back in office.

The only way to end what I think is really a cycle of abuse of our children is to stop it cold turkey. Small reforms are not only ineffective, they're also no match for the powerful forces behind the status quo: the lobbies and unions—and the politicians who are in bed with them. No, if we are going to win this battle—one that is both literally and figuratively a battle for the future of America—then it's going to be won with a plan that no one sees coming.

WHAT COMES NEXT

My plan may be radical, but it's not insane: Soon after we fire the 3.5 million public school teachers, we'll hire the best 3.3 million of them back. Then we'll go out and find the best 200,000 teachers in the world and we'll hire them, too. They'll replace the people who long ago made the mistake of deciding that working in a classroom was a right and not a privilege; the people who hide their poor performance behind tenure and union contracts; and the people who believe that their personal political views deserve a prominent place in their curriculum.

But I'm realistic. I understand that, even given the overwhelming evidence in favor of radical change, it won't come easy. Americans may want the best for their kids, but they also generally favor the status quo. So we're going to have to make the case to our neighbors and friends—and that starts by explaining how we got here in the first place.

Thanks in part to our education system, we tend to think that we're smarter than the stupid guys in the funny wigs who came before us. But that's because we are mistaking technology, progress, and access to information for intelligence. We think that because we know how to use iPhones (but not build them), browse the Internet (but not understand how it works), and use Google (but not really *know* anything), our educational system is working just great. By the same token, we think that those dumb aristocrats who used horses to get around and didn't have electricity were Neanderthals.

It's just not true. Intelligence achieved through education cannot be measured by the future inventions of society. It can only be measured against the rest of the world at that time. And, apples to apples, our Founders were among the best.

At the time of the American Revolution, nine in ten American adults in New England could read and write. That was the highest rate in the civilized world, thanks largely to parents who wanted their kids to read the Bible.

Early Americans heavily favored public education as a method of lifting people up from ignorance. As John Adams wrote in 1775, "Education makes a greater difference between man and man than nature has made between man and brute." After the revolution, seven states immediately wrote provisions about education into their constitutions.

In terms of curriculum, our Founders believed in education in the classics with a heavy emphasis on facts and figures. In other words, learning stuff that's useful, as opposed to "Feeling Special Time" stuff. Jefferson said history had to be the key, since it was only by learning history that people would learn to guard their freedom. More advanced students could take on geography, advanced mathematics, Greek, Latin, and so on.

This was the common perspective at the time. "It is not indeed the fine arts which our country requires," Adams wrote to his wife during the revolution. "[T]he useful, mechanic arts are those which we have occasion for in a young country. . . . I must study politics and war, that my sons may have liberty to study mathematics and philosophy. My sons ought to study mathematics and philosophy, geography, natural history and naval architecture, navigation, commerce and agriculture, in order to give their children a right to study painting, poetry, music, architecture, statuary, tapestry and porcelain."

The Founders wanted local governments—and, unbelievably, parents!—to be in control of their kids' education. Thomas Jefferson wrote, "If it is believed that these elementary schools will be better managed by the governor and council or any other general authority of the government, than by the parents within each ward, it is a belief against all experience."

Go ahead and read that quote a few more times. *A belief against all experience.* Jefferson was too polite to say it this way, but, basically, you're an idiot if you think that some government can educate kids better than parents can. It's common sense. Yet if you try to make that case today it's somehow *you* who are the idiot.

Jefferson didn't stop there—he effectively suggested school vouchers in 1779, and proposed that it should be parents' choice whether to allow their children to go to school (he said it was a mistake to "shock the common feelings by a forcible transportation and education of the infant against the will of his father"). Most important, he said it would be a huge mistake to force people to pay for teachers with whom they didn't agree. "To compel a man to furnish contributions of money for the propagation of opinions which he disbelieves and abhors, is sinful and tyrannical," he wrote.

Unfortunately, a century later, Jefferson's warning disintegrated in the face of the Progressive era. Though he lived and died before the period we now call the Progressive era, one of the leaders in this "progressive education" crusade was

Finland? Really?

Finland's education system is famously effective. Why? Not because they pay more than we do—we actually spend one-third more per pupil than Finland. It's about teacher quality and work ethic. Teachers are only selected from the top 10 percent of graduates of the master's in education program, and students there receive specialized attention and keep longer school hours. Finland doesn't start teaching kids until age seven and they don't focus on homework—instead, they focus on student learning and ensuring that students spend enough time learning to achieve their goals. There are, of course, a lot of differences between the United States and Finland, but it would be nice to focus on the students instead of the teachers (and their unions) for a while.

Horace Mann, a champion for universal public education. Mann, like the Founders, believed that education was of paramount importance. But he wedded education to the notion that *he and people like him should run it.*

One of Mann's goals was to cut out certain brands of religion, including Catholicism, from the public square. He wanted the state to run education in order to unify the population, and he particularly admired the Prussian system, where the state sponsored education from kindergarten through college. There, public education started off as a virtual indoctrination center directed against freedom of religion.

Sound familiar? In *Stop Stealing Dreams*, Seth Godin writes:

> *After a self-financed trip to Prussia, [Mann] instituted the paramilitary system of education he found there, a system he wrote up and proselytized to other schools, first in the Northeast U.S. and eventually around the country.*

Mann's ideas caught on and pretty soon the idea of "public" education became widespread. Obviously, this had a great effect on literacy and the availability of education for the common man, but it also taught the elites that they could rule the masses through the education system itself.

The first person to really understand this, and exploit it, was John Dewey. Dewey was an academic at the University of Michigan, University of Chicago, and Columbia University and his goal was to "reconstruct" American society in the late nineteenth and early twentieth centuries.

Whereas Mann was a well-intentioned American with some good ideas—along with plenty of bad ones—Dewey was a full-on European elite in his thinking. He believed that the American notion of individual rights was empty, and he put far more emphasis on the "right" to food, housing, medical care, and free education. Put it this way: Dewey once said that he was impressed by the "marvelous development of progressive educational ideas and practices under the fostering care of the Bolshevist government."

Dewey was also a supporter of the idea that elites (like himself) should determine how and what people learn. He rejected natural individualism—aka "liberty"—and said that individuals instead had to be *made* free "with the aid and support of conditions, cultural and physical: including in 'cultural,' economic, legal and political institutions as well as science and art."

This was indoctrination, pure and simple. Worse, it was leftist/progressive indoctrination. It would be one thing to "indoctrinate" kids with the values that America stood for (you know: *one nation, under God, with liberty and justice for all*)—but putting them into schools where they'd be fed European elitist propaganda? No thanks.

John Dewey didn't believe in moral admonitions. Like the famous philosopher Rousseau, Dewey believed that kids should be left to their own devices. Want to teach a kid not to murder somebody? Let him murder his friend and then feel bad about it.

Children, he wrote, "should be allowed as much freedom as possible; prohibitions and commands, the result of which either upon themselves or their companions they cannot understand, are bound to be meaningless; their tendency is to make the child secretive and deceitful." The only morality kids should be taught, Dewey believed, is how to get along with others. And the job of the schools was to teach the unity of the people under the nonreligious state.

Even Dewey recognized the value of science and mathematics. He rejected only the teaching of morality and religion. It was later, with the federalization of education, that American educational standards began to drop. When the feds took charge of the educational system—for the noble purpose of ending segregation—they wrecked it. Local control went away. Faraway regulators were making rules for kids they'd never even meet. And the kids simply stopped learning. Dewey's idea of collective, top-down control of education was becoming a reality.

FOLLOW THE MONEY

When it comes to the destruction of American education, there's really only one question that always needs to be asked: who profits?

Take a look at public school primary education:

While the government spent about $2,800 per student in 1961, it now spends well in excess of $10,000 per student, after adjusting for inflation.

In 1961, 14.6 percent of teachers didn't even have a college degree; today, it's less than 1 percent. Meanwhile, more than half of our teachers now have master's or doctorate degrees, as opposed to less than a quarter in 1961. Why? Because the unions negotiated that you can make more money with additional degrees. Unfortunately, degrees don't ensure

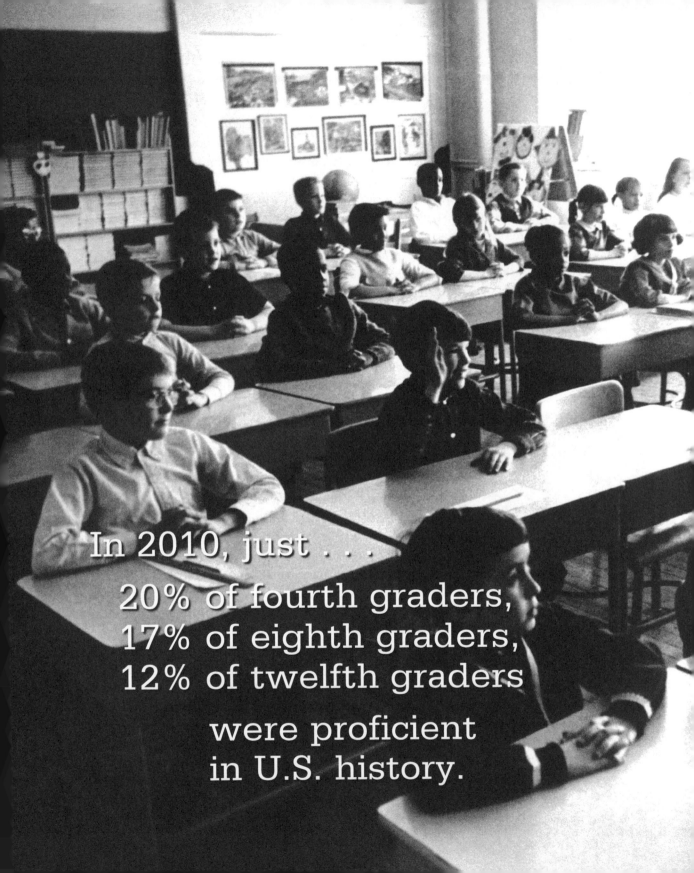

In 2010, just . . .
20% of fourth graders,
17% of eighth graders,
12% of twelfth graders
were proficient
in U.S. history.

quality, and neither do higher salaries. Teachers are now paid over 45 percent more than they were in 1961, after adjusting for inflation.

So, back to the question I originally asked: who profits from this? Certainly not our kids; they're struggling. Teachers are doing better, but no one is accusing them of making *too much* money, by any stretch. So, who is making money and growing their power base off the status quo? Simple: the teachers unions.

When it comes to politics, both sides like to create villains upon which all of our frustrations can be hurled. The right has unions, Jimmy Carter, Hollywood, the media, and Keith Olbermann—and the left has millionaires, George W. Bush, Big Oil, the Koch brothers, and, well, me. In many cases these villains simply make convenient targets, but teachers unions are the exception. In fact, it's difficult to make the case that teachers unions are not *worse* than their reputation.

The arguments and stunning stats and stories about teachers unions have been well covered. I won't waste your time rehashing it all here, other than to say that, at their most basic level, these unions are fundamentally opposed to everything we believe in—both as parents and as Americans.

We're All Winners!
Don't worry, American kids aren't near the bottom of the pack in *every* category! They rank first—*first*—in self-esteem.

Unions work to ensure that teachers have very little incentive to do a good job and suffer no consequences for doing a bad one. It's the very definition of mediocrity, and our test scores only serve to prove the old adage correct: *Garbage in, garbage out.*

Teachers unions have lobbied for teachers to do less and receive more. They've created a system in which educators get paid based on how many degrees they collect instead of on how well they teach. Why should a third grader care whether a teacher has a Ph.D. in astrophysics?

Teachers don't get merit-based raises, they get raises based on longevity. The goal of the game is to simply stay employed—which isn't all that difficult given the tenure system. In fact, most teachers union contracts actually have "last in, first out" terms, meaning that the last teacher hired is the first one fired if layoffs are necessary. It doesn't matter if that most recent hire is the single greatest teacher in the history of education. The contract stipulates that he has to go first, and so he does.

Because everybody loves teachers, few people fight against their unions, even though it's clear that the unions themselves don't make quality of education their

Government Solutions

Even criminal actions sometimes can't get these teachers fired. In New York City, for example (where the union contract runs over two hundred pages), it can take months or years for the city to go through all the steps required in the union contract. Until recently, the teachers accused of wrongdoing reported each school day to a "rubber room" where they would spend their time reading novels or doing crossword puzzles. Five hundred and fifty teachers reported to these rooms each day, costing the city $30 million a year.

Once the existence of these rooms went public the negative publicity was too much for both sides to handle. So, in 2010 a big announcement was made: the rubber rooms would be shut down. Great news, except that, in typical government/union fashion, they did nothing to solve the underlying problem. The teachers will still spend months or years waiting for the contractual process to play out, but instead of reporting to a rubber room, they'll report to the school that is attempting to fire them. Genius.

top priority. Actually, that's putting it mildly. Since this book is about truth, let me put it as bluntly as I can: teachers union leaders generally don't give a darn about kids.

Sound incendiary? It's meant to. But here's the best part: it's not just hatemonger Glenn Beck saying that—the unions themselves are! In 2009, Bob Chanin, the former top lawyer for the National Education Association (America's biggest teachers union), spoke at the NEA's annual meeting about why union members support them:

NEA and its affiliates are effective advocates because we have power.

And we have power because there are more than 3.2 million people who are willing to pay us hundreds of millions of dollars in dues each year, because they believe that we are the unions that can most effectively represent them, the unions that can protect their rights and advance their interests as education employees.

This is not to say that the concern of NEA and its affiliates with closing achievement gaps, reducing dropout rates, improving teacher quality and the like are unimportant or inappropriate. To the contrary. These are the goals that guide the work we do. But they need not and must not be achieved at the expense of due process, employee rights and collective bargaining. That simply is too high a price to pay.

The last part is worth reading again. He wants quality teachers and better education, but not if that means having to hurt the union. That's absurd! Any parents would tell you that they don't care about the bureaucracy, or contracts, or collective bargaining—they care only about results. But here you have a union leader saying that they only care about the results *if* those results can be achieved within the structure of their union contract. The problem is that history has proven

The Not-So-Golden State

In California, the situation is so bad that schools have taken to shifting sexual predators from place to place, just as the Catholic Church did in the bad old days. At Miramonte Elementary School, one teacher who'd been in the system for nearly thirty years was arrested and held on $23 million bail, for, among other things, spoon-feeding "an unknown cloudy-colored liquid substance" to children. The school district actually *paid him $40,000* for the privilege of getting rid of him. They covered over $16,000 in legal fees and another $24,000 or so in back pay. Plus he'll receive full pension and health benefits.

we can't have it both ways. If you don't align the interests of the educators and the educated then you set yourself up for certain failure. Decades' worth of evidence is in: unions are not improving the quality of education.

If you put the data aside you are still left with the commonsense argument as to why union leaders care more about their own organization than anything else: The more teachers the unions have who are employed, the more dues the unions receive. The more dues they get, the more money they have to fund political campaigns. The more politicians they can fund, the more favors they are owed. The more favors they are owed, the more favors they can redeem via legislation that raises spending levels on education and increases their dues. It's a vicious cycle that at no point factors in teacher quality or student progress.

It also can't be overlooked that, given their central role in the education of our kids, unions have an unfair ability to spread their message in the classroom. In fact, the left's favorite "historian," Howard Zinn, advocated exactly that, writing, "If teacher unions want to be strong and well-supported, it's essential that they not only be teacher-unionists but teachers of unionism. We need to create a generation of students who support teachers and the movement of teachers for their rights."

While they've been very successful at meeting that objective, they've been far less successful at creating a generation of something much more important for our future: good students.

WHY YOUR KIDS BECOME SOCIALISTS

Don't get me wrong. There are plenty of great, wonderful public school teachers out there. I know some of them personally. Some even believe in capitalism and are not well represented by their left-leaning union leaders. But the reality is that some significant portion of public school teachers chose to get into the field in part because it was a secure, stable, government job with predictable hours and generous vacations—in other words, the exact opposite of the risks and rewards of entrepreneurship.

Here's how this works in practice, according to Joe Kernen, a CNBC television anchor who relayed a conversation he had with his nine-year-old son, Blake, who attends a New Jersey public school:

BLAKE: My teacher says the recession is the banks' fault.
JOE KERNEN: That's way too simple, Blake. For something as big as this recession, there's a lot of blame to go around.
BLAKE: And my teacher says it's 'cause we care too much about buying stuff, and it might not be so bad if we stopped.
JOE KERNEN: Your teacher said . . . *what*?

Only twenty-one states require students to take an economics course as a high school graduation requirement, and only five states (Georgia, Louisiana, New York, New Jersey, and North Carolina) require entrepreneurship to be a component of a course offered in high schools.

If you think education from kindergarten through high school is in trouble, though, it's nothing compared to college.

Are Unions the Problem?

It's helpful to understand the rationale of those who seem to genuinely want to improve education, but who also support the current union structure. What I've generally found is that their arguments almost always come back to political ideology—they support unions because they fear that "evil capitalists" will somehow take over if these unions are gone. For example, consider this quote from a *Forbes* writer in a column titled "Why I Support the Teachers Unions."

The teachers unions are not always right. No group is. But they represent a democratic approach to our public education system, and if we push them out and usher in an age of for-profit online schools, cheaper labor, and funnel all those saved tax dollars back in the pockets of the wealthiest Americans, we may as well kiss our public schools goodbye.

After spending virtually the entire column arguing that teachers unions are valuable because they protect teachers, whose buy-in and support we need for reform, he finally reveals his real motivations: reach the money quote at the end. He supports teachers unions because he thinks so little about capitalism, freedom of choice, and bringing education back to the local level that he fears for the future without them. In his mind, unions are apparently the only thing preventing us from outsourcing American history teacher jobs to call centers in Mumbai.

THE COLLEGE SCHEME

A college education is a key part of the American Dream, right? Isn't that what we've all been told? You haven't really "made it" in America if you don't have a degree.

I don't buy it. And you shouldn't, either.

In theory, the Dream goes like this: you do well in school, graduate from a good college, and get a great job with which you'll finance a home, family, and, ultimately, the college education of your children. And on and on it goes.

But is that still the reality? More often than not, no— not even close. These days, kids enroll in college, borrow tens or hundreds of thousands of dollars to pay for it, have their worldviews shaped by tenured professors, then leave and begin the often lengthy process of trying to find a job, which often ends up not even being in their area of study.

Maybe it's time to rethink the whole value proposition of a college education.

Average college debt has now climbed to roughly $24,000 a student. And college debt, unlike other debts, doesn't get eliminated by declaring bankruptcy— it follows you around the rest of your life. "Kids become indentured servants," James Altucher, managing director of Formula Capital, says, "taking jobs and pursuing careers they don't necessarily want. Instead, if they had a five-year head start over their peers by not going to college, they could figure out how to make a lot more money—and wouldn't have to deal with massive debt."

"Indentured servants" . . . is it any wonder that progressives have pushed so hard for college to become ingrained as part of "the Dream" in our culture?

Bankruptcy 101

There will be 5.4 million students going to colleges and universities in the United States this fall and about that many American parents wondering how they'll ever meet all the costs.

—ASSOCIATED PRESS, AUGUST 1965

The Unions Get Rich While Your Kids Get Dumb

There is no way to separate the teachers unions from politics. The NEA and the American Federation of Teachers (AFT) make $2 billion in union dues every year. The teachers unions have also gotten fully behind both Obamacare and Occupy Wall Street in order to back the Democrat machine.

In the 2008 election cycle, teachers unions gave $5.4 million to candidates for national office. Ninety-five percent of that went to Democrats. It's no coincidence that the biggest single recipient of Obamacare waivers is the union representing New York City public school teachers.

While earning a college degree does correlate with higher lifetime earnings, it's certainly no guarantee of it. Especially not anymore. And it's definitely not going to guarantee a population with more common sense or basic knowledge. It turns out that, in many cases, kids actually lose basic knowledge as they go through college. At universities like Cornell, Yale, Duke, and Princeton, freshmen did better on a basic civics test than seniors. The Intercollegiate Studies Institute found that going to college made you more likely to favor same-sex marriage, approve of abortion, and disagree with the idea that "anyone can succeed in America with hard work and perseverance."

Peter Thiel, the cofounder of PayPal, has actually started handing out money to smart young kids who agree to leave college and work instead. "Learning is good," he says. "College gives people learning and also takes away future opportunities by loading the next generation down with debt." Thiel points out that education costs have escalated by a factor of three since 1980.

Uncritical Thinking
A recent study by Richard Arum of New York University and Josipa Roksa of the University of Virginia found that one in three students didn't improve at all in critical thinking skills throughout college.

Here's the truth: smart people don't absolutely have to go to college. They certainly should consider it—but, in many cases, they're better off *not* going to college. If instead of drinking beer and being indoctrinated, students spent those four (or five, or six) years gaining real experience, then, by twenty-two, they'd have a great leg up on many of their competitors. That's why Benjamin Franklin apprenticed at a print shop instead of going to college—it was less expensive, and it afforded him the opportunity to learn to do something useful. Or how about Abraham Lincoln? Or Edison? We need more Americans with practical know-how and fewer with multiple degrees in stupid crap nobody cares about, taught by people who hate the country that has made them rich.

By claiming that college is for everyone, we just end up dumbing down the entire system and preventing people from going into the areas where they'll really excel. Widespread access means we have to ensure that everybody can pass and prosper. And that means lower standards so that everybody can feel good about themselves, which, in today's schools, is *way* more important than knowing how to program a computer or develop a vaccine. Sure, Silicon Valley may be hiring applicants from China and India to fill their open slots, but at least our guys can put that gold star on their welfare-sponsored refrigerator in their rent-controlled apartments.

Good Company?
In addition to the nine U.S. presidents who did not graduate from college, neither did Bill Gates, Mark Zuckerberg, John D. Rockefeller, Henry Ford, Michael Dell—or me.

But it gets worse.

Throughout our educational system, teachers and professors are indoctrinating students purposefully into the cult of the Left. Most of these teachers and professors are protected by law and by policy and many enjoy tenure, which grants them the unalienable right to teach any ideas they want to. The education system is the vanguard of the socialist revolution in the United States. And what no one will tell you is that it's been that way for decades.

You're Qualified . . . for the Wrong Job

In his documentary *Waiting for Superman*, former teachers union supporter Davis Guggenheim reported that, by the year 2020, there will be 123 million high-pay, high-skill jobs available throughout the country . . . but just 50 million Americans with the qualifications to fill those jobs.

Until the 1960s, America's universities were the best in the world—and the students who came out led the world in know-how. Going to college was something special. It wasn't a place to play beer pong and smoke pot. Nobody went to college to get the "college experience." People went to college to get an education.

Then the universities became indoctrination centers, with tenured professors spouting insane theories for high pay, lecturing the rest of us on how we're bad Americans because we're not more like the Chinese. While there had always been hints that higher education was a leftist bastion—Woodrow Wilson was, after all, president of Princeton—it wasn't until the 1960s that everything went to hell in a handbasket.

That's when the Frankfurt School took over.

THE MARXIST THOUGHT INVASION

After World War I, a group of German Marxists decided that the best shot for communist success was to infiltrate culture and education. It was a good idea, actually. Once they were firmly ensconced in culture and education they could tear it down with something called "critical theory"—the idea that everything needs to be criticized endlessly. After culture and education had been stripped bare, Marxism could rebuild society in its own image.

Critical theory was a Marxist philosophy brought to the United States by the so-called Frankfurt School. It posited that all of cultural, governmental, and academic institutions had been shaped by a legacy of capitalism. In order for Marxism to flourish, therefore, the current structure had to be torn down from within through incessant criticism—hence the term "critical theory." Critical theory is the foundation for political correctness as well as the ethnic studies movements on campuses across America.

When the Nazis took control in Europe, these Frankfurt School Marxists realized they had best get out of town. Fortunately for them, liberals at Columbia University were ready and willing to open their door. Most of them ended up as professors at major universities. And there they began to apply and teach critical theory.

Critical theory quickly morphed into critical studies—studies that were designed to dismantle the teaching of American history and philosophy, which were considered bourgeois and capitalist subjects. The stuff Adams and Jefferson and Washington wanted taught was thrown out in favor of Black Studies, LGBT Studies, and—well—basically any kind of study that broke us down into special interest groups.

Political correctness also began with the Marxists who took over the universities. Mao actually invented the term; the philosophical friends of the Frankfurt School brought it to our shores. And so students today learn about "Zombies in Popular Media" rather than founding philosophy.

And while it's possible that nobody is offended, it's a near certainty that nobody is learning anything.

DIVERSITY OF OPINION: LEFT AND FAR LEFT

If we fast-forward almost a century it's easy to see what "critical theory" and similar concepts have done to colleges and universities. A recent survey to members of various prestigious American associations (like the American Economic Association, the American Historical Association, etc.) revealed the extent of the damage:

Democrats dominate the social sciences and humanities. Of the fields we sampled, anthropology and sociology are the most lopsided, with Democratic:Republican ratios upwards of 20:1, and economics is the least lopsided, about 3:1. Among social-science and humanities professors up through age 70, the overall Democrat:Republican ratio is probably about 8:1.

In some cases, there isn't even one Republican for every eight or twenty Democrats on the faculty. There are *none*. Zip. Zilch. *Nada*. Nonexistent. The history department at the University of Iowa had twenty-two registered Democrats and zero registered Republicans. The one at Duke University had thirty-two registered Democrats and zero registered Republicans.

But, let's be fair: lots of people don't identify themselves through a political party, so what if we instead asked professors if they identified themselves as "liberal" or "conservative" instead of Republican or Democrat? In that case, "Only

19.7 percent of respondents identify themselves as any shade of conservative, as compared to 62.2 percent who identify themselves as any shade of liberal."

That compares to a general population of American adults that, at the time, was 31.9 percent conservative and 23.3 percent self-identified liberal.

Another, more recent, survey, shows a similar split: around 72 percent of professors teaching at American universities describe themselves as liberal and only 15 percent as conservative, according to a study published by professors at George Mason University a few years back. In elite schools, 87 percent of the faculty referred to themselves as liberal and only 13 percent as conservative.

Okay, but even some self-identified liberals may prefer capitalism to socialism, so let's broaden the question even further. In that case, 24 percent of social sciences professors identified themselves as "radical," and 17.6 percent described themselves as "Marxist." (Unfortunately, the survey doesn't specify how many of the radicals were Marxists, or how many of the Marxists were radicals.)

MY RADICAL IDEA TO TAKE ON THE RADICALS

Before World War II, the German university system was a breeding ground for Nazism. In 1933, Nazi students started burning books, many times with the active help of their professors. Jewish professors and students were ousted, and intellectuals like Martin Heidegger (a forerunner of deconstruction, an offshoot of critical theory) joined up with the Nazis.

After World War II, the Allies had to figure out a way to change the universities in Germany back into places of learning rather than hotbeds of fascism. In the end, they shut down many of the universities completely and rooted out the Nazi influences. Only after the schools had been completely reformed were they allowed to reopen.

I hate to say it, but someone has to: that's exactly what needs to happen to our public universities now.

While there are many good professors, there are also many evil ones. The problem is that the two groups have become so intertwined that it would be impossible to root out only those who have put their ideologies in front of their responsibilities. The only real way to do that is to simply start over.

Why should we allow our universities to not only tolerate, but also celebrate, domestic terrorists like Bill Ayers (who has been barred from entering Canada on several occasions) and Bernardine Dohrn and allow them to mentor young

One economist estimated that Princeton University (endowment: $17 billion) received a federal subsidy of approximately $54,000 per student last year.

people? Why should we allow our universities to consider Ward Churchill (he of the "little Eichmanns" on 9/11) a legitimate scholar? Why should we allow our universities to treat Noam Chomsky's political musings as anything other than the ravings of a Marxist madman? Why should we allow our universities to provide homes and insanely high pay to philosophers of destruction like Frances Fox Piven, the political science professor who suggested a strategy for the "have-nots" to kill the American system of government by overloading government welfare services? And why should we allow our universities to create havens for ideological apologists for communism and socialism to virtually spit on our flag and then hide behind their tenure when asked to defend their actions or speech?

These professors and administrators are the real "fat cats" in America, the real one percent. They often produce nothing but a crop of students who leave their classroom hating America, hating capitalism, and apologizing for our history. They've been in bed with the government and the radical left to delegitimize individual rights and freedoms. They're destroying us. It's that simple. And, worst of all, we're paying them millions of dollars to do it. *We're paying them to destroy us.*

And we're paying them an awful lot of money. The average professor at a public institution of higher education with a doctoral program pulls down in excess of $115,000 per year; at private institutions, they average $151,000. At Harvard the average professor makes almost $200,000; longtime professors with tenure can make much more. Other top universities pay similar salaries: UCLA pays its professors an average of more than $144,000; Berkeley pays nearly that much; so do the universities of North Carolina, Michigan, and Maryland, along with many others.

The problem with those salaries is that virtually all of these colleges collect federal funding, even though some of them also have enormous private endowments. Harvard, for example, has a $32 billion endowment (it in-

Indoctrination Centers

Frances Fox Piven, a professor at the City University of New York, and those like her often use their posts to promote their political views to students. Piven recently wrote: "The challenge to educators, and especially to university educators, seems to me clear. We have both an opportunity and responsibility to try to deal with public-policy issues and fill in the blank space that endangers democracy."

Actually, you have a responsibility to force your students to think for themselves. You don't "fill in the blank space" with your views, you fill it in by giving students an ability to think critically, to understand both sides of an argument and make up their own minds. You don't teach them what to think, you teach them how to think. Oh, by the way, the piece she wrote in which that quote appeared was titled "Crazy Talk and American Politics: or, My Glenn Beck Story."

creased by $4.4 billion in fiscal 2011 alone), but they have lots of company: the University of Chicago has $6.3 billion, Notre Dame has $7.3 billion, MIT has $10 billion, Princeton has $17 billion, and Yale has $19 billion.

That is an unfathomable amount of cash. In fact, even at a rate of $51,000 per year for tuition, room, and board, and assuming no growth in their endowment, Harvard could pay the entire cost of education for every student they admit . . . for the next thirty years. Instead, the upper middle class subsidizes everybody else while Harvard professors get rich and the endowment gets fatter . . . and the college takes in hundreds of millions of dollars in federal funding every year. And that's just the private schools—state schools get tons of taxpayer cash, of course, even though they charge students an arm and a leg to attend.

LESSONS IN PRACTICAL ECONOMICS

While private universities receive most of their public funding via research grants, meaning that most public funding isn't directly tied to what goes on in the classroom, public universities are a different story.

Most public schools are state supported with billions of dollars. But when states' budgets are in disarray from spending too much money on education with too little to show, they don't cut spending—they look to the federal government instead to fix their problem. And that, of course, means that education becomes even more centralized, at the same level that destroyed elementary and secondary public school education. "Individual states are making these individual decisions," lamented former University of Washington president Mark Emmert, "but across the whole country all of a sudden, this amazing asset that we have is eroding rapidly, and there's no one looking at it from a systemic level at the national level." According to the Associated Press, "He compared the situation to individual states deciding they no longer want to maintain highways within their borders, but the whole country needs that interstate highway system."

Oh, how wrong he is.

The federal government is looking at this state problem with greedy eyes. That's why President Obama is pushing further and further into federal funding of educational loans.

But that also gives us the opportunity to fight back. We can't control what happens at Harvard so long as they're not using taxpayer dollars. But we *can* control what happens at our universities if we're paying for them. And as states begin to cut funding, and as the feds start to step in to fill the gap, we can step in with them and demand the sort of change we want to see: a return to teaching of real American history and literature; higher standards in math and science; real progress in breaking the monopoly of progressive thought. We can return power to local communities by using the power of the purse.

BRAVE COWARDS

It's kind of ironic that some of the things that are doing the most damage to our society actually began with good intentions. For example, the idea of giving "lifetime tenure" to professors was based on the same rationale used to justify lifetime tenure for Supreme Court justices: if you want people to be free to pursue real inquiry then you've got to ensure that they are insulated from political attacks. We don't want professors afraid for their jobs if they examine certain controversial subjects in a classroom.

But there's a problem with this logic and we've seen it firsthand with the Supreme Court: If people feel insulated from all pressure, they stop acting rationally. They start living in the realm of theories instead of realities.

America comes with both rights and responsibilities. You have, for example, the right to free speech, but you have the responsibility to not yell "fire" in a crowded theater. If you don't live up to that responsibility, you face certain consequences. It's a simple but effective formula. Unfortunately, tenured professors are completely insulated from it. They can scream fire in their classrooms all they want—and then hide behind their tenure if anyone questions them on it.

I don't know about you but I'm sick of it. You know what, professor? If you really believe in what you're saying, then put your job on the line like the rest of us. What is there to be afraid of—aside from the fact that one day a student will call you out on your lies?

The truth is that you don't really believe in freedom of speech—you only believe in freedom of *your* speech. If you believed in real freedom of speech—the idea that a person can

Theories and Facts

A few months ago, scientists from CERN, the Switzerland home of the Large Hadron Collider, began challenging Einstein's theory of special relativity. The science community was stunned—but the reality is that Einstein's theory was just that: a theory. Unfortunately, many professors don't teach that way. In their classrooms there are no such thing as theories, only absolutes. It's kind of ironic that the greatest thinkers of all time worked to ensure that their ideas were constantly challenged and debated, yet those same ideas are now taken as gospel inside many classrooms.

stand on a soapbox in the town square and shout his opinions—then you would be willing to take the same risk that every other person does.

Tenured professors don't have to be cautious about their arguments or back them up with facts—whatever they say in the classroom is magically the truth. Americans have a "right" to a home? Yep, that's exactly what the Founders wanted. Higher taxes create jobs? Sure, why not. America is a bloodthirsty animal intent on destroying the Middle East so that we can secure their oil? It's all the truth in the ivory tower that is the American university classroom.

PARENTAL SUPERVISION

Progressives have spent the better part of a hundred years pushing their agenda—and they've hijacked everything from our kindergartens to our colleges to do it. The more "educated" we get, the dumber we become. And that has always been the goal. There's a reason that slave masters wanted to keep their slaves illiterate: they understood that true education makes people long for freedom and liberty. Today's slave masters are the professors and unions and bureaucrats in Washington who run our education system.

We need to clean out the system, top to bottom. That means investigating and firing teachers who don't teach our kids, decertifying the teachers unions, cutting off federal funding to institutions with huge endowments, and driving down tuition payments through open competition. It means start-up educational institutions and universities, and new homeschooling and private school options that focus on apprenticeships and hands-on learning.

But most of all (and I can't believe I even have to write this), it means getting parents more involved in the education of their children.

Take control of your kids' future. Don't be passive. Don't just go to parent/teacher conferences and accept what's said. Dig in, question with boldness. *These are our children*. We can never forget that. Despite what some say, no one will ever care about their future more than we do. Not their teachers, not their principals, and certainly not those who run the unions. 🐔

Stomachs or Brains?

It's gotten so bad that schools are now fighting against parents packing their own kids' school lunches. State inspectors in North Carolina actually forced a four-year-old to turn over her lunch for not being sufficiently nutritious. If the schools care so much about what they put in our kids' bodies, they should care just as much about what they put into our kids' heads.

Chapter Twelve

YOUNG SOCIALISTS
WHY OUR KIDS THINK
THEY HATE CAPITALISM

"I was down at the Occupy Wall Street protest today, and never has the divide between the iPhone world and the politics world been so clear: I saw a bunch of people very well-served by their computers and telephones . . . but undeniably shortchanged by our government-run cartel education system."

—Kevin D. Williamson, deputy managing editor of *National Review*

GIVEN THE WAY our formal education system has been hijacked, it almost makes sense that our kids come out pulling the lever for Democrats without giving it another thought. It's frustrating and it's got to change, but at least it's understandable. What I can't understand, however, is how we're losing the capitalism argument. I know *why* we're losing it—our kids are being brainwashed by a bunch of washed-up, stuck-in-the-sixties, tweed-jacket-wearing professors into feeling guilty for being successful—but I still don't get *how* we're losing it.

My daughter is in college right now and every time I go to visit her campus I'm floored by what I see: smartphones stuffed into the pockets of designer jeans; Xboxes and PlayStations connected to flat-screen high-definition televisions; MacBook Airs or iPads in almost all dorm rooms.

College students don't have to leave their dorm rooms or even use a telephone to order pizza or burgers anymore; they can do it via online delivery companies like Seamless. They don't have to go to the mall for jeans or sneakers; they can just go online, comparison-shop for the best price, order, and a few days later they show up at their door. They don't have to go to a theater to catch a movie, or even to a video store; they can just stream them over Netflix.

In other words, college students aren't senior citizens collecting Social Security checks while rocking their way through the afternoon nap on the porch. They're active *consumers*—and are some of the most cutting-edge in the world. They're the ones we ask about the newest fashion trends, which movie to see, or which phones have the best features, or which place to eat has the best food. They love to shop. They love to spend money.

And they are very lucky to be in America.

The only problem is that they don't seem to appreciate any of it very much. Yes, I know that makes me sound like my grandfather, but it's true. After all, our kids could easily be living in the Soviet Union of 1990, where, as a *Washington Post* report put it, "the state-run shops are so barren" that to find a pair of jeans in Moscow a Russian had to resort to bribery or an illegal "black market."

Or they could be living in Equatorial Guinea, where President Obiang Nguema Mbasogo has ruled since seizing power in a military coup in 1979. There, "the government owned the only national radio and television broadcast system, RTVGE. The president's eldest son owned the only private broadcast media." I'm pretty sure our students wouldn't appreciate having *Teen Mom* or *Jersey Shore* replaced with constant reruns of *The Thousand Greatest Things About President Mbasogo*.

And if you think *that* would tick them off, imagine how they'd react if they lived in Turkmenistan, where, the State Department reports, the government of President Gurbanguly Berdimuhamedov "suspended the operation of the privately owned . . . Mobile TeleSystems (MTS), leaving approximately 2.5 million persons—half of the country's population and 80 percent of the mobile-phone users—without use of their mobile phones or access to the Internet."

Of course, all of that pales in comparison to being deprived of pizza, burgers, ice cream, and beer—the essential food groups of college students. But that's exactly what would happen if they lived in North Korea. Because of the failures of the communist economy, food shortages are so severe in North Korea that several studies have found their citizens to be inches shorter than South Koreans.

All of this raises a profound question: Why is it that Third World dictators always have names like Obiang Nguema Mbasogo or Gurbanguly Berdimuhamedov?

No, sorry, I got sidetracked, that's not the profound question, this is: Given how much America's style of free-market capitalism has given to America's youth, why do they resent it so much? It's incredible that we have done such a poor job in explaining and defending capitalism that we are even in this position, but that's the reality. Like it or not, progressives are winning the battle for our kids, teaching them that capitalism is outmoded at best, evil at worst. If we don't reverse the trend quickly there will soon be nothing left of capitalism to defend.

Kids Say the Darnedest Things
One young man at an Occupy Wall Street event, who introduced himself as a veteran of Tahrir Square, summed up the way many young people seem to feel: "They have their laws, they have their debts," he said, "and we have our Revolution."

THE NAME GAME

First, the good news: we have the winning argument. The data, both anecdotal and real, that proves the triumph of capitalism over all other economic systems is on our side; we've just done nothing with it. We've taken for granted that the youth would see the amazing life that capitalism has created for them and want it to continue. But we were wrong. So now it's time to stop being passive and instead get out there and make our case. This can no longer be "the system that brought us to the brink of another Great Depression." It must instead be "the system that has put that iPhone in your pocket, allowed your parents to buy the home you grew up in, and will one day provide you with a meaningful job."

It's pretty clear exactly where we need to focus our attention in this sales effort. A recent Pew poll asked adults for their reaction to certain words. *Socialism* was viewed negatively by 59 percent and positively by 29 percent, while *capitalism* was viewed positively by 52 percent and negatively by 37 percent.

Advantage: capitalism.

So far, so good, but here's the catch: among people ages eighteen to twenty-nine, the results changed dramatically: 43

What's in a Word?

Maybe it's the actual word *capitalism* that's the problem? As you've probably heard me say before, "change the language and you change the argument."

Republican strategist Frank Luntz's polling firm found that "[t]he public . . . prefers capitalism to socialism, but they think capitalism is immoral. And if we're seen as defenders of quote, Wall Street, end quote, we've got a problem."

A Gallup poll found that 86 percent of Americans had a positive image of "free enterprise" but only 61 percent had a positive image of "capitalism." Another survey by the U.S. Chamber of Commerce found that while 65 percent of small business owners had a positive impression of "free enterprise," only 45 percent think capitalism is a good idea—even though they're the same thing.

percent were positive toward socialism, and 43 percent were positive toward capitalism. Meanwhile, 49 percent were negative toward socialism and 48 percent negative toward capitalism. It was virtually a dead heat.

If we didn't already know it intuitively just by looking around, the data proves it conclusively: we are losing the youth. And, once we do, we have lost the essence of America, forever. Remember Reagan's warning: "Perhaps you and I have lived with this miracle too long to be properly appreciative. Freedom is a fragile thing and is never more than one generation away from extinction. It is not ours by inheritance; it must be fought for and defended constantly by each generation, for it comes only once to a people. Those who have known freedom and then lost it have never known it again."

One left-wing professor, writing on the progressive website "Common Dreams," celebrated the ongoing progressive victory in changing the hearts and minds of our youth. "Young people cannot be characterized as a capitalist generation," he wrote. "They are half capitalist and half socialist. Since the socialist leaning keeps rising among the young, it suggests—depending on how you interpret 'socialism'—that we are moving toward an America that is either Center-Left or actually majoritarian socialist."

If you're a lover of capitalism like me, that's hard to hear—but he's absolutely right, that is the way we are moving. Whether it is the young people at Occupy Wall Street rallies or ones that you know in your own life, there's plenty of anecdotal evidence for the idea that capitalism has an image problem with younger Americans.

THE ACCIDENT OF HISTORY

Here's the understatement of the century: World War II was a pretty big deal. Those who lived through it, or bravely fought in it, are likely to never forget that Nazism was short for "National *Socialism*." They are also likely to never forget that it was a really, really, horribly bad idea that eventually cost the lives of millions of innocent people.

The Cold War with the Soviet Union and its puppet states in Eastern Europe was a very big deal, too. The generation of Americans who lived through that likely remember that *U.S.S.R.* was an abbreviation for the "Union of Soviet *Socialist* Republics." That generation also likely remembers that the Soviet Union was such a bad idea that they had to build a wall to keep people in and shoot those who tried to escape.

People who are in college now are too young to remember the U.S.S.R. in its evil-empire heyday, and their history teachers have barely taught them about the American Revolution, let alone modern European history. When our kids think about Russia or Eastern Europe today, the words that likely come to mind are "fashion models" or "billionaires in mega-yachts," not "failed socialist menace" or the "nuclear holocaust."

It's counterintuitive, but it's actually been a disadvantage (at least as far as making this argument is concerned) that no country with a state-run economy has risen to threaten America in recent years the way that Nazi Germany or the Soviet Union once did. There is no "evil empire" anymore that Americans can rally against or compare themselves to. Turkmenistan and Equatorial Guinea aren't exactly the stuff of front-page headlines. Sure, Iran and North Korea are serious threats in terms of their ability to wreak havoc with a nuclear weapon. And China does challenge America, though its economy has grown stronger largely by adding more capitalism, not less. But none of them, at least for now, is even close to the scale of a Nazi Germany or Soviet Russia.

But it's not merely an accident of history that has strengthened support for socialism among our youth. Another big part of the story is the way these young people are being bombarded with anticapitalist messages in popular culture and in schools.

SOCIAL(ISM) STUDIES

It starts the moment a parent brings their child to a playgroup or to a park with a sandbox. The message to children with toys is "share everything," as the line of Robert Fulghum's bestseller *All I Really Need to Know I Learned in Kindergarten* puts it.

That may make for more peaceful playgrounds and playdates, and kids obviously need to learn how to share, but it's easy for that message to be taken to extremes. The children's book *The Rainbow Fish* tells the story of a fish with special shiny scales who decides to give them away to the other fish. According to the book's conclusion, "His most prized possessions had been given away, yet he was very happy." At the end, the rainbow fish is no longer different from the other fishes because he has ripped the scales off his own body to give them to others. One negative (although sadly accurate) review at Amazon.com is titled, "Great for the young communist and socialist."

Children's movies haven't been much better. Disney's *The Muppets,* a family-oriented film that came out in December 2011, has a plot that is summarized on the movie's website thus:

> *On vacation in Los Angeles, Walter—the world's biggest Muppet fan—his brother Gary, and Gary's girlfriend Amy from Smalltown, USA, discover the nefarious plan of oilman Tex Richman to raze the Muppet Theater and drill for the oil recently discovered beneath.*

As one critic wondered, why do these movies never seem to be about nefarious plans by evil poor environmentalists to turn the Muppet Theater into a wildlife refuge or wind farm?

After the books and movies a child finally graduates to school, where, as we covered in the previous chapter, any chance they stood of becoming a pro-capitalist adult quickly vanishes.

One thing that really shocked me as I researched this was the content in the textbooks themselves. It's one thing to have a liberal teacher tell kids what to think, but it's another thing to have a textbook—something that should be completely void of political commentary—blatantly argue against capitalism.

Lawrence Reed, president of the Foundation for Economic Education, looked at high school economics textbooks and found that "errors abound." But that's a huge understatement. I think what he found is less about errors and more about very carefully crafted political speech clearly meant to subtly influence our students. For example:

 "Despite fears by some Americans that governmental tampering with the free enterprise system would be harmful, most government policies have met with success." —from David E. O'Connor's *Economics—Free Enterprise in Action*

 "Under a balanced budget, the government would not be able to do things that many people think it should do, like building roads and providing for the needy." —Henry Billings, *Introduction to Economics*

 "As societies become more complex, the need for government power tends to increase." —Sanford Gordon and Alan Stafford's *Applying Economic Principles*

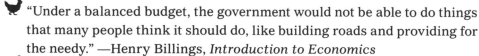

These opinions clearly rub off on students. The Higher Education Research Institute surveys tens of thousands of college students from dozens of different institutions each year when they arrive on campus as freshmen, and then again when they leave as seniors. Here are the results of one recent survey:

Change in Life Goals

Percent of students reporting that the following are "essential" or "very important" to them:	At college entry	At end of college	Change
Becoming involved in programs to clean up the environment	19.9	30.2	+10.3
Helping others who are in difficulty	70.0	76.6	+6.6
Becoming successful in a business of my own	36.2	35.2	-1.0
Being very well-off financially	67.2	59.9	-7.3

Change in Political Values

Students' characterization of their political views:	At college entry	At end of college	Change
Liberal or far left	29.8	39.0	+9.2
Conservative or far right	30.3	23.7	-6.6

In other words, students entered college about evenly split between being liberal and conservative, but after four years of propaganda, the liberals gained a 15-percentage-point advantage. College made the students a lot more likely to want to clean up the environment, but less likely to want to be well-off financially or successful in their own businesses.

The point is that we face an increasingly steep uphill battle. It's not *just* books or *just* movies or *just* liberal teachers and textbooks—it's all of it. To fight back we are going to have to do a lot more than just attack the messengers; we're going to have to attack the message itself.

EARNING IS LEARNING

Most young people have rebellious, anti-authoritarian impulses. They don't like being told what, when, or how to do something. It's ironic, then, that many of these same people embrace a system in which there would be far *more* regulations, many *more* bureaucrats micromanaging their lives, and far *more* rules and restrictions on how things can be done.

And that is the beauty of the free-enterprise movement: it has the word *free* right there in the title. Yet when we think of these "rebellious" youths we don't think of them joining their "Young Republicans" club at school; we think of them camping overnight at Occupy protests or road-tripping to an Obama event.

Why?

Simple: we've done an absolutely terrible job at selling the message. Capitalism isn't "cool." It's not something you fight for or get excited about. *But it can be.* In fact, it *should* be; a free market is the very thing that gives every American kid the hope that they'll achieve their dream. After all, when asked what they want to be when they grow up, very few twelve-year-olds are going to answer "class warrior," or "environmental activist," or "welfare recipient."

But the job of selling this message of freedom of opportunity can't just happen in the classroom (that battle is lost for the foreseeable future) or in the bookstore or cinema—it must happen at home. Parents have an enormous role to play in this effort, not by mandating that little Johnny become the next Milton Friedman (remember, mandates don't work) but by *showing* them what it really means.

I'd love to take my son Raphe out and open up a lemonade stand with him. I'll show him how to market his stand, how to get people to tell others it's the best lemonade they've ever had, and how to change his prices throughout the day based on the demand. I'll tell him that he should work as hard as he can because he'll get to keep every cent he makes; he'll just have to pay me for the supplies.

The following weekend I'll take him out again. This time I'll tell him that, no matter what happens, he'll get to keep just five dollars at the end of the day. If he makes less than that, I'll pay him the difference. If he makes more, he'll give me the excess.

I'm pretty sure this little exercise wouldn't make me Father of the Year, but hopefully it would give my son something tangible to think about as he grows up. It's one thing to hear "redistribution of wealth," and it's another thing entirely to put in a long hard day of work only to have your money taken away.

Another option for parents is foreign travel. Exposing kids to the "real world" outside of America can have a lot of benefits. Seeing the struggles and the challenges of day-to-day life—the shortages, the corruption—can help to drive home the advantages of free enterprise.

Admittedly, a trip like that isn't for everyone; it's a lot riskier than just reading about the country on the Web. And if you wind up detained by Obiang Nguema Mbasogo or Gurbanguly Berdimuhamedov, don't count on me coming to rescue you.

A less aggressive approach is to ensure that our kids spend some time with immigrants who have come to America from countries

If Only We All Had Yachts

One highly successful capitalist had a child who went off to England to study after graduating from high school. He came home "immersed in the idea and ideals of socialism," declaring himself in favor "of all people sharing equally in the world's wealth." The child's mother told him, fine, if that's what he believed, they'd take away his cherished boat, and he could spend his time just fishing off the pier. The defender of capitalism, in this case, was, of all people, Rose Kennedy, and the young socialist was Joe Kennedy Jr., who didn't want to give up the boat, and who later died in World War II.

with much different views on economic freedom. Some of the most enthusiastic defenders of capitalism I've ever met, not to mention its most successful practitioners, are those who came here as legal immigrants or refugees fleeing Castro's Cuba or Communist China or the Soviet Union. They understand firsthand the disadvantages of the system they left behind.

If trips abroad or conversations with immigrants aren't your style, there are plenty of other options. Several volunteer-driven nonprofit organizations teach students about free enterprise by putting them to work. Junior Achievement, founded in 1919, now reaches four million students a year. In New York, hundreds of teams of high school students compete each year to write the best plan for a new business as part of Junior Achievement. Members of the winning teams get three thousand dollars apiece and iPhones, and they get to ring the closing bell on the NASDAQ stock market. The Boy Scouts have an "American Business" merit badge with requirements that include "Run a small business involving a product or service for at least three months. . . . For example: a newspaper route, lawn mowing, sales of things you have made or grow." Millions of Girl Scouts have learned sales and marketing principles selling cookies.

Even a job that seems menial, or a distraction from school, can become valuable training. Warren Buffett, who became the richest businessman in America, got started in high school working newspaper delivery routes for the *Washington Times-Herald*, *Washington Post*, and *Washington Star*. He invested some of his earnings in a business that put pinball machines in barbershops.

By getting personally involved, parents can help make it much more likely that their children grow up to be entrepreneurs rather than Occupiers. It can take some extra work and thought to find books and movies that aren't hostile to capitalism, to keep an eye on what's going on at school, to drive your child to Scout meetings, or to encourage them to apply for that first summer job—but it's more than worth it.

Of course, as any parents reading this already know well, there are never any guarantees. Even well-intentioned parents don't always get it exactly right—Bill Gates's parents were worried when he dropped out of Harvard to pursue founding Microsoft; the president of my production company dropped out of college to pursue his dreams and his mother responded by crying—but the potential payoff is huge: a child who takes care of you in your old age rather than one who lives in your basement.

WHO WANTS TO BE A BILLIONAIRE?

Let's be honest: socialism and cradle-to-grave social policies do have a certain simple emotional appeal, especially when cloaked in the language of "fairness" and "equality." It's easy to see a poor family and imagine how they might be helped by a government program. It's much more abstract and complex to think about the people who might be taxed to fund that program, or about the jobs that could've been created if that program didn't have to be funded, or about the chances that the government program might create perverse incentives or have unintended consequences that could wind up hurting the people it is intended to help.

Capitalism is sometimes harder to defend than other economic systems, but we can never forget that morality is actually at the center of this. One of the most influen-

Learning from Experience

Some of capitalism's most passionate defenders came to America or other Western nations as immigrants after fleeing state-controlled political and economic systems. Among them:

Friedrich Hayek, the author of *The Road to Serfdom* and *The Fatal Conceit*, two books warning of the dangers of centralized government planning, was born in Austria, but in 1938, with Nazi Germany annexing Austria, Hayek became a British citizen.

Ludwig von Mises, an economist of the Austrian School and a close associate of Hayek, also fled the Nazis, arriving in America in 1940.

Rose Friedman, the wife of libertarian economist Milton Friedman, his collaborator on the 1962 book *Capitalism and Freedom,* and his coauthor on *Free to Choose* and *Two Lucky People*, was born in what is now Ukraine before coming to America with her family at age two.

Ayn Rand, the author of the procapitalist novel *Atlas Shrugged* and of the book *Capitalism: The Unknown Ideal*, was born in St. Petersburg, Russia, in 1905, and knew the oppressive rule of both the czar and the Soviet communist thugs that followed. She came to America in 1926.

tial economic thinkers of all time was the Scottish philosopher Adam Smith. His book *An Inquiry into the Nature and Causes of the Wealth of Nations* came out in 1776, the same year that America declared independence from Great Britain. That book described important economic concepts, such as how free trade benefits both sides because of comparative advantage, and how the "invisible hand" of self-interest benefits society overall.

But it was Smith's earlier book, *The Theory of Moral Sentiments*, published in 1759, that is perhaps more important. That book focused on how market rewards encourage virtues such as hard work—what he called "industry"—and trustworthy behavior. He explained this in a section titled "Of the influence and authority of the general Rules of Morality, and that they are justly regarded as the Laws of the Deity." Smith asked, "What is the reward most proper for encouraging *industry*, prudence, and circumspection? Success in every sort of business."

In other words, capitalism is good not only because it is the best system around for generating lots of great stuff that people want to buy, but also because it's the best way to encourage people to work hard and be honest in their dealings. Capitalism is, at its core, survival of the fittest—and a "fit" business is one that not only offers value, but also treats its customers right. That last point is too often missed. There's a lot of attention paid to how capitalism encourages cutthroat competition, but much less attention is paid to how it encourages cooperation—among employees on the same team, between companies and their suppliers, and between entrepreneurs and their financial backers.

Believers in what Adam Smith called "the Laws of the Deity" have come at capitalism from all kinds of angles. The very big deal that the Bible makes out of the Exodus of the Children of Israel from slavery in Egypt, for example, leads to the idea that the individual, not the pharaoh or some modern equivalent, has the ownership of his own labor. The commandment not to steal brings with it the concept that what an individual has worked to produce belongs to that individual.

When it comes right down to it, though, the case for capitalism doesn't require a lot of deep study of the Bible, eighteenth-century Scottish philosophers, or even adventure travel to Equatorial Guinea or Turkmenistan. It just requires our kids to open their minds and eyes to what's standing right in front of them, to just connect the dots and start appreciating that they are among the 0.3 percent of humans who have ever been fortunate enough to live under this kind of freedom.

One thing that might open further their appreciation for capitalism is the fact that it is one of the few economic systems in the world in which a regular kid can be a billionaire in less than a decade. For example, Facebook's twenty-eight-year-old founder, Mark Zuckerberg, is worth more than $20 billion. Under what other economic system can a smart person with a good idea, who isn't the heir to a kingdom, make $20 billion before they're thirty years old?

But maybe the best way to talk about capitalism with our kids is to show them how it's cutting out the middlemen and giving them the power to decide their own destinies. For example, I used to be a Top 40 deejay and I knew very well the long and arduous process that artists went through before their song might eventually be played on my station.

1. Someone with an idea for a song starts a band in their garage.
2. The band might start to audition for local bar owners, hoping one of the places would let them play.
3. If that goes well they might work their way up to a larger bar. People might begin to show up specifically to watch them play—though, aside from friends, family, and flyers, there were few ways to get the word out.
4. With luck, they might make it to a bigger bar and even more people might start showing up, though there were still few ways to get the word out beyond friends and family.
5. With more luck, a talent scout for a record label might happen to see them in that bar one night.
6. That record scout might ask the band to make a "demo tape," which the scout might then play for an executive at the label.
7. If the executive likes the tape, he might offer them a small contract to put an album together.
8. If the album comes out well, and the timing is right, the label might promote the new band to the few chain record stores that monopolized the industry or to a few key radio stations.
9. If the programming director of a radio station hears the song and likes it he might authorize it to be played on the air.
10. If the song is played on the air, listeners might like it and call in to request it. If so, it might go into a heavier rotation, which means it might eventually show up on a *Billboard* chart.

Today, that entire process can be replaced by one talented person with a video camera and a YouTube account. Yes, Bieber, I'm looking at you.

Our kids don't care about the way we used to do things. In fact, they likely resent it. The legacy systems that have been built over decades are meaningless to them. Some executive sitting in some corner office deciding who is going to be successful stands against everything our kids stand for. *And that is exactly how we should be promoting capitalism.* Despite the language games, it's capitalism that encourages progress and the transformation of industries, and it's progressives and socialism that encourage the status quo.

The truth is that our kids love and embrace capitalism perhaps more than any other generation has in our country's history. They just don't know it yet.

It's our job to make sure they do.

Hope My Publisher Isn't Reading This

The same kind of free-market transformation is happening in other industries as well. Take book publishing, for example. Twenty-seven-year-old Amanda Hocking spent years being rejected by book agents and traditional publishing houses. Desperate to make $300 so she could afford a trip to Chicago, Hocking self-published one of her paranormal thrillers by using Amazon.com. She was hoping to sell a few copies; she sold 1.5 million. No agents, no publishers, no bookstores or marketing companies or printing presses or delivery trucks. Just a talented writer who cut out all of the middlemen and took her work directly to the audience.

Chapter Thirteen

ADAPT OR DIE
THE COMING INTELLIGENCE
EXPLOSION

" We don't know a **millionth** of one percent about **anything. "**

—Thomas Edison

THE YEAR IS 1678 and you've just

arrived in England via a time machine. You take out your new iPhone in front of a group of scientists who have gathered to marvel at your arrival. "Siri," you say, addressing the phone's voice-activated artificial intelligence system, "play me some Beethoven."

Dunh-Dunh-Dunh-Duuunnnhhh! The famous opening notes of Beethoven's Fifth Symphony, stored in your music library, play loudly.

"Siri, call my mother."

Your mother's face appears on the screen, a Hawaiian beach behind her. "Hi, Mom!" you say. "How many fingers am I holding up?"

"Three," she correctly answers. "Why haven't you called more—"

"Thanks, Mom! Gotta run!" you interrupt, hanging up.

"Now," you say. "Watch this."

Your new friends look at the iPhone expectantly.

"Siri, I need to hide a body."

Without hesitation, Siri asks: "What kind of place are you looking for? Mines, reservoirs, metal foundries, dumps, or swamps?" (I'm not kidding. If you have an iPhone 4S, try it.)

You respond "Swamps," and Siri pulls up a satellite map showing you nearby swamps.

The scientists are shocked into silence. *What is this thing that plays music, instantly teleports video of someone across the globe, helps you get away with murder, and is small enough to fit into a pocket?*

At best, your seventeenth-century friends would worship you as a messenger of God. At worst, you'd be burned at the stake for witchcraft. After all, as science fiction author Arthur C. Clarke once said, "Any sufficiently advanced technology is indistinguishable from magic."

Now, imagine telling this group that capitalism and representative democracy will take the world by storm, lifting hundreds of millions of people out of poverty. Imagine telling them their descendants will eradicate smallpox and regularly live seventy-five or more years. Imagine telling them that men will walk on the moon, that planes, flying hundreds of miles an hour, will transport people around the world, or that cities will be filled with buildings reaching thousands of feet into the air.

They'd probably escort you to the madhouse.

Unless, that is, one of the people in that group had been a man named Ray Kurzweil.

Kurzweil is an inventor and futurist who has done a better job than most at predicting the future. Dozens of the predictions from his 1990 book *The Age of Intelligent Machines* came true during the 1990s and 2000s. His follow-up book, *The Age of Spiritual Machines*, published in 1999, fared even better. Of the 147 predictions that Kurzweil made for 2009, 78 percent turned out to be entirely correct, and another 8 percent were *roughly* correct. For example, even though every portable computer had a keyboard in 1999, Kurzweil predicted that most portable computers would *lack* a keyboard by 2009. It turns out he was right: by 2009, most portable computers were MP3 players, smartphones, tablets, portable game machines, and other devices that lacked keyboards.

Kurzweil is most famous for his "law of accelerating returns," the idea that technological progress is generally "exponential" (like a hockey stick, curving up sharply) rather than "linear" (like a straight line, rising slowly). In nongeek-speak that means that our knowledge is like the compound interest you get on your bank account: it increases exponentially as time goes on because it keeps building on itself. We won't experience one hundred years of progress in the twenty-first century, but rather *twenty thousand* years of progress (measured at today's rate).

Many experts have criticized Kurzweil's forecasting methods, but a careful and extensive review of technological trends by researchers at the Santa Fe Institute came to the same basic conclusion: technological progress generally tends to be exponential (or even *faster* than exponential), not linear.

So, what does this mean? In his 2005 book *The Singularity Is Near*, Kurzweil shares his predictions for the *next* few decades:

- In our current decade, Kurzweil expects real-time translation tools and automatic house-cleaning robots to become common.
- In the 2020s he expects to see the invention of tiny robots that can be injected into our bodies to intelligently find and repair damage and cure infections.
- By the 2030s he expects "mind uploading" to be possible, meaning that your memories and personality and consciousness could be copied to a machine. You could then make backup copies of yourself, and achieve a kind of technological immortality.

If any of that sounds absurd, remember again how absurd the eradication of smallpox or the iPhone 4S would have seemed to those seventeenth-century scientists. That's because the human brain is conditioned to believe that the past is a great predictor of the future. While that might work fine in some areas, technology is not one of them. Just because it took decades to put two hundred transistors onto a computer chip doesn't mean that it will take decades to get to

Age of the Machines?

"We became the dominant species on this planet by being the most intelligent species around. This century we are going to cede that crown to machines. After we do that, it will be them steering history rather than us."
—JAAN TALLINN, CO-CREATOR OF SKYPE AND KAZAA

Your Brain 2.0

There's no reason to expect that mind uploading can't be achieved with enough technological progress. Nearly all scientists who study the brain think the human mind is, like a computer, basically an information-processing system. But while neurons eventually die, silicon pathways live forever.

four hundred. In fact, Moore's Law, which states (roughly) that computing power doubles every two years, shows how technological progress must be thought of in terms of "hockey stick" progress, not "straight line" progress. Moore's Law has held for more than half a century already (we can currently fit 2.6 *billion* transistors onto a single chip) and there's little reason to expect that it won't continue to.

In 1995, consumers were forced to buy entire albums on CD for $15 to $20. Now? They download only the songs they want for $.99 each.

In 2010, Borders operated more than 500 book and music superstores around the world. Now? There are zero.

But the aspect of his book that has the most far-ranging ramifications for us is Kurzweil's prediction that we will achieve a "technological singularity" in 2045. He defines this term rather vaguely as "a future period during which the pace of technological change will be so rapid, its impact so deep, that human life will be irreversibly transformed."

Part of what Kurzweil is talking about is based on an older, more precise notion of "technological singularity" called an *intelligence explosion*. An intelligence explosion is what happens when we create artificial intelligence (AI) that is better than we are *at the task of designing artificial intelligences*. If the AI we create can improve its *own* intelligence without waiting for *humans* to make the next innovation, this will make it even *more* capable of improving its intelligence, which will . . . well, you get the point. The AI can, with enough improvements, make itself smarter than all of us mere humans put together.

The really exciting part (or the scary part, if your vision of the future is more like the movie *The Terminator*) is that, once the intelligence explosion happens, we'll get an AI that is as superior to us at science, politics, invention, and social skills as your computer's calculator is to you at arithmetic. The problems that have occupied mankind for decades—curing diseases, finding better energy sources, etc.—could, in many cases, be solved in a matter of weeks or months.

Again, this might sound far-fetched, but Ray Kurzweil isn't the only one who thinks an intelligence explosion could occur sometime this century. Justin Rattner, the chief technology officer at Intel, predicts some kind of Singularity by 2048. Michael Nielsen, co-author of the leading textbook on quantum computation, thinks there's a decent chance of an intelligence explosion by 2100. Richard Sutton, one of the biggest names in AI, predicts an intelligence explosion near the middle of the century. Leading philosopher David Chalmers is 50 percent confident an intelligence explosion will occur by 2100. Participants at a 2009 conference on AI tended to be 50 percent confident that an intelligence explosion would occur by 2045.

If we can properly prepare for the intelligence explosion and ensure that it goes well for

The Last Invention

"Let an ultraintelligent machine be defined as a machine that can far surpass all the intellectual activities of any man however clever. Since the design of machines is one of these intellectual activities, an ultraintelligent machine could design even better machines; there would then unquestionably be an 'intelligence explosion,' and the intelligence of man would be left far behind. Thus the first ultraintelligent machine is the last invention that man need ever make."

—I. J. GOOD, STATISTICIAN WHO HELPED ALAN TURING CRACK THE ENIGMA CODE DURING WORLD WAR II humanity, it could be the best thing that has ever happened on this fragile planet. Consider the difference between humans and chimpanzees, which share 95 percent of their genetic code. A relatively small difference in intelligence gave humans the ability to invent farming, writing, science, democracy, capitalism, birth control, vaccines, space travel, and iPhones—all while chimpanzees kept flinging poo at each other.

Likewise, self-improving machines could perform scientific experiments and build new technologies much faster and more intelligently than humans can. Curing cancer, finding clean energy, and extending life expectancies would be child's play for them. Imagine living out your own personal fantasy in a different virtual world every day. Imagine exploring the galaxy at near light speed, with a few backup copies of your mind safe at home on earth in case you run into an exploding supernova. Imagine a world where resources are harvested so efficiently that everyone's basic needs are taken care of, and political and economic incentives are so intelligently fine-tuned that "world peace" becomes, for the first time ever, more than a Super Bowl halftime show slogan.

Intelligent Design?

The thought that machines could one day have superhuman abilities should make us nervous. Once the machines are smarter and more capable than we are, we won't be able to negotiate with them any more than chimpanzees can negotiate with *us*. What if the machines don't want the same things we do?

The truth, unfortunately, is that every kind of AI we know how to build today definitely would *not* want the same things we do. To build an AI that does, we would need a more flexible "decision theory" for AI design and new techniques for making sense of human preferences. I know that sounds kind of nerdy, but AIs are made of math and so math is really important for choosing which results you get from building an AI.

These are the kinds of research problems being tackled by the Singularity Institute in America and the Future of Humanity Institute in Great Britain. Unfortunately, our silly species still spends more money each year on *lipstick research* than we do on figuring out how to make sure that the most important event of this century (maybe of all human history)—the intelligence explosion— actually goes *well* for us.

With self-improving AI we may be able to eradicate suffering and death just as we once eradicated smallpox. It is not the limits of nature that prevent us from doing this, but only the limits of our current understanding. It may sound like a paradox, but it's our brains that prevent us from fully understanding our brains.

TURF WARS

At this point you might be asking yourself: "Why is this topic in this book? What does any of this have to do with the economy or national security or politics?"

In fact, it has *everything* to do with all of those issues, plus a whole lot more. The intelligence explosion will bring about change on a scale and scope not seen in the history of the world. If we don't prepare for it, things could get very bad, very fast. But if we do prepare for it, the intelligence explosion could be the best thing that has happened since . . . *literally* ever.

But before we get to the kind of life-altering progress that would come after the Singularity, we will first have to deal with a lot of smaller changes, many of which will throw entire industries and ways of life into turmoil. Take the music

Beyond Bad Sci-Fi Movies

The "event horizon" of a black hole is the boundary where gravity becomes so strong that you've reached "the point of no return." No rocket in the world would ever be powerful enough to blast you out of the black hole past that point. The Singularity is kind of like that: intelligence explosion is a kind of event horizon because from that moment forward, everything changes and we can't go back. Once the machines are stronger than us, what they want is what happens. So we'd better be careful about precisely specifying (in their code) what they want, before they improve themselves beyond our ability to control them.

business, for example. It was not long ago that stores like Tower Records and Sam Goody were doing billions of dollars a year in compact disc sales; now people buy music from home via the Internet. Publishing is currently facing a similar upheaval. Newspapers and magazines have struggled to keep subscribers, booksellers like Borders have been forced into bankruptcy, and customers are forcing publishers to switch to ebooks faster than the publishers might like.

All of this is to say that some people are already witnessing the early stages of upheaval firsthand. But for everyone else, there is still a feeling that something is different this time; that all of those years of education and experience might be turned upside down in an instant. They might not be able to identify it exactly but they realize that the world they've known for forty, fifty, or sixty years is no longer the same.

There's a good reason for that. We feel it and sense it because it's true. It's happening. There's absolutely no question that the world in 2030 will be a very different place than the one we live in today. But there is a question, a large one, about whether that place will be better or worse.

It's human nature to resist change. We worry about our families, our careers, and our bank accounts. The executives in industries that are already experiencing cataclysmic shifts would much prefer to go back to the way things were ten years ago, when people still bought music, magazines, and books in stores. The future was predictable. Humans like that; it's part of our nature.

But predictability is no longer an option. The intelligence explosion, when it comes in earnest, is going to change *everything*—we can either be prepared for it and take advantage of it, or we can resist it and get run over.

Unfortunately, there are a good number of people who are going to resist it. Not only those in affected industries, but those who hold power at all levels. They see how technology is cutting out the middlemen, how people are becoming empowered, how bloggers can break national news and YouTube videos can create superstars.

And they don't like it.

A BATTLE FOR THE FUTURE

Power bases in business and politics that have been forged over decades, if not centuries, are being threatened with extinction, and they know it. So the owners of that power are trying to hold on. They think they can do that by dragging us backward. They think that, by growing the public's dependency on government, by taking away the entrepreneurial spirit and rewards and by limiting personal freedoms, they can slow down progress.

But they're wrong. The intelligence explosion is coming so long as science itself continues. Trying to put the genie back in the bottle by dragging us toward serfdom won't stop it and will, in fact, only leave the world with an economy and society that are completely unprepared for the amazing things that it could bring.

Robin Hanson, author of "The Economics of the Singularity" and an associate professor of economics at George Mason University,

Reality Check

President Obama was recently asked about unemployment in America and he responded by explaining that automation was impacting the hiring of new workers. "There are some structural issues with our economy where a lot of businesses have learned to become much more efficient with a lot fewer workers. You see it when you go to a bank and you use an ATM, you don't go to a bank teller, or you go to the airport and you're using a kiosk instead of checking in at the gate."

Here's the problem: That's not a "structural issue," that's reality. (In fact, economists have a name for this strange phenomenon that creates jobs and helps the economy grow: "productivity.") You either adapt or you die. ATMs and self-service kiosks aren't the problem—who wouldn't rather go to an ATM than stand in line for a teller? The problem is that our economy is not yet flexible enough to adapt to these changes. If *that* is the structural issue that Obama was talking about then he's exactly right—and if we don't fix it soon, we'll be begging for the days of 9 percent unemployment.

wrote that after the Singularity, "The world economy, which now doubles in 15 years or so, would soon double in somewhere from a week to a month."

That is unfathomable. But even if the rate were much slower, say a doubling of the world economy in *two* years, the shockwaves from that kind of growth would still change everything we've come to know and rely on. A machine could offer the ideal farming methods to double or triple crop production, but it can't *force* a farmer or an industry to implement them. A machine could find the cure for cancer, but it would be meaningless if the pharmaceutical industry or Food and Drug Administration refused to allow it. The machines won't be the problem; humans will be.

And that's why I wanted to write about this topic. We are at the forefront of something great, something that will make the Industrial Revolution look in comparison like a child discovering his hands. But we have to be prepared. We must be open to the changes that will come, because they *will* come. Only when we accept that will we be in a position to thrive. We can't allow politicians to blame progress for our problems. We can't allow entrenched bureaucrats and power-hungry executives to influence a future that they may have no place in.

Many people are afraid of these changes— of course they are: it's part of being human to fear the unknown—but we can't be so entrenched in the way the world works now that we are unable to handle change out of fear for what those changes might bring.

Change is going to be as much a part of our future as it has been of our past. Yes, it will happen faster and the changes themselves will be far more dramatic, but if we prepare for it,

The Progress of Progress

One of the keys to the Singularity (and to most technological progress in general) is that everything will happen in due time. We can embrace and influence progress, but we can't mandate it. Take solar energy, for example. The idea of the sun being a clean energy source for the world is amazing—no one disputes that. But so is the *idea* of flying cars. In neither case has the technology caught up to the reality. Yet, in the case of solar energy, the government has decided that it cannot wait any longer. So, it's provided investments and subsidies and mandates—none of which do much of anything to help the technology itself get better faster.

Looking at the rate of growth, Kurzweil believes that solar power will be ready for mass use in about sixteen years. He writes, "Solar panels are coming down dramatically in cost per watt. And as a result of that, the total amount of solar energy is growing, not linearly, but exponentially. It's doubling every 2 years and has been for 20 years. And again, it's a very smooth curve. There's all these arguments, subsidies and political battles and companies going bankrupt, they're raising billions of dollars, but behind all that chaos is this very smooth progression."

The lesson? Interference by governments in technological progress may be good for winning elections (and certainly, in some cases, the right kind of funding can help speed up innovation), but it does nothing to change the underlying growth curve.

the change will mostly be positive. But that preparation is the key: we need to become more well-rounded as individuals so that we're able to constantly adapt to new ways of doing things. In the future, the way you do your job may change four to five or fifty times over the course of your life. Those who cannot, or will not, adapt will be left behind.

At the same time, the Singularity will give many more people the opportunity to be successful. Because things will change so rapidly there is a much greater likelihood that people will find something they excel at. But it could also mean that people's successes are much shorter-lived. The days of someone becoming a legend in any one business (think Clive Davis in music, Steven Spielberg in movies, or the Hearst family in publishing) are likely over. But those who embrace and adapt to the coming changes, and surround themselves with others who have done the same, will flourish.

When major companies, set in their ways, try to convince us that change is bad and that we must stick to the status quo, no matter how much human inquisitiveness and ingenuity try to propel us forward, we must look past them. We must know in our hearts that these changes will come, and that if we welcome them into our world, we'll become more successful, more free, and more full of light than we could have ever possibly imagined.

Ray Kurzweil once wrote, "The Singularity is near." The only question will be whether we are ready for it.

CITATIONS

Chapter 1
STEP RIGHT UP!
The Progressive Shell Game

PAGE 2: "'the differences between ourselves and our opponents'" Newsmax, *The Greatest Speeches of Ronald Reagan* (West Palm Beach, FL: Newsmax.com, 2002), 41.

PAGE 3: "member of the Senate for multiple years" "How Liberal is John Kerry?" *factcheck.org*, October 19, 2004, http://www.factcheck.org/how_liberal_is_john_kerry.html.

PAGE 4: "'era at the beginning of the 20th century'" "Part I: CNN/YouTube Democratic Presidential Debate Transcript," *cnn.com*, July 23, 2007, http://articles.cnn.com/2007-07-23/politics/debate.transcript_1_new-ideas-issues-don-t-matter-child-care-legislation.

PAGE 6: "'gaining represents benefit to the community'" Ronald J. Pestritto and William J. Atto, eds., *American Progressivism: A Reader* (Lanham, MD: Rowman & Littlefield, 2008), 217. • **"in governmental control is now necessary"** Ronald J. Pestritto and William J. Atto, eds., *American Progressivism: A Reader* (Lanham, MD: Rowman & Littlefield, 2008), 6. • **"'hero is a guy named Teddy Roosevelt'"** "The Second Presidential Debate," *New York Times*, October 7, 2008, http://elections.nytimes.com/2008/president/debates/transcripts/second-presidential-debate.html. • **"'lean in the regulatory leaning is okay.'"** Glenn Beck, "Glenn's revealing interview with Newt Gingrich – Story and Video," *GlennBeck.com* video, 9:27, December 6, 2011, http://www.glennbeck.com/2011/12/06/glenns-revealing-interview-with-newt-gingrich-story-and-video. • **"'fellow progressives of 1791 and '92'"** John Milton Cooper Jr., *Pivotal Decades: The United States, 1900–1920* (New York: Norton, 1990), 170; Edmund Morris, *Colonel Roosevelt* (New York: Random House, 2010), 632. • **"Progressive who hated Japanese immigrants"** Greg Robinson, *By Order of the President: FDR and the Internment of Japanese Americans* (Cambridge, MA: Harvard University Press, 2001), 18, 22–23, 117. • **"in his state into internment camps"** G. Edward White, *Earl Warren: A Public Life* (New York: Oxford University Press, 1982), 67–78.

PAGE 7: **"anti-Semitic congressman John Rankin"** William E. Leuchtenburg, *The FDR Years: On Roosevelt and His Legacy* (New York: Columbia University Press, 1995), 183. • **"'than most any other foreign nation.'"** Robert David Johnson, *The Peace Progressives and American Foreign Relations* (Cambridge, MA: Harvard University Press, 1995), 276. • **"Republican George Norris from the rafters"** Joseph C. Goulden, ed., *Mencken's Last Campaign: H. L. Mencken and the 1948 Election* (Washington: New Republic Book, 1976), 73. • **"delivering a speech in Philadelphia that year"** Mark Sullivan, *Our Times,* vol. 4 (New York: Charles Scribner's Sons, 1939), 472–74. • **"from the Socialist Party of America"** Mel Van Elteren, *Labor and the American Left: An Analytical History* (Jefferson, NC: McFarland., 2011), 67. • **"'on the ruins of public liberty'"** "Washington's Farewell Address 1796," *avalon.law.yale.edu*, Yale Law School, Lillian Goldman Law Library, accessed April 18, 2012, http://avalon.law.yale.edu/18th_century/washing.asp.

PAGE 8: **"'feebleminded and criminal children of weaklings'"** Madison Grant, *The Passing of the Great Race* (New York: Charles Scribner's Sons, 1916), 45. • **"'The book is my Bible'"** Jonathan Peter Spiro, *Defending the Master Race: Conservation, Eugenics, and the Legacy of Madison Grant* (Lebanon, NH: University of Vermont Press, 2009), 357.

PAGE 9: **"'of use to the community or race.'"** Madison Grant, *The Passing of the Great Race* (New York: Charles Scribner's Sons, 1916), 49.

PAGE 10: **"'should be grateful to you for writing it'"** *Atlantic Monthly*, February 1917, 144; *Scribner's Magazine*, July 1917, 32d. • **"Roosevelt's Progressive Party ticket"** Eugene Lyons, *Herbert Hoover: A Biography* (Garden City, NY: Doubleday, 1964), 139. • **"to elect a Democratic Congress"** *New York Times*, April 2, 1920, 17. • **"angled to be his running mate"**

David Pietrusza, *1920: The Year of the Six Presidents* (New York: Carroll & Graf, 2007), 118, 137–39. • **"'unsolicited advice—all of it bad'"** William E. Leuchtenburg, *Herbert Hoover* (New York: Times Books, 2009), 64. • **"'in peacetime in all of history'"** Bill Flax, *The Courage to Do Nothing: A Moral Defense of Markets and Freedom* (Mustang, OK: Tate, 2010), 152. • **"'regimentation without stint or limit.'"** David T. Beito, *Taxpayers in Revolt: Tax Resistance During the Great Depression* (Auburn, AL: Ludwig von Mises Institute, 2009), 163. • **"'country down the path of socialism.'"** William C. Spragens, *Popular Images of American Presidents* (Westport, CT: Greenwood, 1988), 350.

PAGE 11: **"'at its highest level in five years'"** Amity Shlaes, *The Forgotten Man: A New History of the Great Depression* (New York: Harper Perennial, 2008), 94. • **"'for leadership in such times.'"** Arthur A. Ekirch Jr., *Ideologies and Utopias: The Impact of the New Deal on American Thought* (Chicago: Quadrangle Books, 1971); Paul Johnson, *A History of the American People* (New York: HarperCollins, 1998), 741. • **"'sure the economy doesn't collapse.'"** AFP News Agency, "Bush Says Sacrificed Free-Market Principles to Save Economy," *AFP*, December 16, 2008 http://www.google.com/hostednews/afp/article/ALeqM5jyyKrPjYt7VhpS8G8DrRkr18B0hA. • **"less conservative than they already were"** Irving Stone, *They Also Ran* (Garden City: Doubleday & Co., 1966), 365. • **"elements into a single party in 1948"** David M. Jordan, *FDR, Dewey, and the Election of 1944* (Bloomington: Indiana University Press, 2011), 258–60. • **"'on health care, and on housing.'"** Richard Nixon, interviewed by Frank Gannon, "The Nixon/Gannon Interviews," February 9, 1983, Day 1, Tape 6, transcript, The Walter J. Brown Media Archives & Peabody Awards Collection, University of Georgia Special Collections Libraries, http://www.libs.uga.edu/media/collections/nixon/nixonday1.html.

PAGE 12: **"'dime store New Deal.'"** Robert Dallek, *Flawed Giant: Lyndon Johnson and His Times, 1961–1973* (New York: Oxford University Press, 1998), 131.

PAGE 13: **"'our district to the Republican Party.'"** John P. Avlon, *Independent Nation: How Centrism Is Changing the Face of American Politics* (New York: Three Rivers Press, 2004), 166. • **"even LBJ did it in 1968–69"** Thomas Alan Schwartz, *Lyndon Johnson and Europe: In the Shadow of Vietnam* (Cambridge, MA: Harvard University Press, 2003), 205. • **"to tens of millions of Americans"** "General Article: Domestic Politics: American Experience: Nixon," *PBS.org*, accessed April 18, 2012, http://www.pbs.org/wgbh/americanexperience/features/general-article/nixon-domestic. • **"spending skyrocketing 120 percent"** Robert E. Kelly, *The National Debt of the United States 1941 to 2008* (Jefferson, NC: McFarland, 2008). • **"gold standard and devalued the dollar"** Jerry W. Markham *A Financial History of the United States,* vol. 3 (Armonk, NY: M. E. Sharpe, 2002), 38. • **"instituted wage-and-price-controls"** Donald H. Rumsfeld speaking at Tribute to Milton Friedman, May 9, 2002, http://www.defense.gov/speeches/speech.aspx?speechid=216. • **"we [the liberals] get the action.'"** John Micklethwait and Adrian Wooldridge, *The Right Nation: Conservative Power in America* (New York: Penguin Press, 2004), 70. • **"'reconciliation with the Communists abroad.'"** James Reston, "Back to Cuba and the Cold War," *New York Times*, September 27, 1970, E15.

PAGE 14: **"in his own private office"** Margaret MacMillan, *Nixon and Mao: The Week That Changed the World* (New York: Random House, 2008), 9–10. • **"economic policy he instituted in 1922"** Jerry W. Markham *A Financial History of the United States,* vol. 3 (Armonk, NY: M. E. Sharpe, 2002), 38. • **"'Read my lips, no new taxes,'"** Alfred Regnery, *Upstream: The Ascendance of American Conservatism* (New York: Threshold Editions, 2008), 345. • **"an 89 percent approval rating"** Roper Center at the University of Connecticut, "Job Performance Ratings for President Bush (G.H.W.)," Roper Center, *University of Connecticut, ropercenter.uconn.edu,* accessed April 18, 2012, http://bit.ly/IweelD.

PAGE 15: **"37.5 percent in the 1992 election"** Alfred Regnery, *Upstream: The Ascendance of American Conservatism* (New York: Threshold Editions, 2008), 345. • **"spent more on education**

than on Iraq" "**Little-known Fact: Obama's Failed Stimulus Program Cost More Than the Iraq War,**" *Beltway Confidential* blog at *washingtonexaminer.com*, August 23, 2010, http://washingtonexaminer.com/blogs/beltway-confidential/little-known-fact-obama039s-failed-stimulus-program-cost-more-iraq-war. • "**issued just twelve vetoes**" "Vetoes by President George W. Bush," *senate.gov*, http://www.senate.gov/reference/Legislation/Vetoes/BushGW.htm, accessed April 29, 2012. • "**$5.768 trillion to $10.626 trillion**" Mark Knoller, "National Debt Has Increased $4 Trillion Under Obama," *Political Hotsheet, cbsnews.com*, August 22, 2011, http://www.cbsnews.com/8301-503544_162-20095704-503544.html. • "**number of programs had grown to 1,816**" Veronique de Rugy, "Spending Under President George W. Bush" (working paper, Mercatus Center, George Washington University, March 2009), http://bit.ly/IwaIYv.

PAGE 17: "drafting a Constitution in the year 2012" Ariane de Vogue, "Ginsburg Likes S. Africa as Model for Egypt," *Politics: Legal* blog at *abcnews*.com, Feb 3, 2012, http://abcnews.go.com/blogs/politics/2012/02/ginsburg-likes-s-africa-as-model-for-egypt. • "**he wasn't alone: the vote was 96–3**" Steve Benen, "It's Amazing Ginsburg is even on the Bench," *Political Animal* blog at *washingtonmonthly*.com, August 30, 2011, http://bit.ly/IwaUa4.

Chapter 2
THE LIBERTARIAN OPTION
Ending the Progressive Scam

PAGE 22: "'that honors the traditions of our country'" Nancy Pelosi, "Rep. Pelosi's Floor Speech Before the House Health Care Vote," *aolnews.com*, March 21, 2010, http://www.aolnews.com/2010/03/21/rep-pelosis-house-floor-speech-before-health-care-vote. • "**the Founding Fathers had envisioned**" Mark Hemingway, "Harry Reid: The Founding Fathers Would Support Telling Boeing Where They Can Build Factories," *The Blog* blog at *weeklystandard.com*, May 11, 2011, http://www.weeklystandard.com/blogs/harry-reid-founding-fathers-would-support-telling-boeing-where-they-can-build-factories_560885.html. • "**'not give them up for expedience's sake'**" Barack Obama, "Barack Obama's Inaugural Address," transcript, *nytimes.com*, January 20, 2009, http://www.nytimes.com/2009/01/20/us/politics/20text-obama.html.

PAGE 23: "Heritage Foundation Freedom Index" The Heritage Foundation, "2012 Index of Economic Freedom," *heritage.org*, accessed April 13, 2012, http://www.heritage.org/index/default. • "**'economic freedom over the last 10 years.'**" James Gwartney, Robert Lawson, and Joshua Hall, "2011 Economic Freedom Dataset," *Economic Freedom of the World: 2011 Annual Report* Executive Summary (Vancouver, BC: Fraser Institute, 2011), http://www.cato.org/pubs/efw/efw2011/EFW-2011-executivesummary.pdf. • "**'Which comes closer to your own view?'**" Nate Silver, "Poll Finds a Shift Toward More Libertarian Views," *Five Thirty Eight* blog at *nytimes.com*, June 20, 2011, http://fivethirtyeight.blogs.nytimes.com/2011/06/20/poll-finds-a-shift-toward-more-libertarian-views.

PAGE 24: "want the government to cut taxes" "To Help Economy, Voters Want Government To Do More Cutting," *rasmussenreports.com*, December 26, 2011, http://www.rasmussenreports.com/public_content/business/general_business/december_2011/to_help_economy_voters_want_government_to_do_more_cutting. • "**government being the arbiters of morality**" Nate Silver, "Poll Finds a Shift Toward More Libertarian Views," *Five Thirty Eight* blog at *nytimes.com*, June 20, 2011, http://fivethirtyeight.blogs.nytimes.com/2011/06/20/poll-finds-a-shift-toward-more-libertarian-views. • "**John McCain in the general election**" Matt Welch, "Ron Paul's McCain-Like Path to the Nomination," *reason.com*, December 30, 2011, http://reason.com/archives/2011/12/30/ron-pauls-mccain-like-path-to-the-nomina. • "**pretty good place to find libertarians**" "CBS Poll: Independents Prefer Ron Paul Vs Obama," *forbes.com*, January 9, 2012, http://www.forbes.com/sites/kenrapoza/2012/01/09/cbs-poll-independents-prefer-ron-paul-vs-obama.

PAGE 25: "independents has increased in 18 states" Richard Wolf, "Voters Leaving Republican, Democratic Parties in Droves," *USA Today*, December 22, 2011, http://www.usatoday.com/news/politics/story/2011-12-22/voters-political-parties/52171688/1.

PAGE 27: "and against gun rights" Chris Field, "Let's Closely Examine McCain's Record," *humanevents.com*, February 1, 2008, http://www.humanevents.com/article.php?id=24785.

PAGE 28: "Heritage Foundation's Index of Government Dependence" William W. Beach and Patrick D. Tyrrell, "The 2012 Index of Dependence on Government," *Heritage Center for Data Analysis*, *Heritage Foundation*, February 8, 2012, http://www.heritage.org/research/reports/2012/02/2012-index-of-dependence-on-government. • **"if a foreign country had invaded them"** "Just Days After 9/11, Ron Paul Blames America," *rightscoop.com* December 26, 2011, http://www.therightscoop.com/just-days-after-911-ron-paul-blames-america.

PAGE 29: "'they attack us because we're over there'" "Ron Paul in 2007 Republican Primary Debate in Columbia SC," sponsored by *Fox News*, May 15, 2007, http://www.issues2000.org/Archive/2007_GOP_primary_SC_Ron_Paul.htm. • **"241 American soldiers were murdered"** "Beirut Barracks Attack Remembered," *cbsnews.com*, February 11, 2009, http://www.cbsnews.com/2100-202_162-579638.html. • **"'building walls around our own country'"** Newt Gingrich, interview by Wolf Blitzer, *The Situation Room,* CNN online, transcript, December 31, 2011, http://transcripts.cnn.com/TRANSCRIPTS/1112/31/sitroom.01.html.

PAGE 30: **"'measure the cause of all mankind'"** Thomas Paine, *Common Sense* (Bartleby.com, 1999), http://www.bartleby.com/133.

PAGE 31: "over 650 at last count" "Ron Paul says U.S. has Military Personnel in 130 Nations and 900 Overseas Bases," *politifact.com*, September 12, 2011, http://www.politifact.com/truth-o-meter/statements/2011/sep/14/ron-paul/ron-paul-says-us-has-military-personnel-130-nation. • **"extreme fiscal and social conservatives"** Emily Ekins, "Is Half the Tea Party Libertarian?" *reason.com*, September 26, 2011, http://reason.com/poll/2011/09/26/is-half-the-tea-part-libertart.

PAGE 32: "published his results on Politico.com" David Kirby and Emily Ekins, "Tea Party's Other Half," *politico.com*, October 28, 2010, http://www.politico.com/news/stories/1010/44243.html. • **"'Liberty and responsibility are inseparable'"** Friedrich A. Hayek, "The Creative Powers of a Free Civilization," chap. 2 in *The Constitution of Liberty* (Chicago: University of Chicago Press, 1960). • **"'general description also of what libertarianism is'"** Manuel Klausner, "Inside Ronald Reagan: A Reason Interview," *Reason*, July 1975, http://reason.com/archives/1975/07/01/inside-ronald-reagan/singlepage. • **"referred to himself a 'libertarian journalist'"** William F. Buckley, *Happy Days Were Here Again: Reflections of a Libertarian Journalist* (New York: Random House Inc., 1993).

PAGE 33: "'soul of conservatism is libertarianism.'" Manuel Klausner, "Inside Ronald Reagan: A Reason Interview," *Reason*, July 1975, http://reason.com/archives/1975/07/01/inside-ronald-reagan/singlepage.

PAGE 34: "Senator Lee, for example, said:" Mike Lee, "Patriot Act and the Fourth Amendment—Floor Speech," transcript, May 31, 2011, http://www.lee.senate.gov/public/index.cfm/blog?ID=9d699112-5663-4707-a5e7-41f6aafbcadb. • **"We can find a balance there"** Nick Gillespie, Matt Welch, and Jim Epstein, "Sen. Jim DeMint: Why Republicans Must Become More Libertarian," *reason.com*, February 7, 2012, http://reason.com/blog/2012/02/07/sen-jim-demint-why-republicans-must-beco.

PAGE 36: "federal income tax is a libertarian nightmare" "Congressman Scott Garrett Claims Half of All Americans Don't Pay Federal Income Taxes," *politifact.com NJ, The Star Ledger*, February 15, 2012, http://www.politifact.com/new-jersey/statements/2012/feb/29/scott-garrett/congressman-scott-garrett-claims-half-all-american. • **"the people with piercings…"** Benny Johnson, "Van Jones Unloads on Libertarians," *TheBlaze.com*, April 2, 2012, http://www.theblaze.com/stories/van-jones-unloads-on-libertarians-they-hate-the-brown-folk-the-gays-the-lesbians-theyre-anti-immigrant-bigots.

PAGE 37: "'a freedom indistinguishable from selfishness'" Michael Gerson, "Ayn Rand's Adult-Onset Adolescence," *Post Opinions* blog at *washingtonpost.com*, April 21, 2011, http://www.washingtonpost.com/opinions/ayn-rands-adult-onset-adolescence/2011/04/21/AFv2JyKE_story.html. • **"'all are to take a back seat'"** Jeffrey Sachs, "Libertarian Illusions," *Huff Post Politics*, *huffingtonpost.com*, January 15, 2012, http://www.huffingtonpost.com/jeffrey-sachs/libertarian-illusions_b_1207878.html. • **"you have to read about how perfect he is"** Earth Institute at Columbia University, "Full Bio: Jeffrey D. Sachs," *earth.columbia.edu*, accessed April 13, 2012, http://www.earth.columbia.edu/articles/view/1770, accessed April 13, 2012. • **"'determine how likely one is to give'"** Arthur C. Brooks, *Who Really Cares: The Surprising Truth About Compassionate Conservatism* (New York: Basic Books, 2006), 110.

Chapter 3
GEORGE SOROS
The Puppet Master Pulls All the Strings

PAGE 42: "'I am beginning to be able to...'" George Soros, *Soros on Soros: Staying Ahead of the Curve* (New York: John Wiley and Sons, Inc., 1995), 238.

PAGE 44: "'[Q]uite anti-Semitic, and ashamed of being Jewish'" George Soros, interview by Steve Kroft, *60 Minutes*, CBS, December 20, 1998. • **"a future-tense Esperanto verb meaning 'will soar.'"** "The Mind of George Soros; Meet the Esperanto Enthusiast Who Wants to Save the World from President Bush," *The Wall Street Journal*, March 2, 2004. • **"Soros's father purchased forged papers"** Michael T. Kaufman, *Soros: The Life and Times of a Messianic Billionaire* (New York: Knopf, 2002), 27. • **"identifying the family as Christians and bribed"** George Soros, interview by Steve Kroft, *60 Minutes*, CBS, December 20, 1998. • **"Baumbach took the young Soros... to take the possessions of a Jewish family"** Michael T. Kaufman, *Soros: The Life and Times of a Messianic Billionaire* (New York: Knopf, 2002), 37. • **"asked by Steve Kroft about that experience"** George Soros, interview by Steve Kroft, *60 Minutes*, CBS, December 20, 1998.

PAGE 45: "'not only to save ourselves but also to save others'" George Soros, foreword to *Masquerade: Dancing Around Death in Nazi-Occupied Hungary*, by Trivadar Soros (New York: Arcade Publishing, 2001), x. • **"'It's a very happy-making, exhilarating experience'"** George Soros, interview by Steve Kroft, *60 Minutes*, CBS, December 20, 1998.

PAGE 46: "philosopher Professor Karl Popper as his 'tutor'" George Soros, *Soros on Soros: Staying Ahead of the Curve* (New York: John Wiley and Sons, Inc., 1995), 33. • **"'Yet, this is what is happening, both internally and externally'"** David Horowitz and Richard Poe, *The Shadow Party: How George Soros, Hillary Clinton, and Sixties Radicals Seized Control of the Democratic Party* (Nashville: Nelson Current, 2006) 73. • **"'what the Constitution ought to be'"** David Horowitz and Richard Poe, *The Shadow Party: How George Soros, Hillary Clinton, and Sixties Radicals Seized Control of the Democratic Party* (Nashville: Nelson Current, 2006), 69. • **"'bubble of American supremacy' as the greatest threat to world peace"** George Soros, *The Bubble of American Supremacy: The Costs of Bush's War in Iraq* (New York: PublicAffairs, 2004). • **"to save $500,000 and then return to Europe"** Michael T. Kaufman, *Soros: The Life and Times of a Messianic Billionaire* (New York: Knopf, 2002), 83. • **"It was worth more than $1 billion"** "Soros Fund Management Llc—Company Profile, Information, Business Description, History, Background Information on Soros Fund Management Llc," *referenceforbusiness.com*, accessed April 11, 2012, http://www.referenceforbusiness.com/history2/85/Soros-Fund-Management-Llc.html; Peter Schweizer, *Do As I Say (Not As I Do): Profiles in Liberal Hypocrisy* (New York, Doubleday, 2005), 157.

PAGE 47: "'on a global scale.'" George Soros, "America's Global Role: Why the Fight for a Worldwide Open Society Begins at Home," *soros.org*, May 27, 2003, http://www.soros.org/resources/articles_publications/articles/americanprospect_20030527.

PAGE 48: "'I hope you are wrong'" George Soros, *Soros on Soros: Staying Ahead of the Curve* (New York: John Wiley and Sons, Inc., 1995), 15. • **"by his own account, was not constrained by scruples"** George Soros, *The Crisis of Global Capitalism* (New York: Public Affairs, 1998), 75. • **"he pocketed a billion dollars off the trade"** Michael T. Kaufman, *Soros: The Life and Times of a Messianic Billionaire* (New York: Knopf, 2002). • **"'chances of being successful would have been reduced'"** Michael T. Kaufman, *Soros: The Life and Times of a Messianic Billionaire* (New York: Knopf, 2002). • **"convicted him of insider trading"** "Soros Loses Case Against French Insider-Trading Conviction," *Bloomberg Business Week*, October 6, 2011, http://www.businessweek.com/news/2011-10-06/soros-loses-case-against-french-insider-trading-conviction.html.

PAGE 49: "'at a private townhouse in Manhattan'" Karl West, "Man Who Broke the Bank of England, George Soros, 'at Centre of Hedge Funds Plot to Cash in on Fall of the Euro,'" *Daily Mail*, February 27, 2010, http://www.dailymail.co.uk/news/article-1253791/Is-man-broke-Bank-England-George-Soros-centre-hedge-funds-betting-crisis-hit-euro.html. • **"his 'Open Society Foundations' in Hungary"** Open Society Foundation, "About the Open Society Foundation," *soros.org*, accessed April 12, 2012, http://www.soros.org/about. • **"throughout Eastern Europe and Central Asia"** Open Society Foundation, "About: Timeline," *soros.org*, accessed April 12, 2012, http://www.soros.org/about/timeline. • **"In 1993, Soros established the flagship of his network"** Open Society Foundation, "About: Timeline," *soros.org*, http://www.soros.org/about/timeline, accessed April 12, 2012. • **"'whose governments are accountable to its citizens'"** Open Society Foundations, "About the Open Society Foundation," *soros.org*, http://www.soros.org/about, accessed April 12, 2012. **"United States and Israel the chief targets of its 'human rights' protests"** Adrian Karatnycky and Arch Puddington, "The Human-Rights Lobby Meets Terrorism," *NGO Monitor*, March, 2002, http://www.ngo-monitor.org/data/images/File/The_Human_Rights_Lobby_Meets_Terrorism_2003.pdf. • **"more than 70 countries"** Open Societies Foundation "About the Open Society Foundation," *soros.org*, accessed April 12, 2012, http://www.soros.org/about. • **"Open Society Institute is a $1.9 billion operation"** Open Society Institute, tax return, signed by Greg Collier, http://dynamodata.fdncenter.org//990pf_pdf_archive/137/137029285/137029285_200812_990PF.pdf.

PAGE 50: "more than 400 American cities to pledge noncompliance with the Patriot Act;" Bill of Rights Defense Committee "Resolutions Passed and Efforts Underway, By State," *bordc.com*, accessed April12, 2012, http://www.bordc.org/list.php. • **"supporters of communist causes"** Matthew Vadum, "A Constitutional Right to Public Funds," *American Spectator*, November 13, 2009, http://spectator.org/archives/2009/11/13/a-constitutional-right-to-publ/1. • **"four longtime supporters of communist causes"** Center for Constitutional Rights, "Illegal Detentions and Guantanamo," *ccrjustice.org*, accessed April 12, 2012, http://ccrjustice.org/illegal-detentions-and-guantanamo. • **"'so-called war on terror'"** Center for Constitutional Rights, "Illegal Detentions and Guantanamo," *ccrjustice.org*, accessed April 12, 2012, http://ccrjustice.org/illegal-detentions-and-guantanamo. • **"such as the American Immigration Council"** Immigration Policy Center, "Papers Please: Eliminating Birthright Citizenship Would Affect Everyone," *immigrationpolicy.org*, January 4, 2011, http://www.immigrationpolicy.org/just-facts/papers-please-eliminating-birthright-citizenship-would-affect-everyone. • **"Immigrant Legal Resource Center"** William Hawkins and Erin Anderson, *The Open Borders Lobby and the Nation's Security After 9/11* (Los Angeles: Center for the Study of Popular Culture, 2004), 54, http://www.discoverthenetworks.org/guides/Open%20Borders%20Lobby.pdf. • **"the Sentencing Project, which attacks the American prison system as racist"** Sentencing Project, "Racial Disparity," *sentencingproject.org*, accessed April 13, 2012, http://www.sentencingproject.org/template/page.cfm?id=122. • **"the Gamaliel foundation" Gamaliel, "About Gamaliel,"** *gamaliel.org*, accessed April 13, 2012, http://www.gamaliel.org/AboutUs/Mission.aspx. • **"Midwest Academy…'racial justice'"** Midwest Academy "About Us," *midwestacademy.com*, accessed April 13, 2012, http://www.midwestacademy.com/about-us. • **"'actions speak louder than words'"** Ruckus Society, "What We Do," *ruckus.org*, accessed April 13, 2012, http://www.ruckus.org/section.php?id=71. • **"self-declared (former, if you listen to him) communist"** Eliza Strickland, "The New Face of Environmentalism,"

East Bay Express, November 2, 2005, http://www.eastbayexpress.com/gyrobase/the-new-face-ofenvironmentalism/Content?oid=1079539. • **"Washington Post, the Columbia Journalism Review, and ProPublica"** Dan Gainor, "Soros Spends Over $48 Million Funding Media Organizations," *mrc. org*, May 18, 2011, http://www.mrc.org/commentary/soros-spends-over-48-million-funding-media-organizations. • **"National Public Radio, the socialist American Prospect, Inc."** Dan Gainor, "Soros Spends Over $48 Million Funding Media Organizations," *mrc.org*, May 18, 2011, http://www.mrc.org/commentary/soros-spends-over-48-million-funding-media-organizations.

PAGE 51: "Independent Media Institute, and Media Matters For America" Dan Gainor, "Soros-Funded Lefty Media Reach More Than 300 Million Every Month," *mrc.org*, May 25, 2011, http://www.mrc.org/commentary/soros-funded-lefty-media-reach-more-300-million-every-month. • **"Catholics in Alliance for the Common Good"** Catholics in Alliance for the Common Good, "Mission and Vision, FAQ," *catholicsinalliance.org*, accessed April 13, 2012, http://www.catholicsinalliance.org/aboutus. html. • **"'safe and legal abortion services'"** Catholics for Choice, "Abortion," *catholicsforchoice.org*, accessed April 13, 2012, http://www.catholicsforchoice.org/topics/abortion/default.asp. • **"encouraging American troops to desert"** Robert Patterson, *War Crimes: The Left's Campaign to Destroy Our Military and Lose the War on Terror* (New York: Three Rivers Press, 2007), 181. • **"Global Exchange would be sending aid"** Scott Swett and Roger Canfield, "Aid and Comfort – How Leading Democrats Enabled the Iraqi Insurgency in Fallujah," *americanthinker.com*, March 27, 2012, http://www. americanthinker.com/blog/2010/10/aid_and_comfort_how_leading_de.html. • **"given more than $400 million to 'progressive nonprofit organizations'"** Tides, "History," *tides.org*, accessed April 13, 2012, http://web.archive.org/web/20080626103456/http://www.tides.org/about-tides/history/index.html. • **"'the Daddy Warbucks of drug legalization'"** Joseph A. Califano Jr., "Devious Efforts To Legalize Drugs," *The Washington Post*, December 4, 1996. • **"'transform the culture and experience of dying and bereavement'"** Neil Harab, "George Soros' Social Agenda for America," *Capital Research Center Foundation Watch*, April, 2003, https://www.capitalresearch.org/pubs/pdf/x3770435801.pdf. • **"Open Society Institute gave $45 million to PDA"** Open Society Institute, "Project on Death in America – Report of Activities: January 2001-December 2003" (report, Project on Death in America, New York, 2004), http://www.soros.org/resources/articles_publications/publications/report_20041122/a_complete. pdf. • **"such as the United Nations Foundation"** United Nations Foundation, "UN Foundation and UNA-USA Announce Alliance to Strengthen Support for the UN," press release, November 18, 2010, http://www.unfoundation.org/news-and-media/press-releases/2010/un-foundation-and-una-usa-announce-alliance.html. • **"American criminal-justice to an international prosecutor"** Neil A. Lewis, "U.S. Rejects All Support for New Court on Atrocities," *New York Times*, May 7, 2002, http://www.nytimes. com/2002/05/07/world/us-rejects-all-support-for-new-court-on-atrocities.html. • **"'The sovereignty of states must be subordinated to international law and international institutions'"** George Soros, *The Crisis of Global Capitalism* (New York: PublicAffairs, 1998), xxix.

PAGE 52: "'and I take great pride in having contributed to it'" David Holley, "Soros Invests in His Democratic Passion," *Los Angeles Times*, July 5, 2004, http://articles.latimes.com/2004/jul/05/world/ fg-soros5. • **"'setting up a state within a state…'"** David Horowitz and Richard Poe, *The Shadow Party: How George Soros, Hillary Clinton, and Sixties Radicals Seized Control of the Democratic Party* (Nashville: Nelson Current, 2006), 233. • **"trying it in the other country"** "'Puppet Master' Soros has 'Fun' Subversively & Adversely Affecting Societies; Lays Out His Plan for America," *theblaze.com*, November 9, 2010, http://www.theblaze.com/stories/puppet-master-soros-has-fun-subversively-lays-out-his-plan-for-america.

PAGE 53: "'We actually work together as a team'" George Soros, interview by Charlie Rose, *Charlie Rose Show*, PBS, November 30, 1995. • **"serve as a key advisor on the project"** Connie Bruck, "The World According to Soros," *New Yorker*, January 23, 1995. • **"previously funded through one of his foundations"** David Horowitz and Richard Poe, *The Shadow Party: How George Soros, Hillary Clinton, and Sixties Radicals Seized Control of the Democratic Party* (Nashville: Nelson Current, 2006)

93-94. • **"'Soviet Empire is now called the Soros Empire'"** Kyle-Anne Shiver, "George Soros and the Alchemy of 'Regime Change'" *americanthinker.com*, February 27, 2008, http://www.americanthinker.com/2008/02/george_soros_and_the_alchemy_o.html. • **"the diversion of $100 billion out of the country"** Kyle-Anne Shiver, "George Soros and the Alchemy of 'Regime Change,'" *americanthinker.com*, February 27, 2008, http://www.americanthinker.com/2008/02/george_soros_and_the_alchemy_o.html. • **"resign as director of the Harvard Institute in May 1999"** David Horowitz and Richard Poe, *The Shadow Party: How George Soros, Hillary Clinton, and Sixties Radicals Seized Control of the Democratic Party* (Nashville: Nelson Current, 2006) 93-94. • **"deal to acquire a large portion of Sidanko Oil"** Kyle-Anne Shiver, "George Soros and the Alchemy of 'Regime Change,'" *americanthinker.com*, February 27, 2008, http://www.americanthinker.com/2008/02/george_soros_and_the_alchemy_o.html. • **"'was part of the crony stuff that was going on'"** David Horowitz and Richard Poe, *The Shadow Party: How George Soros, Hillary Clinton, and Sixties Radicals Seized Control of the Democratic Party* (Nashville: Nelson Current, 2006), 96. • **"'one of the greatest social robberies in human history'"** Richard Poe, "Remembering Russiagate: Never Have So Few Stolen So Much from So Many," *richardpoe.com*, May 11, 2005, http://www.richardpoe.com/2005/05/11/remembering-russiagate.

PAGE 54: **"recruiting other philanthropies, like the Pew Charitable Trust"** Ryan Sager, "Buying 'Reform': Media Missed Millionaires' Scam," *New York Post*, March 17, 2005. • **"paid off in 2002 with the passage of McCain-Feingold Act"** Ed Morrissey, "Inside McCain's Reform Institute," *captainsquartersblog.com*, March 9, 2005. • **"'both within countries and among countries'"** George Soros, *The Bubble of American Supremacy: The Costs of Bush's War in Iraq* (New York: PublicAffairs, 2004). • **"'requires affirmative action on a global scale'"** George Soros, "America's Global Role: Why the Fight for a Worldwide Open Society Begins at Home," *soros.org*, May 27, 2003, http://www.soros.org/resources/articles_publications/articles/americanprospect_20030527.

PAGE 55: **"'willing to put my money where my mouth is'"** Laura Blumenfeld, "Billionaire Soros Takes on Bush," *Washington Post*, November 11, 2003. • **"than would have been possible prior to September 11"** George Soros, *Soros on Globalization* (New York: Public Affairs, 2002). • **"along with billionaires like Progressive Insurance mogul Peter B. Lewis"** David Horowitz and Richard Lawrence Poe, "The Shadow Party: A Three Part Investigative Report," October 6-11, 2005, http://www.richardpoe.com/2005/10/06/part-1-the-shadow-party. • **"group created by West Coast billionaire Wes Boyd"** David Horowitz and Richard Poe, *The Shadow Party: How George Soros, Hillary Clinton, and Sixties Radicals Seized Control of the Democratic Party* (Nashville: Nelson Current, 2006), 93-94. • **"contributed $23,700,000 of his personal funds"** Open Secrets, "Top Individual Contributors to Federally Focused 527 Organizations, 2004 Election Cycle," *opensecrets.org*, March 12, 2012, http://www.opensecrets.org/527s/527indivs.php?cycle=2004.

PAGE 56: **"most exclusive of all the Shadow Party institutions"** Democracy Alliance, "Membership," *democracyalliance.org*, accessed April 16, 2012, http://www.democracyalliance.org/membership. • **"donate at least $200,000 annually"** Matthew Vadum and James Dellinger, "The Democracy Alliance Does America: The Soros-Founded Plutocrats' Club Forms State Chapters," *Capital Research Center Foundation Watch*, December, 2008, https://www.capitalresearch.org/pubs/pdf/v1228145204.pdf. • **"'the netroots and progressive organizations'"** Working for Us, "About Us," *workingforuspac.org*, accessed April 16, 2012, http://web.archive.org/web/20071023221553/http://www.workingforuspac.org/pages/about.

PAGE 57: **"names of what it called the 'top offenders'"** Working for Us, "Frequently Asked Questions," *workingforuspac.org*, accessed April 16, 2012, http://web.archive.org/web/20081122061556/http://www.workingforuspac.org/pages/faq. • **"Mark Ritchie, an activist supported by ACORN"** Matthew Vadum, "SOS in Minnesota," *The American Spectator,* November 7, 2008, http://spectator.org/archives/2008/11/07/sos-in-minnesota. • **"at least 393 convicted felons voted illegally"** John Fund, "Felons for Franken: Illegal Felon Voters May have Handed Democrats 60-Vote Majority," *Wall Street*

Journal, July 14, 2010, http://online.wsj.com/article/SB10001424052748704518904575365063352229680.html. • **"tallies were updated or corrected, Franken benefited"** Matthew Vadum, "Fighting *Franken*stein," *The American Spectator,* April 14, 2009, http://spectator.org/archives/2009/04/14/fighting-frankenstein. • **"announced that he would support Obama"** Maria Bartiromo, "George Soros: Chairman Soros Fund," *Business Week,* October 22, 2007, www.businessweek.com/magazine/content/07_43/b4055047.htm.

PAGE 58: "Self-defined revolutionary 'communist' Van Jones" Eliza Strickland, "The New Face of Environmentalism," *East Bay Express,* November 2, 2005, http://www.eastbayexpress.com/gyrobase/the-new-face-ofenvironmentalism/Content?oid=1079539. • **"at the Soros-funded Center for American Progress"** Juliet Eilperin, "Former White House Adviser Van Jones Lands New D.C. Gig at Liberal Think Tank," *Washington Post,* February 24, 2010, http://www.washingtonpost.com/wp-dyn/content/article/2010/02/23/AR2010022304889.html.

PAGE 59: "and the League of Conservation Voters" "Carol M. Browner," *topics.nytimes.com,* January 24, 2011, http://topics.nytimes.com/top/reference/timestopics/people/b/carol_m_browner/index.html. • **"appointed to the Obama Economic Recovery Advisory Board"** Chris Cillizza, "Anna Burger to Leave SEIU, Change to Win," *The Fix* blog at *washingtonpost.com,* http://voices.washingtonpost.com/thefix/democratic-party/anna-burger-to-leave-seiu-chan.html. • **"named 'safe school czar'"** Maxim Lott, "Critics Assail Obama's 'Safe Schools' Czar, Say He's Wrong Man for the Job," *foxnews.com,* September 23, 2009, http://www.foxnews.com/politics/2009/09/23/critics-assail-obamas-safe-schools-czar-say-hes-wrong-man-job. • **"among the most frequent visitors to the White House"** Susan Davis, "SEIU's Stern Tops White House Visitor List," *Washington Wire* blog at *wsj.com,* October 30, 2009, http://blogs.wsj.com/washwire/2009/10/30/seius-stern-tops-white-house-visitor-list. • **"need to provide hundreds of billions of dollars'"** Kerry Picket, "New Book Shows How Soros Set Up and Financially Benefited from '09 Stimulus," *Water Cooler* blog at *washingtontimes.com,* November 14, 2011, http://www.washingtontimes.com/blog/watercooler/2011/nov/14/picket-new-book-shows-how-soros-set-and-financiall. • **"from several hundred to several thousand more dollars each year"** Dangelo Gore, "Cap-and-Trade Cost Inflation," *factcheck.org,* May 28, 2009, http://www.factcheck.org/2009/05/cap-and-trade-cost-inflation. • **"admitting that it 'will be painful'"** Robert Mackey and Tom Zeller, Jr. "George Soros on the Clean-Energy Economy," *Green* blog at *nytimes.com,* October 14, 2008, http://green.blogs.nytimes.com/2008/10/14/george-soros-on-the-green-energy-economy. • **"he replied simply, 'Yes'"** Robert Mackey and Tom Zeller, Jr. "George Soros on the Clean-Energy Economy," *Green* blog at *nytimes.com,* October 14, 2008, http://green.blogs.nytimes.com/2008/10/14/george-soros-on-the-green-energy-economy. • **"they would have to retrofit their operations"** Kerry Picket, "EPA Imposes Obama's Cap and Trade Regs – Energy Prices 'Skyrocket'" *Water Cooler* blog at *washingtontimes.com,* August 20, 2011, http://www.washingtontimes.com/blog/watercooler/2011/aug/20/picket-obama-08-energy-prices-will-skyrocket-under. • **"a favorite of Obama's 'regulatory czar'"** Jonathan Weisman and Jess Bravin, "Obama's Regulatory Czar Likely to Set a New Tone," *Wall Street Journal,* January 8, 2009, http://online.wsj.com/article/SB123138051682263203.html. • **"proponent of 'distributive justice'"** Eric A. Posner and Cass R. Sunstein, "Climate Change Justice" (working paper, University of Chicago Law School, Chicago, IL, August 2007).

PAGE 60: "through climate policy than through direct foreign aid'" Eric A. Posner and Cass R. Sunstein, "Climate Change Justice" (working paper, University of Chicago Law School, Chicago, IL, August 2007), 19.

PAGE 61: "It's just right there. I'm telling you'" morgenr, "The Public Plan Deception – It's Not About Choice," *youtube.com,* May 20, 2009, http://www.youtube.com/watch?v=zZ-6ebku3_E. • **"victims turning persecutors'"** George Soros, *The Bubble of American Supremacy: The Costs of Bush's War in Iraq* (New York: PublicAffairs, 2004). • **"bringing Hamas into the peace process'"** George Soros, "On Israel, America, and Aipac," *The New York Review of Books,* April 12, 2007, http://www.nybooks.com/articles/archives/2007/apr/12/on-israel-america-and-aipac. • **"organization**

overwhelmingly made up of Democrats'" Jennifer Rubin, "AIPAC's Chief: Obama Is Wrong about a Bunch of Stuff," *Right Turn* blog at *washingtonpost.com*, March 5, 2012, http://www.washingtonpost.com/blogs/right-turn/post/aipacs-chief-obama-is-wrong-about-a-bunch-of-stuff/2012/03/05/gIQAUlfmsR_blog.html. • "'new direction for American policy in the Middle East'" Jstreet.org, "Privacy Policy," accessed April 17, 2012, http://jstreet.org/privacy_policy.

PAGE 62: "'been an obstacle to peace'" JStreet.org, "Settlements," *jstreet.org*, accessed April 17, 2012, http://jstreet.org/page/settlements. • "objected to Jewish settlements in Jerusalem" Mark Landler and Ethan Bronner, "In Curt Exchange, U.S. Faults Israel on Housing," *New York Times*, November 9, 2010, http://www.nytimes.com/2010/11/10/world/middleeast/10jerusalem.html. • "given a total of $750,000 to J Street" Eli Lake, Soros Revealed as Funder of Liberal Jewish American Lobby," *Washington Times*, September 24, 2010, http://www.washingtontimes.com/news/2010/sep/24/soros-funder-liberal-jewish-american-lobby. • "'change is too sudden and carries too many risks'" George Soros, "Why Obama has to get Egypt Right," *georgesoros.com*, February 3, 2011, http://www.georgesoros.com/articles-essays/entry/why_obama_has_to_get_egypt_right.

PAGE 63: "'at the hand of the believers [i.e., Muslims]'" Sheik Yousuf Al-Qaradhawi, "Allah Willing, the Next Time Will Be at the Hand of the Believers," *memritv.org*, January 30, 2009, http://www.memritv.org/clip_transcript/en/2005.htm. • "'or the sole representative of the Jewish community'" George Soros, "Why Obama has to get Egypt Right," *georgesoros.com*, February 3, 2011, http://www.georgesoros.com/articles-essays/entry/why_obama_has_to_get_egypt_right. • "statement from the group Faith in Public Life" Marcus Feldman, "Fox Still Won't Acknowledge that Americans Support Insurance Coverage for Contraception," *mediamatters.org*, March 1, 2012, http://mediamatters.org/blog/201203010025. • "co-founded by Jim Wallis" Faith in Public Life, "Background," *faithinpubliclife.org*, accessed April 17, 2012, http://web.archive.org/web/20070106034458/http://www.faithinpubliclife.org/about/background.html.

CHAPTER 4
ECONOMIC TERRORISM
FINANCIAL WEAPONS OF MASS DESTRUCTION

PAGE 66: "'aware of the lines in their own hands'" Kevin Freeman, "The Weapons of Our Warfare," *humanevents.com*, January 18, 2012, http://www.humanevents.com/article.php?id=48871.

PAGE 67: "global economy had lost close to $50 trillion" Kevin Hechtkopf, "Summers: $50 Trillion In Global Wealth Has Been Erased," *EconWatch* blog at *cbsnews.com*, March 13, 2009, http://www.cbsnews.com/8301-503983_162-4863891-503983.html. • "compelling evidence of outside manipulation" Bill Gertz, "Financial Terrorism Suspected in 2008 Economic Crash: Pentagon Study Sees Element," *Washington Times*, February 28, 2011, http://www.washingtontimes.com/news/2011/feb/28/financial-terrorism-suspected-in-08-economic-crash. • "'Nobody wants to go there'" Bill Gertz, "Financial Terrorism Suspected in 2008 Economic Crash: Pentagon Study Sees Element," *Washington Times*, February 28, 2011, http://www.washingtontimes.com/news/2011/feb/28/financial-terrorism-suspected-in-08-economic-crash. • "how our enemies might harm our economy" Kevin D. Freeman, *Secret Weapon: How Economic Terrorism Brought Down the U.S. Stock Market and Why "It Can Happen Again"* (Washington, D.C.: Regnery Publishing, Inc., 2012), 180.

PAGE 68: "money, livestock, land, and possessions for the food Joseph had stored" Dr. Gary North, "Was Joseph an Immoral Ruler?" *Biblical Economics Today* 14, no. 2 (Feb./March 1992), http://www.garynorth.com/freebooks/docs/a_pdfs/newslet/bet/9202.pdf. • "Napoleon was also a big fan of economic weaponry" Tor Egil Førland, "The History of Economic Warfare: International Law, Effectiveness, Strategies," *Journal of Peace Research* 30, no. 2 (May 1993) 151-162. • "'chain reaction that eventually led to the attack on Pearl Harbor" Winston S. Churchill, *The Second World War:*

The Grand Alliance, Volume 3 (Boston: Houghton Mifflin Company, 1950) 426-427. • **"counterfeited British currency in the hopes of destroying their economy"** Andreas Schroeder, *Scams!: True Stories From the Edge* (Toronto: Annick Press Ltd., 2004) 72–87; Larry Allen, *The Encyclopedia of Money* (Santa Barbara: ABC-CLIO LLC, 2009), 306. • **"if they did not withdraw their troops from the Suez Canal"** James P. Hubbard, *The United States and the End of British Colonial Rule in Africa, 1941-1968* (Jefferson, NC: McFarland & Company, Inc., 2010) 153–54. • **"oil embargo against the U.S. and Israel in 1973"** U.S. Department of State, Office of the Historian "OPEC Oil Embargo, 1973-1974," *Milestones:1969-1976* in *history.state.gov*, accessed April 6, 2012, http://history.state. gov/milestones/1969-1976/OPEC. • **"break the 'Evil Empire' of the Soviet Union"** Peter Schweizer, *Victory: The Reagan Administration's Secret Strategy That Hastened the Collapse of the Soviet Union* (New York: Atlantic Monthly Press, 1996), xviii. • **"short the British pound and 'break the Bank of England'"** David Litterick, "Billionaire who broke the Bank of England," *The Daily Telegraph*, September 13, 2002, http://www.telegraph.co.uk/finance/2773265/Billionaire-who-broke-the-Bank-of-England.html. • **"North Koreans have been counterfeiting"** David Rose, "North Korea's Dollar Store," *Vanity Fair*, August 5, 2009, http://www.vanityfair.com/politics/features/2009/09/office-39-200909.

PAGE 69: "economic warfare approach against Iran" Pepe Escobar, "US Wants SWIFT War On Iran," *Middle East* blog at *atimes.com*, February 17, 2012, http://www.atimes.com/atimes/Middle_East/ NB17Ak04.html. • **"our national debt could be extinguished within a decade"** "President Clinton: The United States on Track to Pay Off the Debt by End of the Decade," *clinton4nara.gov*, December 28, 2000, http://clinton4.nara.gov/WH/new/html/Fri_Dec_29_151111_2000.html. • **"'Unrestricted Warfare'"** Col. Qiao Liang and Col. Wang Xiangsui, *Unrestricted Warfare: China's Master Plan to Destroy America* (Panama City: Pan American Publishing Company, 2002). • **"'slaves to technology in [our] thinking'"** Col. Qiao Liang and Col. Wang Xiangsui, *Unrestricted Warfare: China's Master Plan to Destroy America* (Panama City: Pan American Publishing Company, 2002), 15. • **"'in the ranks of new concept weapons'"** Col. Qiao Liang and Col. Wang Xiangsui, *Unrestricted Warfare: China's Master Plan to Destroy America* (Panama City: Pan American Publishing Company, 2002), 16.

PAGE 70: "'military thinking and the methods of operation'" Col. Qiao Liang and Col. Wang Xiangsui, *Unrestricted Warfare: China's Master Plan to Destroy America* (Panama City: Pan American Publishing Company, 2002), 122. • **"'that George Soros is not a financial terrorist'"** Col. Qiao Liang and Col. Wang Xiangsui, *Unrestricted Warfare: China's Master Plan to Destroy America* (Panama City: Pan American Publishing Company, 2002), 36. • **"'rather, it will be George Soros'"** Col. Qiao Liang and Col. Wang Xiangsui, *Unrestricted Warfare: China's Master Plan to Destroy America* (Panama City: Pan American Publishing Company, 2002), 39.

PAGE 71: "'social panic, street riots, and a political crisis'" Col. Qiao Liang and Col. Wang Xiangsui, *Unrestricted Warfare: China's Master Plan to Destroy America* (Panama City: Pan American Publishing Company, 2002), 122-123. • **"the Chinese currently holds a staggering $3 trillion in foreign reserves"** "China's Foreign Exchange Reserves, 1977-2011: Foreign-Exchange Reserves Reached US $3.2 Trillion in December 2011," *chinability.com*, accessed April 7, 2012, http://www.chinability.com/ Reserves.htm. • **"(more than $1 trillion by China)"** SWF Institute, "Sovereign Wealth Fund Rankings," *swfinstitute.org,* accessed April 7 2012, http://www.swfinstitute.org/fund-rankings. • **"this wealth has been accumulated since the year 2000"** Tina Aridas, "Largest Sovereign Wealth Funds (SWF) – 2010 Ranking," *gfmag.com*, http://www.gfmag.com/tools/global-database/economic-data/10300-largest-sovereign-wealth-funds-swf-2010-ranking.html (accessed April 7, 2012). • **"'Why then would they shy away from economic warfare?'"** Kevin D. Freeman, *Secret Weapon: How Economic Terrorism Brought Down the U.S. Stock Market and Why It Can Happen Again* (Washington, D.C.: Regnery Publishing, Inc., 2012), 210. • **"vice chairman of the Central Military Commission"** Lev Navrozov, "China's Gen Chi: U.S. Easily Defeated," *newsmax.com*, December 10, 2009, http://www.newsmax. com/navrozov/china-haotian-chi/2009/12/10/id/339799.

PAGE 72: "it was estimated that he had 'several billion' dollars" richwebnews, "Gaddafi's Libya

Wealth Estimated in Several Billions," *allvoices.com*, February 23, 2011, http://www.allvoices. com/contributed-news/8281804-gaddafis-libya-wealth-estimated-in-several-billions. • **"$200 billion in Western markets"** Paul Richter, "Gaddafi Salted Away About $200 Billion," *Sidney Morning Herald*, October 22, 2011, http://news.smh.com.au/breaking-news-world/gaddafi-salted-away-about-200-billion-20111022-1md9z.html. • **"four times the estimated wealth of Warren Buffett"** "The World's Billionaires," *Forbes.com*, http://www.forbes.com/profile/warren-buffett, accessed April 24, 2012. • **"When prices collapsed, so did their economy"** Peter Schweizer, *Victory: The Reagan Administration's Secret Strategy That Hastened the Collapse of the Soviet Union* (New York: Atlantic Monthly Press, 1996), xviii. • **"As the world's largest consumer of oil, the United States"** "The World's Top Consumers and Producers of Oil," *cnn.com*, June 3, 2008, http://www.cnn.com/2008/ US/06/02/oil.map/index.html. • **"'adds almost $60 billion to annual consumer bills'"** Ross DeVol, "The $110 Effect: What Higher Gas Prices Could Really Do to the Economy," *theatlantic.com*, March 13, 2012, http://www.theatlantic.com/business/archive/2012/03/the-110-effect-what-higher-gas-prices-could-really-do-to-the-economy/254386/. • **"$147.50 in mid-2008"** "Timeline: Half a Century of Oil Price Volatility," *reuters.com*, November 20, 2008, http://www.reuters.com/article/2008/11/20/us-oil-prices-idUKTRE4AJ3ZR20081120. • **"estimated $1 trillion in additional dollars was paid by the West"** Kevin D. Freeman, *Secret Weapon: How Economic Terrorism Brought Down the U.S. Stock Market and Why It Can Happen Again* (Washington, D.C.: Regnery Publishing, Inc., 2012), 73.

PAGE 73: "'warranted by ordinary commercial transactions'" Kevin D. Freeman, *Secret Weapon: How Economic Terrorism Brought Down the U.S. Stock Market and Why It Can Happen Again* (Washington, D.C.: Regnery Publishing, Inc., 2012), 73. • **"'They don't know who holds what positions'"** "Did Speculation Fuel Oil Price Swings?" *60 Minutes*, April 14, 2009, http://www.cbsnews. com/video/watch/?id=4713382n. **"'the weapon of oil or Silah al Naft'"** Walid Phares, "OPEC War Against America's Economic Independence?" *counterterrorismblog.org*, October 10, 2008, http:// counterterrorismblog.org/2008/10/opec_war_against_americas_econ.php. • **"'absolute necessity to use that weapon'"** Walid Phares, "OPEC's Heavy Hand" *humanevents.com*, October 10, 2008, http:// counterterrorismblog.org/2008/10/opec_war_against_americas_econ.php. • **"Iran believes this will eventually spell the end for the dollar"** Sharmine Narwani, "How Iran Changed the World," *al-akhbar. com*, February 17, 2012, http://english.al-akhbar.com/node/4308. • **"the rest of the world may agree"** Garry White, "Iran Presses Ahead with Dollar Attack," *The Daily Telegraph*, February 12, 2012, http:// www.telegraph.co.uk/finance/commodities/9077600/Iran-presses-ahead-with-dollar-attack.html. • **"'force down the price of a security or commodity by sustained selling'"** *dictionary.com*, "Bear Raid," http://dictionary.reference.com/browse/bear+raid (accessed April 8, 2012).

PAGE 74: "'once in 4 billion years'" Vedant Misra, Marco Lagi, and Yaneer Bar-Yam, "Evidence of Market Manipulation in the Financial Crisis" (report, New England Complex Systems Institute, Cambridge, MA, January 3, 2012), http://necsi.edu/research/economics/bearraid.pdf. • **"'hitting the U.S. economy through all possible means'"** James Pethokoukis, "Al Qaeda's Failed War on the U.S. Economy," *Money* blog at *usnews.com*, September 11, 2008, http://money.usnews.com/money/ blogs/capital-commerce/2008/09/11/al-qaedas-failed-war-on-the-us-economy. • **"'the destruction of the American economy'"** James Pethokoukis, "Al Qaeda's Failed War on the U.S. Economy," *Money* blog at *usnews.com*, September 11, 2008, http://money.usnews.com/money/blogs/capital-commerce/2008/09/11/al-qaedas-failed-war-on-the-us-economy.

PAGE 75: "'through all possible means.'" James Pethokoukis, "Al Qaeda's Failed War on the U.S. Economy," *Money* blog at *usnews.com*, September 11, 2008, http://money.usnews.com/money/blogs/ capital-commerce/2008/09/11/al-qaedas-failed-war-on-the-us-economy.

PAGE 76: "'the end of our economic system and our political system as we know it'" "Rep. Kanjorski: $550 Billion Disappeared in 'Electronic Run on the Banks'," *liveleak.com*, February 7, 2009, http:// www.liveleak.com/view?i=ca2_1234032281. • **"perpetrators aren't always caught"** Zachary A. Goldfarb, "SEC Faults Its Handling Of Tips on Short Sales," *Washington Post*, March 19, 2009, http://

www.washingtonpost.com/wp-dyn/content/article/2009/03/18/AR2009031803459.html. • **"linked to naked short selling"** Gary Matsumoto, "Naked Short Sales Hint Fraud in Bringing Down Lehman (Update 1)," *bloomberg.com*, March 19, 2009, http://www.bloomberg.com/apps/news?pid=newsarchive &sid=aB1jlqmFOTCA.

PAGE 77: **"could tank major companies"** Andy Kessler, "Have We Seen the Last of the Bear Raids?: The Short-Sellers Probably Saved Us Five to 10 Years of Poor Bank Earnings," *Wall Street Journal*, March 26, 2009, http://online.wsj.com/article/SB123802165000541773.html. • **"financial weapons of mass destruction"** James B. Kelleher, "Buffett's 'Time Bomb' Goes off on Wall Street,"*reuters.com*, September 18, 2008, http://www.reuters.com/article/2008/09/18/us-derivatives-credit-idUSN1837154020080918. • **"also pumping trillions of dollars into the system"** David Goldman, "CNNMoney.com's Bailout Tracker," *cnn.com*, November 16, 2009, http://money.cnn.com/news/storysupplement/economy/bailouttracker. • **"U.S. dollar as the world's reserve currency"** Keith B. Richburg "China, Other Developing BRICS Nations Seek Change in Global Economic Order," *Washington Post*, April 14, 2011, http://www.washingtonpost.com/world/china-other-developing-brics-nations-seek-change-in-global-economic-order/2011/04/14/AFarMgdD_story.html. • **"infiltrate...the stock market and several key utilities"** "Napolitano: Hackers 'Came Close to Shutting Down Critical Infrastructure," *homelandsecuritynewswire.com*, October 28, 2011, http://www. homelandsecuritynewswire.com/napolitano-hackers-came-close-shutting-down-critical-infrastructure. • **"hackers to infiltrate...NASA"** Defense Systems Staff, "IG Finds more than 5,400 Cybersecurity Incidents at NASA," *defensesystems.com*, March 6, 2012, http://defensesystems.com/articles/2012/03/06/agg-nasa-cyberattack.aspx.

PAGE 78: **"likely a single group acting on behalf of a government"** John Ribeiro, "McAfee on a Mammoth Cyberattack, Hackers Compromised 72 Organizations Since 2006," *networkworld.com*, August 3, 2011, http://www.networkworld.com/news/2011/080311-mcafee-hackers-compromised-72-organizations.html. • **"including our satellite systems"** Melanie Eversley, "'Suspicious Events' with Satellite Confirmed," *USA Today*, October 28, 2011, http://content.usatoday.com/communities/ondeadline/post/2011/10/nasa-confirms-satellites-were-hacked/1. • **"plans for their own advantage"** Tom Gjelten, "U.S. Not Afraid to Say It: China's the Cyber Bad Guy," *npr.org*, February 18, 2012, http://www.npr.org/2012/02/18/147077148/chinas-hacking-of-u-s-remains-a-top-concern. • **"disseminated it to anyone in the world"** *US v. Sergey Aleynikov*, 737 F.Supp.2nd 173 (2010). • **"convicted of stealing trade secrets"** Patricia Hurtado, "Ex-Goldman Programmer Freed After Theft Conviction Thrown Out," *bloomberg.com*, February 18, 2012, http://www.bloomberg.com/news/2012-02-17/ex-goldman-programmer-s-conviction-overturned-on-appeal.html. • **"a 'disruptive scheme' to surgically target the American economy"** Robert Wenzel, "Paulson: Russia Tried to Get China to Blow Up Fannie and Freddie," *economicpolicyjournal.com*, January 29, 2010, http://www. economicpolicyjournal.com/2010/01/paulson-russia-tried-to-get-china-to.html. • **"emergency authority to prop up these companies"** Michael McKee and Alex Nicholson, "Paulson Says Russia Urged China to Dump Fannie, Freddie Bonds," *bloomberg.com*, January 29, 2010, http://www.bloomberg.com/apps/news?pid=newsarchive&sid=afbSjYv3v814. • **"held nearly $500 billion of those bonds, did not sell"** Aaron Back, "Much Ado in China About Fannie and Freddie," *China Real Time* blog at *wsj.com*, February 12, 2011, http://blogs.wsj.com/chinarealtime/2011/02/12/much-ado-in-china-about-fannie-and-freddie.

PAGE 79: **"closure of the file-sharing website Megaupload"** Rebecca Seales, "'This Is Just the Beginning: Hacking Group Anonymous Takes Over Greek Ministry of Justice Website and Warns Other Governments Are in Its Sights," *Daily Mail*, February 3, 2012, http://www.dailymail.co.uk/news/article-2095950/This-just-beginning-Hacking-group-Anonymous-launches-cyber-attack-Greek-Ministry-Justice.html. • **"This is JUST the BEGINNING"** Rebecca Seales, "'This Is Just the Beginning: Hacking Group Anonymous Takes Over Greek Ministry of Justice Website and Warns Other Governments Are in Its Sights," *Daily Mail*, February 3, 2012, http://www.dailymail.co.uk/news/

article-2095950/This-just-beginning-Hacking-group-Anonymous-launches-cyber-attack-Greek-Ministry-Justice.html. • **"'Yes, yes, yes' he says, almost gleefully"** John Arlidge, "George Soros on the Coming U.S. Class War," *Newsweek*, January 23, 2012, http://www.thedailybeast.com/newsweek/2012/01/22/george-soros-on-the-coming-u-s-class-war.html.

PAGE 80: "accused of short-selling American stocks" Adam Cohen, "How Bin Laden Funds His Network" *Time*, September 23, 2001, http://www.time.com/time/magazine/article/0,9171,175972,00.html. • **"'reaches $640 billion of losses'"** Daveed Gartenstein-Ross, "Death by a Thousand Cuts," *Foreign Policy*, November 23, 2010, http://www.foreignpolicy.com/articles/2010/11/23/death_by_a_thousand_cuts. • **"'enrolled in doctoral programs'"** Peter Bergen and Swati Pandey, "The Madrassa Myth" *New York Times*, June 14, 2005, http://www.nytimes.com/2005/06/14/opinion/14bergen.html. • **"something of an egomaniac"** Patrick Roberts, "Bin Laden had a Donald Trump-Sized Ego but Looked Like a Broken Old Man," *Irish Central*, May 8, 2011, http://www.irishcentral.com/story/news/people_and_politics/bin-laden-had-a-donald-trump--sized-ego-but-looked-like-a-broken-old-man-121462604.html. • **"did not list 'concrete targets'"** "Al-Qaeda Plotting Against European Economy," *Borneo Bulletin*, August 26, 2011.

PAGE 81: "'bin Laden boasted of it on the world stage'" Daveed Gartenstein-Ross, "Don't Get Cocky, America: Al Qaeda Is Still Deadly Without Osama bin Laden," *Foreign Policy*, May 2, 2011, http://www.foreignpolicy.com/articles/2011/05/02/dont_get_cocky_america. • **"'slaves to technology in their thinking'"** Qiao Liang and Wang Xiangsui, *Unrestricted Warfare: China's Master Plan to Destroy America* (Los Angeles: Pan American Publishing Company, 2002).

Chapter 5
THE AMERICAN DREAM IS A LIE

PAGE 84: "'more than anything else, is the American Dream.'" Arthur Edson, "The American Dream—Home of Your Own," *The Associated Press*, August 27, 1947, http://bit.ly/Ko5R7u.

PAGE 86: "'have their basic needs met'" Madonna Gauding, "Occupy Wall Street Redefines the American Dream," *OccasionalPlanet.org*, November 26, 2011, http://www.occasionalplanet.org/2011/11/26/occupy-wall-street-redefines-the-american-dream. • **"'individual farm ownership'"** "'Farm Dream' Plan Urged by Roosevelt," *Hartford Courant*, February 17, 1937. • **"'work and become great'"** Ira Wolfert, "How an Immigrant Boy Made Way to Place on Supreme Court Bench," *Milwaukee Journal*, January 8, 1939. • **"won the Pulitzer Prize ten years earlier"** Pulitzer.org, "1922 Winners," *Pulitzer.org*, http://www.pulitzer.org/awards/1922 (accessed March 31, 2012). • **"The Epic of America"** Jim Cullen, *The American Dream: A Short History of an Idea that Shaped a Nation* (New York: Oxford University Press, 2003), 4. • **"'circumstances of birth or position'"** James Truslow Adams, *The Epic of America* (Boston: Little, Brown & Co., 1931), 374.

PAGE 87: "'imperfectly even among ourselves'" Jim Cullen, *The American Dream: A Short History of an Idea that Shaped a Nation* (New York: Oxford University Press, 2003), 374-75. • **"is the American dream'"** Arthur Edsen, "The American Dream--Home of Your Own," *Dubuque Telegraph-Herald*, August 27, 1947. • **"'rising wage scale' of average workers"** James Truslow Adams, *The Epic of America* (Boston: Little, Brown & Co., 1931), 379. • **"'observer of the political scene'"** Merrill D. Peterson, *The Jefferson Image in the American Mind* (New York: Oxford University Press, 1960), 373. • **"'was his supporting theory'"** Elizabeth A. Brennan and Elizabeth C. Clarage, *Who's Who of Pulitzer Prize Winners* (Phoenix: Oryx Press, 1999), 281.

PAGE 88: "'of the institutions he creates'" "Ike Warns U.S. Dream May Turn into Nightmare," *St. Petersburg Times*, October 25, 1949. • **"'good and evil you shall not eat'"** 1 Genesis 2:16-17 (New Revised Standard Version). • **"'Republican House and Senate'"** "Text of Nixon's Address to the

Republican Club Dinner Here; Cites Nation's Prosperity Puts Case in Nutshell Calls Democrats Reactionary to Keep Individuals Free on Racial Minorities Praises 'Practical Leaders'" *New York Times*, February 14, 1956, http://query.nytimes.com/gst/abstract.html?res=F50612F93F58157B93C6A81789D 85F428585F9. • **"'all men are created equal'"** Jim Cullen, *The American Dream: A Short History of an Idea that Shaped a Nation* (New York: Oxford University Press, 2003), 126. • **"'by the peddlers of despair'"** "'Peddlers of Despair,'" *Eugene Register-Guard*, October 15, 1964.

PAGE 89: "'for the purpose of increasing what he has'" Jim Powell, "Alexis de Tocqueville: How People Gain Liberty and Lose It," *The Freeman* 46, no. 7 (July 1996), http://www.thefreemanonline. org/featured/alexis-de-tocqueville-how-people-gain-liberty-and-lose-it/. • **"'Life, Liberty and the pursuit of Happiness'"** John R. Vile, *The Constitutional Convention of 1787: A Comprehensive Encyclopedia of American Founding,* Volume 2 (Santa Barbara, CA: ABC-CLIO, Inc., 2005), 518. • **"'whatever God intends he should become'"** Ronald Reagan, *The Creative Society: Some Comments on Problems Facing America* (New York: Devin-Adair, 1968), 41. • **"'brokerage firm that bears his name'"** Christopher Gardner, "Biography," *ChrisGardnerMedia.com*, http://www.chrisgardnermedia. com/about/bio (accessed March 31, 2012).

PAGE 90: "'Hyper-Charge the American Dream Movement'" Campaign for America's Future, "2011 Take Back the American Dream Conference Agenda," *ourfuture.org*, http://www.ourfuture.org/ conference/agenda (accessed April 1, 2012). • **"'because of economic problems'"** "The American Dream: Many Have Lost Faith, Study Reveals," *St. Petersburg Evening Independent*, March 1, 1978. • **"'is becoming just that—a dream'"** Bob Ferri, "Literally the American Dream," *Portsmouth Daily Times*, January 12, 1982. • **"'the home in which they grew up'"** "American Dream Is Still Strong," *Spartanburg Herald-Journal*, May 23, 1984. • **"'the poor get poorer'"** "American Dream Fading for Young as Rich Get Richer, and Poor Get Poorer," *Salt Lake City Deseret News*, September 5-6, 1988. • **"'tax the wealthy'"** Michael Graham, "Will 'Generation Gimme' Ever Work for the American Dream," *MichaelGraham.com*, December 2, 2011, http://michaelgraham.com/archives/will-ldquo-generation-gimme-rdquo-ever-work-for-the-american-dream.

PAGE 91: "'financial security…on top'" Michael F. Ford, "Five Myths About the American Dream," *Washington Post*, January 6, 2011, http://www.washingtonpost.com/opinions/five-myths-about-the-american-dream/2011/11/10/gIQAP4t0eP_story.html. • **"'money is a worthy end in itself'"** Michael F. Ford, "Five Myths About the American Dream," *Washington Post*, January 6, 2011, http://www. washingtonpost.com/opinions/five-myths-about-the-american-dream/2011/11/10/gIQAP4t0eP_story.html. • **"'only 31% of the population overall'"** Xavier University Center for the Study of the American Dream, "The American Dream: The Second Annual State of the American Dream Survey" (survey findings, Xavier University, March 2011), http://www.xavier.edu/americandream/programs/documents/ Final-American-Dream-Survey-PowerPoint.pdf.

PAGE 92: "'God-given ability will take you'" Jennifer L. Hochschild, *Facing Up to the American Dream: Race, Class, and the Soul of the Nation* (Princeton: Princeton University Press, 1995), 18. • **"'success of our great nation'"** Nancy Pelosi, interviewed by Brian Wingfield, "Nancy Pelosi on the American Dream," *Forbes.com*, March 22, 2007, http://www.forbes.com/2007/03/20/nancy-pelosi-dream-oped-cx_bw_dream0307_0322pelosi.html. • **"'meaning of the 'American Dream'?'"** Max Frankel, "'Brain' Counts Russian Queries; U.S. Cigarette Price Tops List," *New York Times,* August 5, 1959. • **"'Obama team could be bringing it to an end'"** Star Parker, "Parker: The End of the American Dream," *ScrippsNews.com*, February 20, 2009, http://www.scrippsnews.com/node/41099. • **"'those at the bottom of society'"** Nicolaus Mills, "American Dream Is About Equality, Not Wealth," *CNN. com*, July 8, 2011, http://articles.cnn.com/2011-07-08/opinion/mills.debt.dream_1_american-dream-james-truslow-adams-puritans. • **"'universal suffrage and education'"** Max Frankel, "'Brain' Counts Russian Queries; U.S. Cigarette Price Tops List," *New York Times,* August 5, 1959. • **"'the American nightmare'"** Fox News, "Van Jones: Death to the 'Great White Suburbs'," *FoxNews.com*, March 22, 2012, http://nation.foxnews.com/van-jones/2012/03/22/van-jones-death-great-white-suburbs.

Chapter 6
BORDERING ON INSANITY
Drugs, Terrorists, and Murder in Our Backyard

PAGE 96: "'You will be met by an overwhelming response'" Alejandro Martinez-Cabrera, "U.S. Warns Mexican Cartels on Cross-Border Violence," *reuters.com*, January 31, 2011, http://www.reuters.com/article/2011/01/31/us-usa-mexico-napolitano-idUSTRE70U5TB20110131.

PAGE 97: "when bodies are burned or put into buckets of quicklime" "51 Bodies Found at Mexico Dumping Ground," *cbsnews.com*, July 24, 2010, http://www.cbsnews.com/2100-202_162-6709785.html. • **"if the violence crosses some imaginary line"** Alejandro Martinez-Cabrera, "U.S. Warns Mexican Cartels on Cross-Border Violence," *reuters.com*, January 31, 2011, http://www.reuters.com/article/2011/01/31/us-usa-mexico-napolitano-idUSTRE70U5TB20110131.

PAGE 98: "La Nacha controlled much of the Juárez heroin, morphine, and marijuana trade" Elaine Carey and Jose Carlos Cisneros Guzman, "The Daughters of La Nacha: Profiles of Women Traffickers," *NACLA Report on the Americas*, May-June, 2011, https://nacla.org/sites/default/files/A04403025_8.pdf.

PAGE 99: "where he's serving three consecutive life terms" John Lee, "Camarena Figure Gets 3 Life Terms," *Los Angeles Times*, May 9, 1991, http://articles.latimes.com/1991-05-09/local/me-1914_1_honduran-juan-matta-ballesteros.

PAGE 101: "'dangerous cartel operating in Mexico'" Michael Ware, "Los Zetas Called Mexico's Most Dangerous Drug Cartel," *cnn.com*, August 6, 2009, http://articles.cnn.com/2009-08-06/world/mexico.drug.cartels_1_los-zetas-drug-cartels-drug-war?_s=PM:WORLD. • **"'lack the extensive training and discipline of older members'"** Samuel Logan, "Los Zetas: Evolution of a Criminal Organization," *ISN Security Watch,* March 11, 2009, *http://www.isn.ethz.ch/isn/Current-Affairs/Security-Watch-Archive/Detail/?id=97554.*

PAGE 103: "movie piracy in Mexico costs Hollywood at least $590 million annually" Michael White, "Hollywood: Organized Crime Goes to the Movies," *Bloomberg Businessweek*, April 7, 2011, http://www.businessweek.com/magazine/content/11_16/b4224016208623.htm. • **"'with profits reaching $2.2 million a day'"** Lucas Urdaneta, "Familia, 'Pirateria' and the Story of Microsoft's 'CSI' Unit," *insightcrime.org*, February 10, 2011, http://insightcrime.org/insight-latest-news/item/540-microsoft-familia-michoacana-selling-pirated-software. • **"and a calf for up to $20,000"** Liliana Alcántara, "Robo de Ganado, Nuevo Negocio del Crimen," *El Universal*, September 6, 2010, http://www.eluniversal.com.mx/primera/35497.html. • **"seven major tunnels along the San Diego border with Mexico"** Douglas Stanglin, "More Than 32 Tons of Pot Seized in San Diego-Tijuana Tunnel," *USA Today*, November 30, 2011, http://content.usatoday.com/communities/ondeadline/post/2011/11/more-than-32-tons-of-pot-seized-in-border-tunnel-linking-san-diego-and-tijuana.

PAGE 104: "It was also lighted and ventilated" Douglas Stanglin, "More Than 32 Tons of Pot Seized in San Diego-Tijuana Tunnel," *USA Today*, November 30, 2011, http://content.usatoday.com/communities/ondeadline/post/2011/11/more-than-32-tons-of-pot-seized-in-border-tunnel-linking-san-diego-and-tijuana. • **"meet a grisly fate in some Arizona lettuce field"** Peter O'Dowd, "In Risky Twist, Using Ultralight Planes To Drop Drugs," *npr.org*, May 26, 2011, http://www.npr.org/2011/05/26/136644297/in-risky-twist-using-ultralight-plans-to-drop-drugs. • **"made of a plaster and cocaine mixture"** Robin Emmott, "Mexico Drug Smugglers Make Jesus Statue of Cocaine," *reuters.com*, May 30, 2008, http://www.reuters.com/article/2008/05/30/us-mexico-drugs-idUSN3031343320080530. • **"hollowed out and filled with packages of cocaine"** Robin Emmott, "Mexico Finds Cocaine Haul Hidden in Frozen Sharks," *reuters.com*, June 17, 2009, http://www.reuters.com/article/2009/06/17/us-mexico-drugs-idUSN1631193420090617. • **"swallowing dozens of little drug-filled balloons"** Mariano Castillo, "Authorities: Woman Carried 91 Heroin Pellets in Body," *cnn.com*, January 6, 2011, http://articles.cnn.com/2011-01-06/us/michigan.drug.mule_1_heroin-pellets-internal-carriers-cbp-news-release.

PAGE 105: "equipped with lighting and ventilation." "Big Mexican border drug tunnel between San Diego and Tijuana discovered," *The Associated Press*, December 1, 2011, http://www.silive.com/news/index.ssf/2011/12/big_mexican_border_drug_tunnel.html.

PAGE 106: "Juan García Ábrego, is also serving multiple life sentences" Dane Schiller, "Ex-Cartel Boss is Doing Harder Time Now in Feds' Supermax," *Houston Chronicle*, May 18, 2011, http://www.chron.com/news/houston-texas/article/Ex-cartel-boss-is-doing-harder-time-now-in-feds-1690243.php. • **"the Mexican government kept many details surrounding the massacre to themselves"** Gary Moore, "Unraveling Mysteries of Mexico's San Fernando Massacre," *insightcrime.org*, September 19, 2011, http://insightcrime.org/insight-latest-news/item/1583-unravelling-mysteries-of-mexicos-san-fernando-massacre.

PAGE 107: "'an act of terrorism has been committed'" Sylvia Longmire, "Calling Casino Attack In Mexico An 'Act Of Terror': Rhetoric Or Rethinking?" *hstoday.com*, September 1, 2011, http://www.hstoday.us/briefings/correspondents-watch/single-article/calling-casino-attack-in-mexico-an-act-of-terror-rhetoric-or-rethinking/eacdae763fccc24686651bdb4fe41bd6.html. • **"partly blame the United States for the attack"** William Booth, "Mexico Blames US Drug Culture, Guns for Casino Massacre," *Washington Post*, August 26, 2011, http://www.washingtonpost.com/world/americas/calderon-mexico-casino-fire-deaths-act-of-terrorism/2011/08/26/gIQAmnVEgJ_story.html. • **"police department issued a confidential memo"** Tucson Police Department, "International Terrorism Situational Awareness: Hezbollah," Tucson Urban Area security initiative, September 20, 2010, http://publicintelligence.info/AZ-Hezbollah.pdf.

PAGE 108: "help of his cousin, who was a member of Hezbollah" Tucson Police Department, "International Terrorism Situational Awareness: Hezbollah," Tucson Urban Area Security Initiative, September 20, 2010, http://publicintelligence.info/AZ-Hezbollah.pdf. • **"'jeopardize those operations'"** "Terrorist Group Setting Up Operations Near Border," *10news.com*, KGTV, May 4, 2011, http://www.10news.com/news/27780427/detail.html.

PAGE 109: "Middle Eastern terrorist organizations" Sylvia Longmire, "Border Security: Hezbollah Presence in the United States is No Surprise*," hstoday.us*, January 10, 2012, http://www.hstoday.us/focused-topics/border-security/single-article-page/hezbollah-presence-in-the-united-states-is-no-surprise/2e1af4c017be5f75d5a5da67329b6b91.html.

PAGE 110: "assassinate the Saudi Arabian ambassador to the United States" Charlie Savage and Scott Shane, "Iranians Accused of a Plot to Kill Saudis' U.S. Envoy," *New York Times*, October 11, 2011, http://www.nytimes.com/2011/10/12/us/us-accuses-iranians-of-plotting-to-kill-saudi-envoy.html.

PAGE 112: "come from our neighbor to the south" U.S. Department of Justice, National Drug Intelligence Center, *National Drug Threat Assessment 2011*, report, August 2011, http://www.justice.gov/ndic/pubs44/44849/44849p.pdf. • **"long-term drug abuse killed an estimated 37,485 Americans"** Kenneth D. Kochanek and others, "Deaths: Preliminary Data for 2009," *National Vital Statistics Reports*, 59, no. 4 (March 16, 2011), www.cdc.gov/nchs/data/nvsr/nvsr59/nvsr59_04.pdf. • **"largest meth labs ever discovered in the United States"** Andria Simmons, "Half-ton of Meth Seized in Norcross 'Superlab'," *Atlanta Journal-Constitution*, November 30, 2010, http://www.ajc.com/news/gwinnett/half-ton-of-meth-759047.html. • **"creates five pounds of toxic waste"** Foundation for a Drug-Free World "What Is Meth Made from?" *drugfreeworld.org*, accessed April 19, 2012, http://www.drugfreeworld.org/drugfacts/crystalmeth/what-is-meth-made-from.html.

PAGE 113: "discovered in North Carolina, Tennessee, Colorado, and Michigan" Dr. John Gettman, "Marijuana Production in the United States," *Bulletin of Cannabis Reform*, December 2006, http://www.drugscience.org/Archive/bcr2/MJCropReport_2006.pdf. • **"Chequamegon-Nicolet National Forest in northern Wisconsin"** Mark Rockwell, "Mexican Nationals Get 10 years for Marijuana Growing Operations in Wisconsin Forest," *Government Security News*, February 6, 2012, http://www.gsnmagazine.com/node/25582. • **"Sheriffs' deputies, hikers, and hunters have been shot at"** United

States Attorney Benjamin B. Wagner, Eastern District of California, "Lassen County Marijuana Growers Present At Fatal Shootout Sentenced To 15 Years Imprisonment On Drug And Firearms Convictions," press release, January 11, 2012, http://www.justice.gov/usao/cae/news/docs/2011/01-11-11LassenMarijuana.html.

PAGE 114: "'better now than it has ever been.'" Stephanie Condon, "Napolitano: Border Security Better Than Ever," *cbsnews.com*, March 25, 2011, http://www.cbsnews.com/8301-503544_162-20047102-503544.html.

PAGE 115: "'whether perpetrated in Mexico or the U.S.'" Kristin M. Finklea, William J. Krouse, and Mark A. Randol, *Southwest Border Violence: Issues in Identifying and Measuring Spillover Violence*, Congressional Research Service, report for Congress, August 25, 2011, http://www.fas.org/sgp/crs/homesec/R41075.pdf. • **"between cartel members in the United States"** Kristin M. Finklea, William J. Krouse, and Mark A. Randol, *Southwest Border Violence: Issues in Identifying and Measuring Spillover Violence*, Congressional Research Service, report for Congress, August 25, 2011, http://www.fas.org/sgp/crs/homesec/R41075.pdf. • **"'the border is better now than it's ever been'"** Stephanie Condon, "Napolitano: Border Security Better Than Ever," *cbsnews.com*, March 25, 2011, http://www.cbsnews.com/8301-503544_162-20047102-503544.html.

Page 116: "She also says that overall violent crime is down across the southwest" Stephanie Condon, "Napolitano: Border Security Better Than Ever," *cbsnews.com*, March 25, 2011, http://www.cbsnews.com/8301-503544_162-20047102-503544.html. • **"'violence on the other side of the border'"** Nina Mandell, "Woman in El Paso Struck by Stray Bullet That May Have Come from Ciudad Juarez, Mexico," *NY Daily News,* February 22, 2012, http://articles.nydailynews.com/2012-02-22/news/31088760_1_stray-bullet-juarez-police-ciudad-juarez. • **"he had sold it and kept the money"** Laurie Merrell, "Chandler Beheading Tied to Mexican Drug Cartel," *Arizona Republic*, March 2, 2011, http://bit.ly/IO4DUJ. • **"grandfather owed a cartel over one million dollars"** Jeff German, "Suspect Pleads Guilty in Drug Cartel Kidnapping," *Las Vegas Review-Journal*, January 18, 2011, http://www.lvrj.com/news/suspect-pleads-guilty-in-drug-cartel-kidnapping-114175549.html. • **"throats slit in northern Alabama by men working for the Gulf cartel"** Pauline Arrillaga, "Grisly Slayings Brings Mexican Drug War to US," *Arizona Republic*, April 18, 2009, http://www.azcentral.com/news/articles/2009/04/18/20090418drugwar-fightathome18-ON.html. • **"while responding to a cartel-related kidnapping call"** Lynn Brezosky, "Hidalgo Sheriff Says Shooting 'Spillover' from Drug War," *San Antonio Express-News*, November 4, 2011, http://www.mysanantonio.com/news/article/Hidalgo-sheriff-has-no-doubt-deputy-s-shooting-2245516.php. • **"happened on a McAllen, Texas, highway"** "Sources: Fatal Gunshots on McAllen Expressway Point to Gulf Cartel," *Monitor*, September 27, 2011, http://www.themonitor.com/articles/mcallen-55174-point-expressway.html. • **"near the Hollywood sign"** Veronica M. Cruz, "Link Probed Between LA Body Parts, Local Corpse," *Arizona Daily Star*, January 20, 2012, http://azstarnet.com/news/local/crime/link-probed-between-la-body-parts-local-corpse/article_5040a9ab-1435-5824-b363-2e52c2d2adeb.html.

Page 118: "from the branches to mark their conquests" Mariela Rosario, "'Rape Trees' Found Along US Southern Border," *Latina*, March 11, 2009, http://www.latina.com/lifestyle/news-politics/rape-trees-found-along-southern-us-border. • **"are sexually abused in some way"** Mariela Rosario, "The Steep Price of Immigration for Latin American Women," *Latina*, March 17, 2009, http://www.latina.com/lifestyle/news-politics/steep-price-immigration-latin-american-women. • **"fifty-one Guatemalan nationals, including six children"** "More Than 50 People Found in Phoenix Drop House," Associated Press, June 29, 2010, http://www.newsvine.com/_news/2010/06/29/4584646-more-than-50-people-found-in-phoenix-drop-house. • **"broken ribs, cuts, and bruises"** Jennifer Thomas and Jared Dillingham, "Illegal immigrants tortured in drop house," *azfamily.com*, December 8, 2011, http://www.azfamily.com/news/local/18-people-found-inside-an-Avondale-drop-house-135242228.html.

PAGE 119: "from persecution by another group" Alejandro Martínez-Cabrera, "Law Inhibits Many Mexican Asylum Cases," *El Paso Times*," July 31, 2011, http://www.elpasotimes.com/news/ci_18587920.

PAGE 120: "More than forty-seven thousand people have been killed" Damien Cave, "Mexico Updates Death Toll in Drug War to 47,515, but Critics Dispute the Data," *New York Times*, January 11, 2012, http://www.nytimes.com/2012/01/12/world/americas/mexico-updates-drug-war-death-toll-but-critics-dispute-data.html.

Chapter 7
THE NEW POLICE STATE
Big Brother Is All Grown Up

PAGE 126: "'It has a vaguely Teutonic ring'" Peggy Noonan, "Rudy's Duty," Opinion Journal, *wsj.com*, June 14, 2002, http://www.peggynoonan.com/article.php?article=149. • **"the act has been misused on numerous occasions"** David Johnston, "Justice Department Says F.B.I. Misused Patriot Act," *nytimes.com*, March 9, 2007, http://www.nytimes.com/2007/03/09/washington/09cnd-fbi.html.

PAGE 127: "would have caused it to expire" Jim Abrams, "Patriot Act Extension Signed By Obama," Huff Post Politics, *huffingtonpost.com*, May 27, 2011, http://www.huffingtonpost.com/2011/05/27/patriot-act-extension-signed-obama-autopen_n_867851.html • **"ability to monitor individual actions"** Jim Abrams, "Patriot Act Extension Signed By Obama," Huff Post Politics, *The Huffington Post* online, May 27, 2011, http://www.huffingtonpost.com/2011/05/27/patriot-act-extension-signed-obama-autopen_n_867851.html. • **"'temporary government program.'"** Lanny Ebenstein, *Milton Friedman: A Biography* (New York: Palgrave MacMillian), 194. • **"dropped at the first opportunity"** Gail Russell Chaddock, "Patriot Act: Three Controversial Provisions that Congress Voted to Keep," *csmonitor.com*, May 27, 2011, http://www.csmonitor.com/USA/Politics/2011/0527/Patriot-Act-three-controversial-provisions-that-Congress-voted-to-keep.

PAGE 128: "'it is the creed of slaves'" *Encyclopedia Britannica Online*, s. v. "William Pitt, the Elder," accessed April 29, 2012, http://www.britannica.com/EBchecked/topic/462131/William-Pitt-the-Elder/462131suppinfo/Supplemental-Information. • **"'hobgoblins, all of them imaginary'"** Howard Zinn, *A People's History of the United States* (New York: HarperCollins, 1980), 647. • **"authorizing the internment of American citizens."** "Executive Order 9066," National Archives, http://www.archives.gov/historical-docs/todays-doc/index.html?dod-date=219, accessed April 24, 2012.

PAGE 129: "'to internal and less dangerous areas'" Franklin D. Roosevelt, February 19, 1942, Executive Order 9066, "Authorizing the Secretary of War to Prescribe Military Areas," *fdrlibrary.marist.edu*, accessed April 11, 2012, http://bit.ly/IAETs8. • **"'and to hell with habeas corpus'"** "The Perilous Fight: Asian Americans," *pbs.org*, accessed April 11, 2012, http://www.pbs.org/perilousfight/social/asian_americans. • **"allowed him to criminalized political dissent"** "Alien and Sedition Acts," *Library of Congress*, Primary Documents in American History, accessed April 10, 2012, http://www.loc.gov/rr/program/bib/ourdocs/Alien.html. • **"set up military tribunals for civilians"** David Greenberg, "Lincoln's Crackdown," *slate.com*, November 30, 2001, http://www.slate.com/articles/news_and_politics/history_lesson/2001/11/lincolns_crackdown.html. • **"Wilson argued that this power was"** "Wilson and Censorship of the Press," *The woodrowwilson.org*, accessed April 11, 2012, http://www.woodrowwilson.org/wilson-and-censorship-of-the-press. • **"generally being restored after each crisis"** Brian A. Jackson, ed., *The Challenge of Domestic Intelligence in a Free Society* (Rand Corporation, 2009), 90.

PAGE 130-131: "until the danger is over." "The Perilous Fight: Asian Americans," *pbs.org*, accessed April 11, 2012, http://www.pbs.org/perilousfight/social/asian_americans.

PAGE 132: "cost between $400,000 to $500,000" Gregg Carlstrom, "Interactive: How much did 9/11 cost the U.S?" *aljazeera.com*, September 1, 2011, http://www.aljazeera.com/indepth/spotlight/the911decade/2011/08/201183083713316460.html.

PAGE 133: "threat to civil liberties Americans face" Erik Kain, "The National Defense Authorization Act if the Greatest Threat to Civil Liberties Americans Face," *forbes.com*, December 5, 2011, http://www.dailymail.co.uk/travel/article-2062646/Naked-airport-X-ray-body-scanners-banned-Europe-cancer-fears.html. • **"because of cancer concerns"** Sarah Gordon, "Europe bans 'naked' airport scanners over cancer fears," *dailymail.co.uk*, November 17, 2011, http://www.dailymail.co.uk/travel/article-2062646/Naked-airport-X-ray-body-scanners-banned-Europe-cancer-fears.html. • **"absolutely staggering price tag"** Dana Priest and William M. Arkin, "Top Secret America: A Hidden World, Growing Beyond Control," *washingtonpost.com*, July 19, 2010, http://projects.washingtonpost.com/top-secret-america/articles/a-hidden-world-growing-beyond-control. • **"much of its effort domestically"** Jane Mayer, "The Secret Sharer," *newyorker.com*, May 23, 2011, http://www.newyorker.com/reporting/2011/05/23/110523fa_fact_mayer. • **"our country has changed"** Radley Balko, "A Decade After 9/11, Police Departments Are Increasingly Militarized," Huff Post Crime, *huffingtonpost.com*, September 12, 2011, http://www.huffingtonpost.com/2011/09/12/police-militarization-9-11-september-11_n_955508.html. • **"disregard of the First"** Spying on First Amendment Activity—State-by-State. *American Civil Liberties Union* online, accessed April 11, 2012, http://www.aclu.org/maps/spying-first-amendment-activity-state-state. • **"and Fourth"** David K. Shipler, "Free to Search and Seize," *The New York Times* online, June 22, 2011, http://www.nytimes.com/2011/06/23/opinion/23shipler.html. • **"thanks to a law passed in 2005"** Glenn Greenwald, "The Digital Surveillance State: Vast, Secret, and Dangerous, *cato-unbound.org,* August 9, 2010, http://readersupportednews.org/off-site-news-section/53-53/2638-greenwald-the-digital-surveillance-state-vast-secret-and-dangerous.

PAGE 134: "warrantless domestic surveillance" Charlie Savage and James Risen, "Federal Judge Finds N.S.A. Wiretaps were Illegal," *nytimes.com*, March 31, 2010, http://www.nytimes.com/2010/04/01/us/01nsa.html. • **"warrantless wiretapping a felony"** Greenwald, "The Digital Surveillance State: Vast, Secret, and Dangerous, http://www.cato-unbound.org/2010/08/09/glenn-greenwald/the-digital-surveillance-state-vast-secret-and-dangerous. • **"have their communications intercepted,"** Roger Wollenberg, "NSA Has Massive Database of Americans' Phone Calls," *usatoday.com*, May 11, 2006, http://www.usatoday.com/news/washington/2006-05-10-nsa_x.htm. • **"completely changed his mind"** "Restrict Warrantless Wiretaps," The Obameter, *politifact.com*, accessed April 10, 2012, http://www.politifact.com/truth-o-meter/promises/obameter/promise/180/end-warrantless-wiretaps.

PAGE 135: "'outweighed by real-life benefits.'" Eric Lichtblau, "Police Are Using Phone Tracking as a Routine Tool," *nytimes.com*, March 31, 2012, http://www.nytimes.com/2012/04/01/us/police-tracking-of-cellphones-raises-privacy-fears.html. • **"seized his laptop and mobile phone"** House v. Napolitano et al. Case No. 1:11-cv-10852-DJC (March 28, 2012), *justia.com*, http://law.justia.com/cases/federal/district-courts/massachusetts/madce/1:2011cv10852/136563/24, accessed April 24, 2012. • **"Fourth Amendment doesn't apply there"** Katherine A. Helm and Joel Cohen, "The Risks of Taking Your Electronic Devices Abroad," *law.com*, February 13, 2012, http://www.law.com/jsp/article.jsp?id=1202542075808&The_Risks_of_Taking_Your_Electronic_Devices_Abroad. • **"and in an ongoing manner"** Katherine A. Helm and Joel Cohen, "The Risks of Taking Your Electronic Devices Abroad," *law.com*, February 13, 2012, http://www.law.com/jsp/article.jsp?id=1202542075808&The_Risks_of_Taking_Your_Electronic_Devices_Abroad. • **"Western interests and civilians"** Patrick Sawer and David Barrett, "Detroit Bomber's Mentor Continues to Influence British Mosques and Universities," *telegraph.co.uk*, January 2, 2010, http://bit.ly/IjOk1M.

PAGE 136: "fiery, angry jihadi loon" Ted Jeory, "Library Ban on Sermons of Hate," *express.co.uk*, January 10, 2010, http://www.express.co.uk/posts/view/150772/Library-ban-on-sermons-of-hate. • **"administration in American history"** Barack Obama, "Transparency and Open Government," Memorandum for the Heads of Executive Departments and Agencies, *Whitehouse.gov*, accessed April 11, 2012, http://www.whitehouse.gov/the_press_office/TransparencyandOpenGovernment. • **"least transparent administrations"** Josh Gerstein, "Obama Least Transparent of Last 6 Administrations," *nation.foxnews.com*, March 5, 2012, http://nation.foxnews.com/president-obama/2012/03/05/obama-least-transparent-last-6-administrations. • **"bemoaned by plenty of Democrats"** Conor Friedersdorf, "The Obama Administration's Abject Failure on Transparency," *theatlantic.com*, February 2012, http://www.theatlantic.com/politics/archive/2012/02/the-obama-administrations-abject-failure-on-transparency/252387/. • **"privately deciding his fate"** Charlie Savage, "Secret U.S. Memo Made Legal Case to Kill a Citizen," *nytimes.com*, October 8, 2011, http://www.nytimes.com/2011/10/09/world/middleeast/secret-us-memo-made-legal-case-to-kill-a-citizen.html. • **"that Awlaki would die"** Glenn Greenwald, "Anwar al-Awlaki: Execution by Secret WH Committee," *salon.com*, October 6, 2011, http://www.salon.com/2011/10/06/execution_by_secret_wh_committee/singleton. • **"We don't know what the criteria"** Mark Hosenball, "Secret Panel Can Put Americans On 'Kill List,'" *reuters.com* online, October 5, 2011, http://www.reuters.com/article/2011/10/05/us-cia-killlist-idUSTRE79475C20111005. • **"the answer of course is"** Micah Zenko, "The Obama Administration and Targeted Killings: 'Trust us,'" *Global Public Square* blog at *cnn.com*, March 7, 2012, http://globalpublicsquare.blogs.cnn.com/2012/03/07/the-obama-administration-and-targeted-killings-trust-us. • **"was also blown up"** Hakim Almasmari, "Official: Drone Attack Kills Al-Awlaki's Son in Yemen," *cnn.com*, October 15, 2011, http://articles.cnn.com/2011-10-15/middleeast/world_meast_yemen-drone-attack_1_anwar-al-awlaki-drone-attack-drone-strike. • **"the size of five Capitol buildings"** James Bamford, "The NSA Is Building the Country's Biggest Spy Center (Watch What You Say)," *wired.com*, March 15, 2012, http://www.wired.com/threatlevel/2012/03/ff_nsadatacenter/all/1.

PAGE 137: **"approximately one yottabyte"** "Megabytes, Gigabytes, Terabytes… What are They?" *whatsabyte.com*, accessed April 11, 2012, http://www.whatsabyte.com. • **"to the complete disregard for it"** Jane Mayer, "The Secret Sharer," *newyorker.com*, May 23, 2011, http://www.newyorker.com/reporting/2011/05/23/110523fa_fact_mayer. • **"'abuse of authority in government'"** Joe Davidson, "Whistleblowers May Have a Friend in the Oval Office," *washingtonpost.com*, December 11, 2008, http://www.washingtonpost.com/wp-dyn/content/article/2008/12/10/AR2008121003364_pf.html. • **"whistleblowers in recent history"** Mark Benjamin, "WikiLeakers and Whistle-Blowers: Obama's Hard Line," *time.com*, March 11, 2011, http://www.time.com/time/nation/article/0,8599,2058340,00.html.

PAGE 138: **"Bush is probably like, Whoa"** Matthew Harwood, "NSA whistle-blower: Obama 'worse than Bush,'" *salon.com*, March 7, 2012, http://www.salon.com/2012/03/07/nsa_whistle_blower_obama_worse_than_bush. • **"'not reasonably possible to identify the number.'"** Pete Yost, "National Intelligence Office Unsure How Many Calls, Emails, Monitored," Huff Post Denver, *huffingtonpost.com*, July 28, 2011, http://www.huffingtonpost.com/2011/07/28/national-intelligence-office-wiretaps_n_912799.html.

PAGE 139: **"threatened or arrested"** Farnaz Fasshini "Iranian Crackdown Goes Global," *The Wall Street Journal*, December 3, 2009, http://online.wsj.com/article/SB125978649644673331.html. • **"turnkey totalitarian state."** James Bamford, "The NSA Is Building the Country's Biggest Spy Center," *Wired.com*, March 15, 2012, http://www.wired.com/threatlevel/2012/03/ff_nsadatacenter/all/1 • **"deserve neither liberty nor safety"** *Historical Review of Pennsylvania* (London: R. Griffiths, 1759). • **"'false choice'"** Erik Dahl, "Domestic Intelligence Today: More Security but Less Liberty?" *hsah.com,* http://www.hsaj.org/?fullarticle=7.2.8.

PAGE 140: **"managed to board a plane"** Lindsey Ellerson, "Obama: Intelligence Community Failed to 'Connect the Dots' in a 'Potentially Disastrous Way,'" *Political Punch* blog at *abcnews.go.com*, January 5, 2010, http://abcnews.go.com/blogs/politics/2010/01/obama-intelligence-community-failed-to-connect-the-dots-in-a-potentially-disastrous-way. • **"'is a simple database search.'"** Mario Aguilar, "Scary Fast Surveillance System Scans 36 Million Faces a Second," *gizmodo.com*, March 23, 2012, http://gizmodo.com/5895831/scary-fast-surveillance-system-scans-36-million-faces-a-second. • **"'took a long pause and replied, 'London?''"** Howard Kurtz, "James Clapper's Intel Slip," *thedailybeast.com*, December 21, 2010, http://www.thedailybeast.com/articles/2010/12/21/how-did-james-clapper-obamas-intel-chief-not-know-about-a-major-bomb-plot.html.

PAGE 141: "they could access her account," Louis Peitzman, "Student Sues School District Over Illegal Search of Her Facebook Page," *gawker.com*, March 10, 2012, http://gawker.com/5892221/student-sues-school-district-over-illegal-search-of-her-facebook-page. • **"log into their Facebook accounts"** "Facebook Passwords of Applicants Demanded by Colleges, Government Agencies," Huff Post Tech, *huffingtonpost.com*, March 6, 2012, http://www.huffingtonpost.com/2012/03/06/facebook-passwords-colleges_n_1323759.html. • **"online behavior can be monitored"** Bob Sullivan, "Government Agencies, Colleges Demand Applicants' Facebook Passwords," *redtape.msnbc.msn.com*, March 6, 2012, http://redtape.msnbc.msn.com/_news/2012/03/06/10585353-govt-agencies-colleges-demand-applicants-facebook-passwords.

Chapter 8
JIM WALLIS AND THE ATTEMPTED HIJACKING OF RELIGION

PAGE 144: "'politicians adjust to the change in the wind'" Jim Wallis, *God's Politics: Why the Right Gets It Wrong and the Left Doesn't Get It* (New York: HarperCollins Publishers, 2006), 22.

PAGE 147: "'evils which vex our civilization shall disappear'" Mark Tooley, *Methodism and Politics in the 20th Century* (Fort Valley: Bristol House, 2012), 13-14. • **"'rich men of America'"** Mark Tooley, *Methodism and Politics in the 20th Century* (Fort Valley: Bristol House, 2012), 15. • **"'abatement of poverty'"** Gene TeSelle, "The Social Creed of 1908 Updated for 21st Century," *pubtheo.com*, May 8, 2009, http://www.pubtheo.com/page.asp?PID=1362. • **"Other groups...also went on to endorse the creed"** Robert Moats Miller, *American Protestantism and Social Issues 1919-1939* (Chapel Hill: University of North Carolina Press, 1958), 31.

PAGE 148: "'conceive to be the good of humanity'" Robert Moats Miller, *American Protestantism and Social Issues 1919-1939* (Chapel Hill: University of North Carolina Press, 1958), 41. • **"'high a percentage of Socialists as can the ministry'"** Robert Moats Miller, *American Protestantism and Social Issues 1919-1939* (Chapel Hill: University of North Carolina Press, 1958), 64. • **"'economic processes for the common good'"** Robert Moats Miller, *American Protestantism and Social Issues 1919-1939* (Chapel Hill: University of North Carolina Press, 1958), 64. • **"'twilight of the gods of capitalism'"** Robert Moats Miller, *American Protestantism and Social Issues 1919-1939* (Chapel Hill: University of North Carolina Press, 1958), 67, 75, 82.

PAGE 149: "'an act of blasphemy'" Edmund W. Robb and Julia Robb, *Betrayal of the Church: Apostasy and Renewal in the Mainline Denominations* (Westchester: Crossway Books, 1986), 121, 132, 133. • **"which hailed him as 'Brother Ortega'"** Mark Tooley, *Methodism and Politics in the 20th Century* (Fort Valley: Bristol House, 2012), 276. • **"enthusiastically met with Fidel Castro at the Cuban Mission to the UN"** National Council of Churches, "End Embargo Against Cuba, Agree Castro, U.S. Church Leaders," news release, October 26, 1995. • **"one of the seven largest Mainline Protestant churches"** The Association of Religion Data Archives, *TheARDA.com*. • **"By 2012, it was less than one in fifteen"** Yearbook of American & Canadian Churches 2011 (Nashville: Abingdon Press, 2011), 363-373.

PAGE 153: "'made some difference in the outcome of the default debate'" Jim Wallis, "The Moral Default," *sojo.net*, August 4, 2011, http://sojo.net/sojomail/2011/08/04. • **"'discussions on the role of religion in politics'"** Laurie Goodstein, "Without a Pastor of His Own, Obama Turns to Five," *New York Times*, March 14, 2009, http://www.nytimes.com/2009/03/15/us/politics/15pastor.html. • **"'to control the destiny of Indochina had been thwarted'"** Ronald H. Nash, *Why the Left Is Not Right: The Religious Left: Who They Are and What They Believe* (Grand Rapids: Zondervan, 1996), 58.

PAGE 154: "'The community organizing stuff is real'" Laurie Goodstein, "Without a Pastor of His Own, Obama Turns to Five," *New York Times*, March 14, 2009, http://www.nytimes.com/2009/03/15/

us/politics/15pastor.html. • **"Honorary Chair of the Democratic Socialists of America"** Jim Wallis, *God's Politics: Why the Right Gets It Wrong and the Left Doesn't Get It* (New York: HarperCollins Publishers, 2006), back cover. • **"public Lenten fast to protest 'cuts'"** Amy Sullivan, "Religious Leaders Launch Fast to Protest Budget Cuts," *Swampland* blog at *time.com*, March 28, 2011, http://swampland.time.com/2011/03/28/religious-leaders-launch-fast-to-protest-budget-cuts. • **"'will go to bed hungry each night if these cuts pass'"** Justin Ruben, "Why I'm Fasting Against the Budget Cuts," *dailykos.com*, April 1, 2011, http://www.dailykos.com/story/2011/04/01/962436/-Why-I-m-Fasting-Against-the-Budget-Cuts-.

PAGE 155: "'future of poor and vulnerable people have crossed a moral line'" Jim Wallis, "Why I Am Beginning to Fast Today," *God's Politics* blog at *sojo.net*, March 28, 2011, http://sojo.net/blogs/2011/03/28/why-i-am-beginning-fast-today. • **"'attacked for 'declaring war' on the safety net'"** Brian Riedl, "Myths of Tax Cuts for Rich, Spending Cuts for Poor," *Heritage.org*, May 3, 2011, http://www.heritage.org/research/commentary/2011/05/myths-of-tax-cuts-for-rich-spending-cuts-for-poor. • **"'they will continue to go hungry'"** "Hungerfast to End on Easter Sunday; Budget Protest Continues," *womenthrive.org*, April 21, 2011, http://www.womenthrive.org/index.php?option=com_content&task=view&id=963&Itemid=46.

PAGE 156: "'hurts veterans and the elderly and the children and women's rights'" "The Day – Moby and MoveOn Protest Budget Cuts on the Poor," *moveon.org*, April 11, 2011, http://front.moveon.org/why-were-fasting-against-the-immoral-budget. • **"as 'bullies,' 'corrupt,' and 'hypocrites'"** Jim Wallis, "Woe to You, Legislators!" *huffingtonpost.com*, April 14, 2011, http://www.huffingtonpost.com/jim-wallis/woe-to-you-legislators_b_849300.html. • **"'commitment to civil discourse in our nation's public life'"** Jim Wallis and Chuck Colson, "Conviction and Civility: We Should Not Lose This Moment for Reflection and Renewal," *christianitytoday.com*, January 1, 2011, http://www.christianitytoday.com/ct/2011/januaryweb-only/convictioncivility.html. • **"'isn't just irresponsible — it's immoral'"** Jim Wallis, "Breaking: Obama Meets with Faith Leaders on Budget Crisis," *God's Politics* blog at *sojo.net*, July 20, 2011, http://sojo.net/blogs/2011/07/20/breaking-obama-meets-faith-leaders-budget-crisis.

PAGE 157: "'ask them to pray for him'" Ambreen Ali, "Christian Coalition Asks Obama to Protect the Poor During Meeting," *Roll Call*, July 20, 2011, http://www.rollcall.com/news/christian_coalition_asks_obama_to_protect_the_poor_during_meeting-207508-1.html. • **"protest 'fasts' between Palm Sunday and Easter."** Thomas C. Reeves, *The Empty Church: The Suicide of Liberal Christianity*, (New York: Free Press, 1996).

PAGE 158: "'so we're with him on that'" Ambreen Ali, "Christian Coalition Asks Obama to Protect the Poor During Meeting," *Roll Call*, July 20, 2011, http://www.rollcall.com/news/christian_coalition_asks_obama_to_protect_the_poor_during_meeting-207508-1.html. • **"'fiscal responsibility and shared sacrifice'"** United States Conference of Catholic Bishops, "U.S. Bishops Join with Other Christian Leaders to Call for 'Circle of Protection' Around Programs for Poor People," news release, April 28, 2011, http://old.usccb.org/comm/archives/2011/11-085.shtml. • **"'did not use a government credit card'"** Christians for a Sustainable Economy, "CASE's Letter to the President," *case4america.org*, accessed April 3, 2012, http://www.case4america.org/cases-letter-to-the-president. • **"'engines of both Wall Street and the Kremlin'"** Katherine Mangu-Ward, "God's Democrat," *Weekly Standard*, April 11, 2005, http://www.weeklystandard.com/Content/Public/Articles/000/000/005/441oqlsg.asp.

PAGE 159: "'hurricane of human suffering'" Mark Tooley, "Sojourn to the Center: Has Religious-Left Activist Jim Wallis Gone Moderate?" *Touchstone* 15, no. 3 (2002), http://www.touchstonemag.com/archives/article.php?id=15-03-054-r. • **"'anchors our nation in a common humanity'"** Jim Wallis, *God's Politics: Why the Right Gets It Wrong and the Left Doesn't Get It* (New York: HarperCollins Publishers, 2006), 19. • **"'not just off the welfare rolls'"** Mark Tooley, "Our Savior, the Democrats," *Weekly Standard*, June 13, 2011, http://www.weeklystandard.com/articles/our-savior-democrats_573260.html.

PAGE 160: "'My hope is that we will have a partnership'" Mark Tooley, "Sojourn to the Center: Has Religious-Left Activist Jim Wallis Gone Moderate?" *Touchstone* 15, no. 3 (2002), http://www. touchstonemag.com/archives/article.php?id=15-03-054-r. • **"'inclined to give Mr. Bush a chance'"** Mark Tooley, "Sojourn to the Center: Has Religious-Left Activist Jim Wallis Gone Moderate?" *Touchstone* 15, no. 3 (2002), http://www.touchstonemag.com/archives/article.php?id=15-03-054-r. • **"'no moral compass'"** Mark Tooley, "Sojourn to the Center: Has Religious-Left Activist Jim Wallis Gone Moderate?" *Touchstone* 15, no. 3 (2002), http://www.touchstonemag.com/archives/article.php?id=15-03-054-r. • **"'$150,000 in 2011 through his foundation'"** Marvin Olasky, "There He Goes Again: Jim Wallis' Sojourners Accepts $150,000 More from Atheist George Soros," *World* magazine, October 22, 2011, http://www.worldmag.com/articles/18750.

PAGE 161: "'Just bad theology'" "Is America a Christian Nation: And Does It Matter?" *lifetreecafe.com*, March 4, 2012, http://www.lifetreecafe.com/topics/030412.

PAGE 162: "'We've been talking faith and politics for a long time'" Julia Duin, "Clergy Offer Obama Counsel," *Washington Times*, January 22, 2009, http://www.washingtontimes.com/news/2009/jan/22/clergy-offer-obama-counsel. • **"'This White House wants our advice'"** Jim Wallis, "A Renewed Faith in Public Life," *On Faith* blog at *washingtonpost.com*, January 25, 2009, http://onfaith.washingtonpost.com/onfaith/panelists/jim_wallis/2009/01/a_renewed_faith_in_public_life.html. • **"'We are in danger of losing the moral core of the health care debate'"** Jim Wallis, "The Moral Core of the Health-Care Debate," *sojo.net*, August 20 2009, http://sojo.net/blogs/2009/08/20/moral-core-health-care-debate.

PAGE 163: "'American exceptionalism, theologically, is a heresy'" Billy Hallowell, "Lib Pastor Jim Wallis: 'American Exceptionalism…Is a Heresy…& It's Very Dangerous'," *theblaze.com*, March 8, 2012, http://www.theblaze.com/stories/lib-pastor-jim-wallis-american-exceptionalism-is-a-heresy-its-very-dangerous. • **"'And I signed up to be a follower of Jesus'"** Connor Ewing, "Wallis Sparks Controversy at Christian Music Festival," *theird.org*, July 15, 2010, http://www.theird.org/page.aspx?pid=1558. • **"more a 'movement person' supposedly akin to Martin Luther King"** Mark Tooley, "Our Savior, the Democrats," *Weekly Standard*, June 13, 2011, http://www.weeklystandard.com/articles/our-savior-democrats_573260.html.

PAGE 164: "'American foreign policy has made the world much better'" Mark Tooley, "Exceptional America?" *American Spectator*, April 8, 2011, http://spectator.org/archives/2011/04/08/exceptional-america. • **"'holding the wealthy and powerful accountable'"** Jim Wallis, "Praying for Peace and Looking for Jesus at #OccupyWallStreet," *Huffington Post*, October 6, 2011, http://www.huffingtonpost.com/jim-wallis/occupy-wall-street-looking-for-jesus_b_998381.html. • **"'those services for women who seek it'"** "Sojourners' Statement on Obama Administration's Contraception Policy Change," *God's Politics* blog at *sojo.net*, February 10, 2012, http://sojo.net/blogs/2012/02/10/sojourners-statement-obama-administrations-contraception-policy-change.

PAGE 165: "'more than they're paying now'" Napp Nazworth, "Progressive Evangelical Jim Wallis Agrees Debt Is Moral Issue," *Christian Post*, April 4, 2012, http://www.christianpost.com/news/jim-wallis-responds-to-christians-for-a-sustainable-economy-letter-55769.

PAGE 166: "'so small that I hadn't remembered them'" Sarah Pulliam Bailey, "Wallis Admits to Soros Funding," *Politics* blog at *christianitytoday.com*, August 20, 2010, http://blog.christianitytoday.com/ctpolitics/2010/08/wallis_admits_t.html.

Chapter 9
CHANGE THE MEDIA, CHANGE THE WORLD

PAGE 170: "'It will be the fast beating the slow.'" "The Big Idea," *fastcompany.com,* http://www.fastcompany.com/node/653619, accessed April 29, 2012.

PAGE 172: "front page of the Drudge Report" "The Face of CBS to Sign Off," *drudgereport.com*, November 24, 2004, http://www.drudgereportarchives.com/data/2004/11/24/20041124_001000.htm.

PAGE 175: "culture at CBS News in the early 1980s" Peggy Noonan, *What I Saw at the Revolution: A Political Life in the Reagan Era* (New York: Random House, 2006), 24-25, http://books.google.com/books?id=Ff8oVIxKcSoC&pg=PA24.

PAGE 177: "'accountability of government...'" Peter Johnson, "Katrina Rekindles Adversarial Media," *Media Mix column at usatoday.com*, September 5, 2005, http://www.usatoday.com/life/columnist/mediamix/2005-09-05-media-mix_x.htm.

PAGE 179: "'not Woodward and Bernstein on our side'" Michael Calderone, "Conservatives At CPAC Search For The Right's Woodward And Bernstein," *huffingtonpost.com*, February 13, 2012, http://www.huffingtonpost.com/2012/02/13/cpac-conservative-media-journalism_n_1272327.html.

PAGE 180: "journalism make it into that income group" Robert Gebeloff and Shaily Dewan, "What the Top 1% of Earners Majored In," *Economix* blog at *nytimes.com*, January 18, 2012, http://economix.blogs.nytimes.com/2012/01/18/what-the-top-1-of-earners-majored-in.

PAGE 181: "'non-traditional' sources of news" Michelle Malkin, "Announcing Twitchy.com," *michellemalkin.com*, http://michellemalkin.com/2012/03/07/announcing-twitchy-com, accessed April 29, 2012.

PAGE 186: "mainstream media remains a lure" Roy Greenslade, "Journalism Students Don't Read Newspapers," *Greenslade* blog at *guardian.co.uk*, October 12, 2010, http://www.guardian.co.uk/media/greenslade/2010/oct/12/cityuniversity-journalism-education.

Chapter 10
THE ISLAMIST AGENDA
Facts Over Fear

PAGE 190: "'the State of Islam established.'" Oren Kessler, "Muslim Brotherhood Text Reveals Scope of Radical Creed," *jpost.com*, February 9, 2011, http://www.jpost.com/MiddleEast/Article.aspx?id=207415.

PAGE 192: "'that was not prohibited'" *Sharia Law and American State Courts: An Assessment of State Appellate Cases*, Center for Security Policy, report, May 20, 2011, 474, http://shariahinamericancourts.com/wp-content/uploads/2011/06/Sharia_Law_And_American_State_Courts_1.4_06212011.pdf. • **"when she resists his sexual advances"** Ahmad ibn Naqib al-Misri, *Reliance of the Traveller: A Classic Manual of Islamic Sacred Law*, trans. and ed. Nuh Ha Mim Keller, rev. ed. (Beltsville, MA: Amana Publications, 1994) 535, 619. • **"New Jersey family court"** US Constitution, art. VI, sec. 2. • **"giving the woman the protection she was seeking"** *S.D. v. M.J.R.*, 2 N.J. 3d, 412 (2010).

PAGE 193: "irrespective of where they live" William Boykin and others, *Shariah: The Threat to America, An Exercise in Competitive Analysis, Report of Team B II* (Washington, DC: Center for Security Policy Press, 2012), 57. • **"'North American environment'"** Fiqh Council of North America, "History of the Fiqh Council," *fiqhcouncil.org*, accessed April 23, 2012, http://www.fiqhcouncil.org/node/13. • **"'and students in this language'"** Ahmad ibn Naqib al-Misri, *Reliance of the Traveller: A Classic Manual of Islamic Sacred Law*, trans. and ed. Nuh Ha Mim Keller, rev. ed. (Beltsville, MA: Amana Publications, 1994) xvii, http://www.bysiness.co.uk/Classical_Other/reliance.htm. • **"'conforms to the practice and faith of the orthodox Sunni community'"** Ahmad ibn Naqib al-Misri, *Reliance of the Traveller: A Classic Manual of Islamic Sacred Law*, trans. and ed. Nuh Ha Mim Keller, rev. ed. (Beltsville, MA: Amana Publications, 1994) xv, http://www.bysiness.co.uk/Classical_Other/reliance.htm.

PAGE 194: "a boy not until age fifteen" Iran Bulletin, "Islamic Republic of Iran and Penal Codes," *iran-bulletin.org*, accessed April 23, 2012, http://www.iran-bulletin.org/political_islam/punishmnt.html. • **"Beating and raping one's wife is authorized"** Ahmad ibn Naqib al-Misri, *Reliance of the Traveller: A Classic Manual of Islamic Sacred Law*, trans. and ed. Nuh Ha Mim Keller, rev. ed. (Beltsville, MA: Amana Publications, 1994), 541. • **"woman's testimony in court is valued at half that of a man"** Qur'an 2:282. • **"amputation of a thief's right hand"** Ahmad ibn Naqib al-Misri, *Reliance of the Traveller: A Classic Manual of Islamic Sacred Law*, trans. and ed. Nuh Ha Mim Keller, rev. ed. (Beltsville, MA: Amana Publications, 1994), 613. • **"'Whoever a Muslim changes his/her religion, kill him/her'"** Amjaonline "The Shari'ah ruling on Apostasy (Reddah)," April 17, 2006, Sheikh Hatem Mohammad Al-Haj Aly. • **"against nonbelievers is required of all adherents"** Ahmad ibn Naqib al-Misri, *Reliance of the Traveller: A Classic Manual of Islamic Sacred Law*, trans. and ed. Nuh Ha Mim Keller, rev. ed. (Beltsville, MA: Amana Publications, 1994), 599. • **"death sentence mandate for apostates"** Ahmad ibn Naqib al-Misri, *Reliance of the Traveller: A Classic Manual of Islamic Sacred Law*, trans. and ed. Nuh Ha Mim Keller, rev. ed. (Beltsville, MA: Amana Publications, 1994), 595-596.

PAGE195: "'not freely performing their religious obligation as Muslims'" Toni Johnson, "Islam: Governing Under Sharia," *cfr.org*, October 24, 2011, http://www.cfr.org/religion/islam-governing-under-sharia/p8034. • **"'it would be doomed from the start'"** Imran A. Nyazee, *Theories of Islamic Law: The Methodology of Ijtihad* (Chicago: KAZI, 1995).

PAGE 196: "those decisions conflict with Constitutional protections" *Sharia Law and American State Courts: An Assessment of State Appellate Cases*, Center for Security Policy, report, May 20, 2011, http://shariahinamericancourts.com/wp-content/uploads/2011/06/Sharia_Law_And_American_State_Courts_1.4_06212011.pdf. • **"laws of the Middle East in the past 11 years"** Dr. Ihsan Al-Khatib, "Shari'a Law and American Courts: An Interview with Abed Awad, Esq." *Shariainamerica.com*, January 23, 2012, http://shariainamerica.com/2012/01/23/Sharia-Law-and-American-Courts-An-Interview-with-Abed-Awad-Esq.

PAGE 197: "'I am going to dismiss the charge'" The Counter Jihad Report, "Impeach Pennsylvania's Sharia Judge," *counterjihadreport.com*, March 6, 2012, http://counterjihadreport.com/tag/judge-mark-martin. • **"insult directed against the Prophet Muhammad"** Ahmad ibn Naqib al-Misri, *Reliance of the Traveller: A Classic Manual of Islamic Sacred Law*, trans. and ed. Nuh Ha Mim Keller, rev. ed. (Beltsville, MA: Amana Publications, 1994) 597, 713, 724. • **"'the state of Michigan's constitution'"** American Islamic Leadership Coalition "American Muslims Speak Out Against the Enforcement of Shari'ah Law in America," press release, September 7, 2011, http://americanislamicleadership.org/AILC_Response_MI.

PAGE 198: "integrating shariah into yet another element of society" William Boykin and others, *Shariah: The Threat to America, An Exercise in Competitive Analysis, Report of Team B II* (Washington, DC: Center for Security Policy Press, 2012), 265. • **"an Israeli company on grounds that it is impure"** William Boykin and others, *Shariah: The Threat to America, An Exercise in Competitive Analysis, Report of Team B II* (Washington, DC: Center for Security Policy Press, 2012), 267. • **"are fighting in the cause of Allah"** William Boykin and others, *Shariah: The Threat to America, An Exercise in Competitive Analysis, Report of Team B II* (Washington, DC: Center for Security Policy Press, 2012), 267.

PAGE 199: "'in an alien and rival system...'" Gregory Katz, "Archbishop: UK Should Allow Shariah," *The Associated Press*, February 7, 2008, http://www.foxnews.com/wires/2008Feb07/0,4670,BritainShariahLaw,00.html.

PAGE 200: "the largest Muslim charity in America" Gretel C. Kovach, "Five Convicted in Terrorism Financing Trial," NY Times, November 24, 2008, http://www.nytimes.com/2008/11/25/us/25charity.html. • **"organization Hamas under the guise of zakat"** US Department of the Treasury, Office of

Foreign Assets Control, *Specially Designated Nationals and Blocked Persons*, 112th cong., 2nd sess., http://www.treasury.gov/ofac/downloads/t11sdn.pdf. • **"goal of re-establishing the global caliphate'"** William Boykin and others, *Shariah: The Threat to America, An Exercise in Competitive Analysis, Report of Team B II* (Washington, DC: Center for Security Policy Press, 2012), 119.

PAGE 201: "'at the very latest,' Europe will be predominately Islamic" Christopher Caldwell, "Islamic Europe?" *Weekly Standard*, October 4, 2004, http://www.weeklystandard.com/Content/Public/Articles/000/000/004/685ozxcq.asp. • **"'is to dominate in Europe'"** Christopher Caldwell, "Islamic Europe?" *Weekly Standard*, October 4, 2004, http://www.weeklystandard.com/Content/Public/Articles/000/000/004/685ozxcq.asp?page=2. • **"'become integrated into their European host nations'"** Soeren Kern, "European 'No-Go' Zones for Non-Muslims Proliferating: 'Occupation Without Tanks or Soldiers,'" *gatestoneinstitute.org*, August 22, 2011, http://www.gatestoneinstitute.org/2367/european-muslim-no-go-zones.

PAGE 202: "in predominantly Muslim neighborhoods" Soeren Kern, "European 'No-Go' Zones for Non-Muslims Proliferating: 'Occupation Without Tanks or Soldiers,'" *gatestoneinstitute.org*, August 22, 2011, http://www.gatestoneinstitute.org/2367/european-muslim-no-go-zones. • **"exact addresses and satellite maps"** GIS Urban Policy, "Atlas Sensitive Urban Areas (ZUS)," SIG of the Secretariat General of the VIC, accessed April 24, 2012, http://sig.ville.gouv.fr/Atlas/ZUS. • **"non-Muslims can avoid these areas"** GIS Urban Policy, "Atlas Sensitive Urban Areas (ZUS)," SIG of the Secretariat General of the VIC, accessed April 24, 2012, http://sig.ville.gouv.fr/Atlas/ZUS. • **"is completely out of the picture"** DerWesten, "Even in Urban Districts the Police are Afraid," *derwesten.de*, January 8, 2011, http://www.derwesten.de/politik/in-problemvierteln-fuerchtet-sich-sogar-die-polizei-id4926287.html.

PAGE 203: "under the guise of charity" Gretel C. Kovach, "Five Convicted in Terrorism Financing Trial," *NY Times*, November 24, 2008, http://www.nytimes.com/2008/11/25/us/25charity.html. • **"'just as his predecessors did back in the early 1960s'"** Brad Knickerbocker, "Why is Glenn Beck Freaking Out Over Egypt and a Caliphate?" *Vox* blog at *csmonitor.com*, February 12, 2011, http://www.csmonitor.com/USA/Elections/Vox-News/2011/0212/Why-is-Glenn-Beck-freaking-out-over-Egypt-and-a-caliphate.

PAGE 204: "'guidance, instruction, truth and justice.'" MEMRI, "Muslim Brotherhood General Guide Muhammed Badi: Our Ultimate Goal, Establishing a Global Islamic Caliphate, Can Only Be Achieved Gradually and Without Coercion," *memri.org*, February 10, 2012, http://www.memri.org/report/en/print6075.htm.

PAGE 205: "'is made victorious over all other religions'" *United States v. Holy Land Foundation*, 445 F.3d 771 (5th Cit. 2006) http://www.txnd.uscourts.gov/judges/hlf2/09-25-08/Elbarasse%20Search%203.pdf. • **"contacts between CAIR and the FBI"** Richard C. Powers, letter to Jon Kyl, April 28, 2009, http://www.investigativeproject.org/documents/misc/265.pdf. • **"because the Brotherhood pledged they would not seek the presidency"** David D. Kirkpatrick, "Islamist Group Breaks Pledge to Stay Out of Race in Egypt," *New York Times*, March 31, 2012, http://www.nytimes.com/2012/04/01/world/middleeast/brotherhood-chooses-a-candidate-in-egypt.html. • **"(...Brotherhood wouldn't seek the presidency), for president"** David D. Kirkpatrick, "Islamist Group Breaks Pledge to Stay Out of Race in Egypt," *NY Times*, March 31, 2012, http://www.nytimes.com/2012/04/01/world/middleeast/brotherhood-chooses-a-candidate-in-egypt.html. • **"'We have no desire at all to monopolize power'"** David D. Kirkpatrick, "Islamist Group Breaks Pledge to Stay Out of Race in Egypt," *NY Times*, March 31, 2012, http://www.nytimes.com/2012/04/01/world/middleeast/brotherhood-chooses-a-candidate-in-egypt.html.

PAGE 206: "'affiliates of the Muslim Brotherhood to support terrorists'" *United States v. Sabri Benkahla*, 530 F.3d 300 (4th cir. 2008) 530 F.3d 300, http://www.investigativeproject.org/documents/case_docs/542.pdf. • **"met with Islamist 'grievance group' leaders from CAIR"** CAIRtv, "Video: CAIR Meets with FBI, NJ Officials on NYPD Muslim Spying," *youtube.com*, March 5, 2012, http://www.youtube.com/watch?v=IkvJRR71Ebk. • **"'speaking on an Arab-American radio show to**

assuage concerns'" Niraj Warikoo, "FBI Ditches Training Materials Criticized as Anti-Muslim," *usatoday.com*, February 20, 2012, http://www.usatoday.com/news/nation/story/2012-02-20/fbi-anti-muslim-training/53168966/1. • **"'make them slaves to Allah'"** Brigitte Gabriel, *They Must Be Stopped: Why We Must Defeat Radical Islam and How We Can Do It,* 1st ed. (New York: St. Martin's Press, 2008), 117.

PAGE 207:"establishing the caliphate is their religious duty" Hizb ut-Tahrir, "Home," *hizbuttahrir.org*, accessed April 25, 2012, http://english.hizbuttahrir.org. • **"'motivating force behind fundamentalist Islam'"** Jim Murk, *Islam Rising* (Springfield, MO: 21st Century Press, 2006), 15. • **"they who are truly iniquitous!"** Qur'an 24:55.   http://www.islamicity.com/QuranSearch/ (24:55) (Sura Al-Nur, verse 55). • **"'the symbol of Muhammad, will be supreme everywhere'"** Ronald de Valderano, "Terror: The War Against the West," *Imprimis*, November, 1988, http://www.hillsdale.edu/news/imprimis/archive/issue.asp?year=1988&month=11.

PAGE 208:"'your theories are just wacky'" "Shields and Brooks on GOP Candidates' Plausibility, Egypt's Bottom-up Revolution," *PBS NewsHour*, PBS, February 11, 2011, http://www.pbs.org/newshour/bb/politics/jan-june11/shieldsbrooks_02-11.html. • **"through jihad against the apostate rulers and their removal"** Brigitte Gabriel, *They Must Be Stopped: Why We Must Defeat Radical Islam and How We Can Do It,* 1st ed. (New York: St. Martin's Press, 2008), 123.

PAGE 209: "is the highest of our aspirations" Senate Committee on Homeland Security and Governmental Affairs, *Report on the Roots of Violent Islamist Extremism and Efforts to Counter It: The Muslim Brotherhood*, 110th Cong., 2nd sess., 2008, http://www.investigativeproject.org/documents/testimony/353.pdf, and http://counterterrorismblog.org/2008/07/steven_emerson_statement_for.php. • **"in 1963 they created their first American front"** William Boykin and others, *Shariah: The Threat to America, An Exercise in Competitive Analysis, Report of Team B II* (Washington, DC: Center for Security Policy Press, 2012), 117. • **"organization at the University of Illinois, Urbana: the Muslim Student Association"** Muslim Students Association, "Our History: MSA National: Serving Islam and Muslims Since 1963," *msanational.org*, accessed April 26, 2012, http://msanational.org/about-us.

PAGE 210: "'And remember, you read it here first'" Brad Knickerbocker, "Why is Glenn Beck Freaking Out Over Egypt and a Caliphate?" *Vox* blog at *csmonitor.com*, February 12, 2011, http://www.csmonitor.com/USA/Elections/Vox-News/2011/0212/Why-is-Glenn-Beck-freaking-out-over-Egypt-and-a-caliphate/(page)/2. • **"threats from radical Islamists in America and abroad"** William J. Federer, *What Every American Needs to Know About the Qur'an: A History of Islam and the United States* (St. Louis: Amerisearch, 2007), 18.

PAGE 211: "'This is, and I do not use the term lightly, looney tunes'" Matt Schneider, "Chris Matthews: Glenn Beck's Theories Are 'Looney Tunes' Trying To Distract Us from Thought," *mediaite.com*, February 2, 2011, http://www.mediaite.com/tv/chris-matthews-glenn-becks-theories-are-looney-tunes-trying-to-distract-us-from-thought. • **"Allah tear his organs asunder"** Memri Blog, "On Jihadi Forum, Incitement Against American Islamic Forum for Democracy Director," *thememriblog.org*, January 25, 2012, http://www.thememriblog.org/blog_personal/en/41602.htm.

Chapter 11
EDUCATION
Radical Ideas to Defeat the Radicals

PAGE 216: "will help us reach that goal" George H. W. Bush, "State of the Union Address," January 28, 1992, transcript, *usa-presidents.info*, http://www.usa-presidents.info/union/bush-4.html. • **"not just spend more money"** William Jefferson Clinton, "State of the Union Address," February 17, 1993, *usa-presidents.info*, http://www.usa-presidents.info/union/clinton-1.html. • **"or having more public school**

choice" Bill Clinton, "State of the Union Address," *usa-presidents.info*, January 25, 1994, http://www. usa-presidents.info/union/clinton-2.html. • **"have the opportunity to renew our skills"** "1995 State Of The Union Address," Politics, *washingtonpost.com*, January 24, 1995, http://www.washingtonpost.com/ wp-srv/politics/special/states/docs/sou95.htm. • **"let politics stop at the schoolhouse door"** "Text of President Clinton's 1998 State of the Union Address," *washingtonpost.com,* January 27, 1998, http:// www.washingtonpost.com/wp-srv/politics/special/states/docs/sou98.htm. • **"that every single child can learn"** Bill Clinton, "State of the Union Address," January 27, 2000, *usa-presidents.info,* http:// www.usa-presidents.info/union/clinton-8.html. • **"education reform so that no child is left behind"** George W. Bush, "State of the Union Address," January 29, 2002, *usa-presidents.info,* http://www. usa-presidents.info/union/gwbush-2.html. • **"They need more reform"** "Full Transcript: Obama's 2012 State of the Union Address," *usatoday.com*, January 24, 2012, http://www.usatoday.com/news/ washington/story/2012-01-24/state-of-the-union-transcript/52780694/1. • **"competition called Race to the Top"** The White House Office of the Press Secretary, "Remarks by the President in State of Union Address," press release, January 25, 2011, http://www.whitehouse.gov/the-press-office/2011/01/25/ remarks-president-state-union-address.

PAGE 217: "in science and 14th out of 15 in math" "American Children Trail in Math and Science," *New York Times* online, February 06, 1992, http://www.nytimes.com/1992/02/06/us/american-children-trail-in-math-and-science.html, accessed April 12, 2012. • **"they were doing forty years ago"** Fawn Johnson, "Parsing the Nation's Report Card," *Education Experts* blog at *nationaljournal.com,* November 7, 2011, http://education.nationaljournal.com/2011/11/parsing-the-nations-report-car.php, accessed April 12, 2012. • **"spent some \$2 trillion on education"** Andrew J. Coulson, "The Impact of Federal Involvement in America's Classrooms," *cato.org*, February 10, 2011, http://www.cato.org/publications/ congressional-testimony/impact-federal-involvement-americas-classrooms.

PAGE 218-219: "'education system the best in the world...'" Jimmy Carter, "Department of Education Organization Act Statement on Signing S. 210 Into Law." *The American Presidency Project*, October 17, 1979, http://www.presidency.ucsb.edu/ws/index.php?pid=31543#axzz1tU039auy.

PAGE 220: "per student since 1970 in real dollars" Gary W. Patterson, Jr., comment on Audrey Spalding, "The U.S. Education System Wrongly Penalizes Good Teachers, Won't Fire Bad Teachers," *policymic.com*, accessed April 19, 2012, http://www.policymic.com/articles/3257/the-u-s-education-system-wrongly-penalizes-good-teachers-won-t-fire-bad-teachers.

PAGE 221: "parents who wanted their kids to read the Bible" Hannah Barker and Simon Burrows, eds., *Press, Politics and the Public Sphere in Europe and North America 1760–1820* (New York: Cambridge University Press, 2002), 141. • **"nature has made between man and brute"** *The Letters of John and Abigail Adams* (New York: Penguin, 2004), 117. • **"people would learn to guard their freedom"** Meg Brulatour, "Transcendental Ideas: Education; Background for the State of Education in New England: Post-Revolutionary War to Mid-19th Century." *American Transcendentalism Web,* accessed April 19, 2012 http://www.vcu.edu/engweb/transcendentalism/ideas/edhistory.html.

PAGE 222: "architecture, statuary, tapestry and porcelain" "In a Second Revolution," *Life*, December 26, 1960. • **"time learning to achieve their goals"** Erkki Aho, Kari Pitkänen, and Pasi Sahlberg, "Policy Development and Reform Principles of Basic and Secondary Education in Finland since 1968" (working paper series, Education, World Bank, Washington, D.C. May 2006), http://bit.ly/ICRqeC. • **"it is a belief against all experience"** James Bryant Conant, *Thomas Jefferson and the Development of American Public Education* (Berkeley: University of California Press, 1962), 118. • **"the infant against the will of his father"** Tom Shuford, "Jefferson on Public Education: Defying Conventional Wisdom," *educationnews.org*, June 28, 2007, http://www.educationnews.org/articles/jefferson-on-public-education-defying-conventional-wisdom.html, accessed April 19, 2012. • **"and abhors, is sinful and tyrannical"** David Kirkpatrick, "Thomas Jefferson on Education," *heartland.org*, November 1, 2005, http://news.heartland.org/newspaper-article/2005/11/01/thomas-jefferson-education, accessed February 2012.

PAGE 223: "from kindergarten through college" Matthew J. Brouillette, "The 1830s and 40s: Horace Mann, the End of Free-Market Education, and the Rise of Government Schools," Mackinac Center for Public Policy, July 16, 1999, http://www.mackinac.org/2035. • **"and eventually around the country"** Seth Godin, "Stop Stealing Dreams: What is School For?" *sethgodin.com*, accessed April 19, 2012, http://www.sethgodin.com/sg/docs/StopStealingDreamsSCREEN.pdf. • **"fostering care of the Bolshevist government"** Charles A. Morse, "How Communist is Public Education?" *enterstageright. com*, March 25, 2002, http://www.enterstageright.com/archive/articles/0302/0302publiced.htm. • **"institutions as well as science and art"** John Dewey, "The Future of Liberalism," Address to the American Philosophical Association, December 28, 1934, http://www.heritage.org/initiatives/first-principles/primary-sources/john-dewey-on-liberalisms-future.

PAGE 224: "be left to their own devices" Chiemeka Utazi, "Child Education in Rousseau's Concept," *scribd.com*, November 11, 2003, http://scr.bi/ICP2EN. • **"tendency is to make the child secretive and deceitful"** John Dewey, *The Middle Works, 1899-1924, Volume 8: Essays and Miscellany in the 1915 Period and German Philosophy and Politica and Schools of To-Morrow*, ed. Jo Ann Boydson (Carbondale, IL: Southern Illinois University Press, 1979), 226. • **"people under the nonreligious state"** Rev. John A. Hardon, S.J., "John Dewey—Radical Social Educator," *Catholic Educational Review*, October 1952, http://www.ewtn.com/library/HOMESCHL/JNDEWEY2.HTM • **"people under the nonreligious state"** Rev. John A. Hardon, S.J., "John Dewey—Radical Social Educator," *Catholic Educational Review*, October 1952, http://www.ewtn.com/library/HOMESCHL/JNDEWEY2.HTM. • **"per student, after adjusting for inflation"** "Fast Facts," National Center for Education Statistics, *nces. ed.gov*, accessed April 19, 2012, http://nces.ed.gov/fastfacts/display.asp?id=66.

PAGE 225: "In 2010, just…" "The Nation's Report Card: U.S. History 2010," *National Center for Education Statistics*, June 14, 2011, http://nces.ed.gov/pubsearch/pubsinfo.asp?pubid=2011468.

PAGE 226: "in 1961, after adjusting for inflation" Robert Franciosi, *The Rise and Fall of American Public Schools* (New York: Praeger, 2004), 24; U.S. Department of Education, National Center for Education Statistics, *Digest of Education Statistics, 2010* (NCES 2011-015), Table 188 and Chapter 2; National Center for Education Statistics, *nces.ed.gov*, http://nces.ed.gov/fastfacts/display.asp?id=28.

PAGE 227: "steps required in the union contract" Michael Winerip, "Teachers Get Little Say in a Book About Them," *New York Times*, August 28, 2011, http://www.nytimes.com/2011/08/29/education/29winerip.html. • **"costing the city $30 million a year"** Jennifer Medina, "Teachers Set Deal with City on Discipline Process," *New York Times*, April 15, 2010, http://www.nytimes.com/2010/04/16/nyregion/16rubber.html. **"school that is attempting to fire them"** Jennifer Medina, "Teachers Set Deal with City on Discipline Process," *New York Times*, April 15, 2010, http://www.nytimes.com/2010/04/16/nyregion/16rubber.html, accessed April 19, 2012. • **"simply is too high a price to pay"** "Teachers Union Big Wig Says It's Not About Kids, It's About Power!," *foxnews.com*, February 23, 2011, http://nation.foxnews.com/culture/2011/02/23/teachers-union-big-wig-says-its-not-about-kids-its-about-power.

PAGE 228: "receive full pension and health benefits" Kristen Gosling, "Mark Berndt Paid to Resign from School District Following Sex Scandal," *ksdk.com*, February 10, 2012, http://www.ksdk.com/news/article/302979/28/Teacher-in-Los-Angeles-sex-scandal-paid-to-resign, accessed February 2012.

PAGE 229: "kiss our public schools goodbye" Erik Kain, "Why I Support the Teachers Unions," *forbes. com*, September 28, 2011, http://onforb.es/KoUsJ5.

PAGE 230: "$2 billion in union dues every year" Chris Edwards, "State and Local Fiscal Reforms," Conference on State and Local Government Finance and Economic Turbulence, Federal Reserve Bank of St. Louis, April 9, 2010, http://www.cato.org/speeches/chrisedwards-state-fiscal.pdf. • **"order to back the Democrat machine"** Steven Greenhouse, "N.E.A. Advances Endorsement for Obama in 2012," *The Caucus* blog at *nytimes.com*, May 6, 2011, http://thecaucus.blogs.nytimes.com/2011/05/06/n-e-a-advances-endorsement-for-obama-in-2012. • **"percent of that went to Democrats"** "Teachers Unions," *Influence & Lobbying, opensecrets.org,* accessed April 19, 2012, http://www.opensecrets.org/

industries/indus.php?ind=l1300. • **"New York City public school teachers"** Fred Lucas, "New York City Teachers Union Is Largest Recipient of Obamacare Waiver; Parent AFT Union Spent $1.9 Million on Obama Election," *cnsnews.com*, January 31, 2011, http://cnsnews.com/news/article/new-york-city-teachers-union-largest-recipient-obamacare-waiver-parent-aft-union-spent. • **"movement of teachers for their rights"** "Teaching About Labor Issues and the Wisconsin Worker Fight Back," *rethinkingschools. org,* accessed April 19, 2012, http://rethinkingschools.org/news/WIProtestTeachingResources.shtml. • **"climbed to roughly $24,000 a student"** Chris Taylor, "Is College Worth It?" *Money* blog at *reuters. com*, September 15, 2011, http://blogs.reuters.com/reuters-money/2011/09/15/is-college-worth-it. • **"wouldn't have to deal with massive debt"** Chris Taylor, "Is College Worth It?" *Money* blog at *reuters.com*, September 15, 2011, http://blogs.reuters.com/reuters-money/2011/09/15/is-college-worth-it. • **"America with hard work and perseverance"** T. Kenneth Cribb Jr., "The Shaping of the American Mind" (report, Intercollegiate Studies Institute, Wilmington, DE, December 2009), http://bit.ly/ICPtil.

PAGE 231: **"critical thinking skills throughout college"** "A Lack of Rigor Leaves Students 'Adrift' in College," *npr.org*, February 9, 2011, http://www.npr.org/2011/02/09/133310978/in-college-a-lack-of-rigor-leaves-students-adrift, accessed February 2012. • **"escalated by a factor of three since 1980"** Linsey Davis, "Facebook and PayPal's Peter Thiel Pays College Students to Drop Out," *abcnews.com*, May 26, 2011, http://abcn.ws/ICPvaa, accessed February 2012.

PAGE 232: **"Americans with the qualifications to fill those jobs"** "Prepared Students," *waitingforsuperman.com*, accessed February 2012, http://www.waitingforsuperman.com/action/theme/students.

PAGE 233: **"rather than founding philosophy"** Caroline Evans, "Back to School: 10 Completely Real College Courses That Sound Totally Fake," *Random Ephemera* blog at *houstonpress.com*, August 3, 2011, http://blogs.houstonpress.com/artattack/2011/08/back_to_school_20_completely_r.php. • **"Democrat:Republican ratio is probably about 8:1"** Daniel B. Klein and Charlotta Stern, "Liberal Versus Conservative Stinks," *Society* 45, no. 6 (2008): 488-495, doi: 10.1007/s12115-008-9150-0; Daniel B. Klein and Charlotta Stern, "Democrats and Republicans in Anthropology and Sociology: How Do they Differ on Public Policy Issues?" *The American Sociologist* 35, no. 4 (2004): 79-86, DOI: 10.1007/s12108-004-1025-2 http://www.springerlink.com/content/e942vnq7aumnwynu. • **"Democrats and zero registered Republicans"** "More Iowa Rationalizations," *History News Network* blog at *hnn. us*, George Mason University, December 13, 2007, http://hnn.us/blogs/entries/45545.html.

PAGE 234: **"identify themselves as any shade of liberal"** Scott Jaschik, "Red Grader, Blue Grader," *insidehighered.com*, May 20, 2011, http://www.insidehighered.com/news/2011/05/20/study_finds_differences_in_republican_and_democratic_grading_patterns. • **"liberal and only 13 percent as conservative"** Howard Kurtz, "Most College Profs Lean Left, Study Says," *Seattle Times*, March 30, 2005, http://seattletimes.nwsource.com/html/education/2002224341_professors30.html. • **"reformed were they allowed to reopen"** Mark. W. Clark, *Beyond Catastrophe: German Intellectuals and Cultural Renewal After World War II, 1945-1955* (Lanham, MD: Lexington Books, 2006), 55. • **"from entering Canada on several occasions"** "Bill Ayers Again Barred from Entering Canada," *Canada Newswire*, June 15, 2011, http://www.newswire.ca/en/story/726585/bill-ayers-again-barred-from-entering-canada.

PAGE 235: **"$54,000 per student last year."** Richard Vedder, "Princeton Reaps Tax Breaks as State Colleges Beg," *bloomberg.com*, March 18, 2012, accessed April 29, 2012, http://www.bloomberg.com/news/2012-03-18/princeton-reaps-tax-breaks-as-state-colleges-beg.html.

PAGE 236: **"Maryland, along with many others"** Scott Jaschik, "Murky Picture for Faculty Salaries," *insidehighered.com*, April 13, 2009, http://www.insidehighered.com/news/2009/04/13/aaup. • **"$4.4 billion in fiscal 2011 alone"** "Harvard Endowment Rises $4.4 Billion to $32 Billion," *Harvard Magazine*, September 22, 2011, http://harvardmagazine.com/2011/09/harvard-endowment-rises-to-32-billion, accessed February 2012. • **"and Yale has $19 billion"** Dan Berman, "Top 10 Richest Colleges: The Biggest Endowments," *advisorone.com*, October 24, 2011, http://www.advisorone.com/2011/10/24/

top-10-richest-colleges-the-biggest-endowments. • **"dollars in federal funding every year"** Radhika Jain, "Federal Government a Financial 'Lifeline' for Physics Department," *Crimson*, October 26, 2011, accessed February 2012, http://www.thecrimson.com/article/2011/10/26/physics-department-federal-funds. • **"a systemic level at the national level"** Donna Gordon Blankinship, "Public Universities Look Toward Federal Government as Another Source to Replace State Dollars," *Minneapolis Star Tribune*, April 16, 2010, http://www.startribune.com/templates/Print_This_Story?sid=91072159. • **"country needs that interstate highway system"** Donna Gordon Blankinship, "Public Universities Look Toward Federal Government as Another Source to Replace State Dollars," *startribune.com*, April 16, 2010, http://www.startribune.com/templates/Print_This_Story?sid=91072159.

PAGE 238: "challenging Einstein's theory of special relativity" Tamara Cohen, "Einstein Wrong Again! New Experiment Confirms Doubts over His Speed of Light Theory," *dailtmail.co.uk*, November 18, 2011, http://www.dailymail.co.uk/sciencetech/article-2063163/Einstein-speed-light-2nd-set-scientists-particles-CAN-travel-faster-light.html.

PAGE 239: "her lunch for not being sufficiently nutritious" Matt Willoughby, "State Inspectors Searching Children's Lunch Boxes: This Isn't China, Is It?," *nccivitas.org*, February 14, 2012, http://www.nccivitas.org/2012/state-inspectors-searching-childrens-lunch-boxes-this-isnt-china-is-it.

Chapter 12
YOUNG SOCIALISTS
Why Our Kids Think They Hate Capitalism

PAGE 240-241: Image courtesy of the Everett Collection, Copyright 2012. Used under license from Shutterstock.com.

PAGE 242: "'government-run cartel education system.'" Kevin Williamson, "Jobs Agenda," *nationalreview.com*, October 5, 2011, http://www.nationalreview.com/corner/279321/jobs-agenda-kevin-d-williamson.

PAGE 244: "'the state-run shops are so barren...black market'" David Remnick, "'Soviet Union's Shadow Economy' – Bribery, Barter, Black-Marker Deals Are the Facts of Life," *Seattle Times*, September 22, 1990, http://bit.ly/Ij3swn. • **"'owned the only private broadcast media'"** U.S. Department of State, Bureau of Democracy, Human Rights, and Labor, "2010 Human Rights Report: Equatorial Guinea," report, April 8, 2011, http://www.state.gov/j/drl/rls/hrrpt/2010/af/154344.htm. • **"'or access to the Internet,'"** U.S. Department of State, Bureau of Democracy, Human Rights, and Labor, "2010 Human Rights Report: Turkmenistan," report, April 8, 2011, http://www.state.gov/j/drl/rls/hrrpt/2010/sca/154488.htm. • **"inches shorter than South Koreans."** Carl Bialik, "The Korean Height Gap," *wsj.com*, October 15, 2008, http://blogs.wsj.com/numbersguy/the-korean-height-gap-431.

PAGE 245: "'and we have our revolution.'" Buck Sexton, *Occupy: American Spring* (New York: Mercury Ink, 2012)." • **"*Socialism* was viewed negatively by 59 percent..."** Pew Research Center, "'Socialism' Not So Negative, 'Capitalism' Not So Positive," pewresearch.org, May 4, 2010, http://pewresearch.org/pubs/1583/political-rhetoric-capitalism-socialism-militia-family-values-states-rights. • **"Only 45 percent think capitalism is a good idea"** Frank Newport, "Socialism Viewed Positively by 36% of Americans,"*gallup.com*, February 4, 2010, http://www.gallup.com/poll/125645/Socialism-Viewed-Positively-Americans.aspx.

PAGE 246: "'and then lost it have never known it again.'" Ronald Reagan, "First Inaugural Address 33rd Governor, Republican 1967-1975," *governors.library.ca.gov*, January 5, 1967, http://governors.library.ca.gov/addresses/33-Reagan01.html. • **"'Center-Left or actually majoritarian socialist.'"** Charles Derber, "Capitalism: Big Surprises in Recent Polls," *commondreams.org*, May 18, 2010, http://www.commondreams.org/view/2010/05/18-3.

PAGE 247: "Great for the young communist and socialist." Greg Mankiw, "The Rainbow Fish, Revised," *gregmankiw.blogspot.com*, July 27, 2011, http://gregmankiw.blogspot.com/2011/07/rainbow-fish-revised.html.

PAGE 248: "as one critic wondered" "Oil Baron Tex Richman," *futureofcapitalism.com*, December 3, 2011, http://www.futureofcapitalism.com/2011/12/oil-baron-tex-richman. • "errors abound" Lawrence Reed, "Are High School Economics Textbooks Reliable?," *times-herald.com*, December 08, 2011, http://bit.ly/Ij315q.

PAGE 249: "Here are the results" Ray Franke, Sylvia Ruiz, et al., Higher Education Research Institute, "Findings from the 2009 Administration of the College Senior Survey (CSS): National Aggregates," report, February 2010, http://www.heri.ucla.edu/PDFs/pubs/Reports/2009_CSS_Report.pdf.

PAGE 251: "'sharing equally in the world's wealth.'" Rose Kennedy, *Times to Remember* (Garden City, NY: Doubleday, 1974), 172–73. • **"got to ring the closing bell on the NASDAQ…"** NASDAQ OMX Education Foundation, Junior Achievement of New York, "Junior Achievement of New York Announces the Top Three Winning High School teams of the 2011 Business Plan Competition," press release, June 5, 2011, http://bit.ly/Ij2Kzc. • **"'sales of things you have made or grow.'"** Boy Scouts of America, "American Business," *scouting.org*, 2010, http://bit.ly/Ij2PTA. • **"put pinball machines in barbershops."** Alice Schroeder, *The Snowball: Warren Buffett and the Business of Life* (New York: Bantam Books, 2008).

PAGE 252: "dropped out of Harvard" Joel Dreyfuss, "Gates Meets Gates: Our Editor-in-Chief Quizzes the Microsoft Founder on His Passion About Education," *theroot.com*, July 28, 2011, http://www.theroot.com/views/gates-meets-gates.

PAGE 253: "Success in every sort of business." Adam Smith, "The Theory of Moral Sentiments: Part III: Of the Foundation of our Judgments concerning our own Sentiments and Conduct, and of the Sense of Duty Consisting of One Section Chap. IV: Of the Nature of Self-deceit, and of the Origin and Use of general Rules," in *The Theory of Moral Sentiments,* 6th ed. (London, A. Millar, 1790, 6th Edition), http://www.marxists.org/reference/archive/smith-adam/works/moral/part03/part3c.htm.

PAGE 254: "worth more than $20 billion." Matthew G. Miller and Peter Newcomb, "Slim Beats Gates in Global Daily Ranking of Billionaires," *bloomberg.com*, Mar 5, 2012, http://www.bloomberg.com/news/2012-03-05/slim-beats-gates-in-global-daily-ranking-of-billionaires.html.

PAGE 255: "she sold 1.5 million." Ed Pilkington, "Amanda Hocking, the Writer Who Made Millions by Self-Publishing Online," *guardian.co.uk*, January 12, 2012, http://www.guardian.co.uk/books/2012/jan/12/amanda-hocking-self-publishing.

Chapter 13
ADAPT OR DIE
The Coming Intelligence Explosion

PAGE 258: "'one percent about anything'" Inez N. McFee, *Famous Americans For Young Readers: The Story of Thomas A. Edison* (New York: Barse & Hopkins, 1922), 6.

PAGE 260: "another 8 percent were roughly correct" Ray Kurzweil, "How My Predictions are Faring," *e426.org*, October 1, 2010, http://www.e426.org/pdf/kurzweilai.pdf.

PAGE 261: "criticized Kurzweil's forecasting methods" Robert U. Ayres, review of *The Singularity is Near: When Humans Transcend Biology,* by Ray Kurzweil, *Technological Forecasting and Social Change* 73 (February 2006): 95-100, doi:10.1016/j.techfore.205.12.002; Theodore Modis, "The

Singularity Myth," *Technological Forecasting and Social Change* 73 (February 2006): 104-112; Tesseleno C. Devezas, discussion of *The Singularity is Near: When Humans Transcend Biology,* by Ray Kurzweil, *Technological Forecasting and Social Change* 73 (February 2006): 112-121. • **"(or even faster than exponential), not linear"** Bela Nagy, J. Doyne Farmer, Jessika E. Trancik, Quan Minh Bui, "Testing Laws of Technological Progress" (working paper, Santa Fe Institute, Santa Fe, NM, September 2, 2010), http://tuvalu.santafe.edu/~bn/workingpapers/NagyFarmerTrancikBui.pdf; Bela Nagy, J. Doyne Farmer, Jessika E. Trancik, John Paul Gonzales, "Superexponential Long-term Trends in Information Technology," *Technical Forecasting and Social Change* 78 (October 2011): 1356-1364. • **"will take decades to get to 400"** Michael Kanellos, "Moore's Law to Roll On for Another Decade," *news.cnet.com,* February 10, 2003, http://news.cnet.com/2100-1001-984051.html. • **"not 'straight line' progress"** Michael Kanellos, "Moore's Law to Roll On for Another Decade," *news.cnet.com,* February 10, 2003, http://news.cnet.com/2100-1001-984051.html. • **"2.6 billion transistors onto a single chip"** "Computing Power and Stockmarkets: Moore and More," *Graphic Detail* blog at *economist. com,* November 29, 2011, http://www.economist.com/blogs/dailychart/2011/11/computing-power-and-stockmarkets. • **"basically an information-processing system"** Jose Luis Bermudez, "The Prehistory of Cognitive Science," chapter 1 in *Cognitive Science: An Introduction* (New York: Cambridge University Press, 2010).

PAGE 264: "human life will be irreversibly transformed" Raymond Kurzweil, *The Singularity is Near: When Humans Transcend Biology* (New York: Penguin, 2005), 7. • **"called an intelligence explosion"** Irving John Good, "Speculations Concerning the First Ultraintelligent Machine," *Advances in Computers,* 6 (1965), 31-88; David J. Chalmers, "The Singularity: A Philosophical Analysis," *Journal of Consciousness Studies,* 17 (2010), 7-65; Luke Muelhauser, Anna Salamon, "In Intelligence Explosion: Evidence and Import," in *The Singularity Hypothesis: A Scientific and Philosophical Assessment,* ed. Amnon Eden, Johnny Soraker, Jim Moor, and Eric Steinhart. • **"predicts some kind of Singularity by 2048"** Janet Harris, "Intel Predicts Singularity by 2048," *Tech News* in *techwatch. com,* August 22, 2008, http://www.techwatch.co.uk/2008/08/22/intel-predicts-singularity-by-2048/; Justin Rattner, "The Future of Moore's Law and Intel's Methods of Microchip Design," *Singularity Institute* video, *singinst.org,* October 2008, http://singinst.org/media/singularitysummit2008/justinrattner. • **"chance of an intelligence explosion by 2100"** Michael Nielsen, "What should a reasonable person believe about the Singularity?" *michaelnielsen.org,* January 12, 2011, http://michaelnielsen.org/blog/what-should-a-reasonable-person-believe-about-the-singularity. • **"near the middle of the century"** Shane Legg, "Sutton on Human Level AI," *Vetta Project,* May 9, 2011, http://www.vetta.org/2011/05/sutton-on-human-level-ai. • **"an intelligence explosion will occur by 2100"** David J. Chalmers, "The Singularity: A Philosophical Analysis," *Journal of Consciousness Studies,* 17 (2010), 7-65. • **"would occur by 2045"** Seth D. Baum, Ben Goertzel, Ted G. Goertzel, "How Long Until Human-Level AI? Results from an Expert Assessment," *Technological Forecasting and Social Changes,* 78 (January 2011): 185-195. • **"'last invention that man need ever make,'"** I. J. Good, "Speculations Concerning the First Ultraintelligent Machine" (Academic Press, 1965), http://www.stat.vt.edu/tech_reports/2005/GoodTechReport.pdf.

PAGE 265: "would not want the same things we do" Daniel Dewey, "Learning What to Value," in *Artificial General Intelligence: 4th International Conference, AGI 2011, Mountain View, CA, USA, August 3-6, 2011, Proceedings,* ed. Jurgen Schmidhuber, Kristinn R. Thorisson, Moshe Looks (Springer, 2011), 309-314. • See also: Eliezer Yudkowsky, "Artificial Intelligence as a Positive and Negative Factor in Global Risk," in *Global Catastrophic Risks,* ed. Nick Bostrom, Milan M. Ćirković (New York: Oxford University Press, 2008), 308-345; See also: Luke Muehlhauser, Louie Helm, "The Singularity and Machine Ethics," in *The Singularity Hypothesis: A Scientific and Philosophical Assessment,* ed. Amnon Eden, Johnny Soraker, Jim Moor, Eric Steinhart. • **"making sense of human preferences"** Luke Muehlhauser, "So You Want to Save the World," *lukeprog.com,* March 2, 2012, http://lukeprog. com/SaveTheWorld.html. • For more on the Singularity Institute for Artificial Intelligence, see: http://

singinst.org. • For more on the Future of Humanity Institute, see: http://www.fhi.ox.ac.uk. • **"ever happened on this fragile planet"** Michael Anissimov, "The Benefits of a Successful Singularity," *acceleratingfuture.com*, July 6, 2011, http://www.acceleratingfuture.com/michael/blog/2011/07/the-benefits-of-a-successful-singularity-2.

PAGE 267: "instead of checking in at the gate" "Obama Blames ATMs for High Unemployment," *fox nation* at *foxnews.com*, June 14, 2011, http://nation.foxnews.com/president-obama/2011/06/14/obama-blames-atms-high-unemployment.

PAGE 268: "somewhere from a week to a month" Robin Hanson, "Economics of the Singularity," in *IEEE Spectrum Special Report: The Singularity, spectrum.ieee.org*, June 2008, http://spectrum.ieee.org/robotics/robotics-software/economics-of-the-singularity.